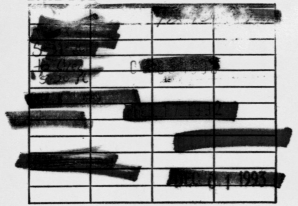

ESSAYS ON THE
EIGHTEENTH CENTURY

DAVID NICHOL SMITH

ESSAYS ON THE EIGHTEENTH CENTURY

Presented to

DAVID NICHOL SMITH

in honour of
his seventieth birthday

OXFORD
AT THE CLARENDON PRESS
1945

OXFORD UNIVERSITY PRESS
AMEN HOUSE, E.C. 4
London Edinburgh Glasgow New York
Toronto Melbourne Capetown Bombay
Calcutta Madras
HUMPHREY MILFORD
PUBLISHER TO THE UNIVERSITY

PRINTED IN GREAT BRITAIN

PREFACE

THIS book is a tribute to David Nichol Smith, Merton Professor of English Literature in the University of Oxford. It was planned and prepared in bad times, and the names of many who would wish to have been associated with it are missing from the table of contents. The absence of any contributors from the Dominions and from France is particularly to be regretted. But Harvard and Yale are here as well as Oxford; the Huntington Library, Smith College, and Columbia as well as Durham, Reading, and London. It is the privilege of the University of Oxford to attract students and scholars from all parts of the world; and there can be few who have gone there in the past thirty-five years to read English who have not reason to remember the name of Nichol Smith with gratitude and affection, whether they have come to know him in the Schools or the Bodleian, in generous converse at Merton College, or in the hospitable house and book-lined study at 20 Merton Street. A journey abroad by such a man is like a triumphal progress, with a friend and pupil to welcome him in every place of learning. This book, incomplete as it may be, is yet a witness to the truth of Bacon's remark that there cannot but be a noble and generous brotherhood contracted among men by learning and illumination.

It is right to offer to David Nichol Smith a book of essays on the eighteenth century. The list of his writings shows indeed that he has written on English and French literature before Dryden and after Johnson, but from his student days at Edinburgh and the Sorbonne his main interest has been in the ages of Dryden, Swift and Pope, and Johnson. First in the University of Glasgow, then in Armstrong (now King's) College, Newcastle, and (since 1908) in Oxford, he has expounded the merits of eighteenth-century literature even when it was not fashionable to do so. There was a time when his seemed to be almost the only voice insisting that 'if Pope be not a poet, where is poetry to be found?' Perhaps he has been a little surprised, and sometimes a little dismayed, that his favourite studies and authors should have become the vogue, for there is no man whose nature is more free from display and affectation. But in fashion or out of it he has proclaimed the

truth about the eighteenth century as he saw it with a judgement and knowledge upon which those who know him or his
work have come to depend. This book will not be worthy of
its aim if it does not help its readers to know more about the
eighteenth century than they did.

'What should books teach but the art of living?' The
eighteenth century has indeed become a part of him. What was
innate and what has been acquired it would be hard to say: but
certainly his preference for sense rather than nonsense, his
care for ease and perspicuity in all that he has written, his love
of good conversation (prolonged to any hour if it is good
enough), his Johnsonian fondness for biographical study and
for finding the man behind the book, his reluctance (faint
but unmistakable and equally Johnsonian) to let the Whig
dogs have the best of it, his sympathy with the manlier virtues
in life and literature, and, above all, his judicious summing up of
books and of men, all remind us of the eighteenth century. His
own exacting scholarship is of a later age, but in its unobtru-
siveness and its good taste it carries us back again to an earlier
day.

From Frontispiece to Index this book is the work of his
friends. There are not many of them who have not had occasion to acknowledge their debt to him in their published
writings, for few scholars have spent their time so generously
and so effectively in assisting the work of others. Yet the books
which mention his name, many as they are, are but a few of
those which have been clarified by his candid scrutiny. If
during the last thirty or forty years the Clarendon Press has
earned an enviable reputation as the publisher of works on
English literature and of editions of the English classics, it
owes that reputation to no one man more than to him. It is,
then, altogether fitting that the imprint 'Oxford At the Clarendon Press' should appear on the title-page, and that the
Delegates of the Press together with their Secretary and the
Printer and Publisher to the University should join with
artist and writers in honouring the seventieth birthday of
David Nichol Smith.

J. S.
F. P. W.

CONTENTS

ADDISON

C. S. LEWIS

'I HAVE always', said Addison, 'preferred cheerfulness to mirth. The latter I consider as an act, the former as an habit of the mind';[1] or again, 'Though I am always serious, I do not know what it is to be melancholy.'[2] These sentences pretty well give us the measure, if not of the man, yet of the work; just as the limpidity of their style, conveying a distinction of almost scholastic precision in such manner that even a 'tea-table' could not fail to understand it, gives us the measure of his talent. They serve also to mark the most profound difference between the Whig essayist and his two great Tory contemporaries.

Swift and Pope were by no means always serious and they knew very well what it was to be melancholy. One would have found more mirth in their conversation than in Addison's: not only epigram and repartee, but frolic and extravaganza—even buffoonery. It is true that they regarded satire as a 'sacred weapon', but we must not so concentrate on that idea as to forget the sheer *vis comica* which brightens so much of their work. Swift's 'favourite maxim was *vive la bagatelle*'.[3] *Gulliver* and the *Dunciad* and the whole myth of Scriblerus have missed their point if they do not sometimes make us 'laugh and shake in Rabelais' easy chair'. Even their love of filth is, in my opinion, much better understood by schoolboys than by psychoanalysts: if there is something sinister in it, there is also an element of high-spirited rowdiness. Addison has a sense of humour; the Tories have, in addition, a sense of fun. But they have no 'habit' of cheerfulness. Rage, exasperation, and something like despair are never far away. It is to this that they owe their sublimity— for Pope, no less than Swift, can be sublime. We suspect that the picture he paints of himself is historically false—

> Yes, I am proud; I must be proud to see
> Men not afraid of God, afraid of me.

But it is a sublime poetical image. The picture of surly, contemptuous virtue had often been attempted before—in Chapman's Bussy and Clermont, in Dryden's Almanzor, in Wycherley's Manly, even in the Christ of *Paradise Regained*; but I would

---

[1] *Spectator*, 381. [2] Ibid. 26. [3] Johnson, *Life of Swift*.

give Pope the palm, for in Milton the discrepancy between
the known historical character of his Hero and the 'Senecal
man' he has painted is more shocking than that between the real
and the imagined Pope. There is nothing of so high a reach
in Addison. The grandeur of 'cynical asperity' is a flower
that grows only in a tropical climate, and in passing to
Addison's world we pass to a world where such things are impossible. Surly virtue is not cheerful nor equable: in the long
run it is not, perhaps, perfectly consistent with good sense.

This contrast between Addison and the Tories comes out
with special clarity in their treatment of enemies. For the Tories,
every enemy—whether it be the Duchess of Marlborough or
only a Shakespearian editor found guilty of some real English
scholarship—becomes a grotesque. All who have, in whatever
fashion, incurred their ill will are knaves, scarecrows, whores,
bugs, toads, bedlamites, yahoos; Addison himself a smooth
Mephistopheles. It is good fun, but it is certainly not good sense;
we laugh, and disbelieve. Now mark Addison's procedure.
The strength of the Tory party is the smaller country gentry
with their Jacobite leanings and their opposition to the moneyed
interest. All the material for savage satire is there. Addison
might have anticipated Squire Western (as he did later in the
Freeholder) and painted merely the block-headed, fox-hunting
sot, the tyrant of his family and his village. Instead, with the
help of Steele, he invents Sir Roger de Coverley. The measure
of his success is that we can now think of Sir Roger for a long
time without remembering his Toryism; when we do remember
it, it is only as a lovable whimsy.

In all our journey from London to his house, we did not so much
as bait at a Whig inn. This often betrayed us into hard beds and
bad cheer; for we were not so inquisitive about the inn as the inn-
keeper; and provided our landlord's principles were sound, did not
take any notice of the staleness of his provisions.

As a natural consequence, Mr. Spectator soon 'dreaded entering
into an house of any one that Sir Roger had applauded for an
honest man'.[1] It is so beautifully done that we do not notice it.
The enemy, far from being vilified, is being turned into a dear
old man. The thought that he could ever be dangerous has been
erased from our minds; but so also the thought that anything
he said could ever be taken seriously. We all love Sir Roger;

[1] *Spectator*, 126.

but of course we do not really attend to him as we do—well, to Sir Andrew Freeport. All through the century which Addison ushered in, England was going to attend more and more seriously to the Freeports, and the de Coverleys were to be more and more effectually silenced. The figure of the dear old squire dominates—possibly, on some views, corrupts—the national imagination to the present day. This is indeed to 'make a man die sweetly'. That element in English society which stood against all that Addison's party was bringing in is henceforth seen through a mist of smiling tenderness—as an archaism, a lovely absurdity. What we might have been urged to attack as a fortress we are tricked into admiring as a ruin.

When I say 'tricked' I am not implying that Steele and Addison calculated the whole effect of their creation just as I have set it down. The actual upshot of their work is obvious; their conscious intentions are another matter. I am inclined to think that Addison really loved Sir Roger—with that 'superior love' which, in England, the victorious party so easily accords to the remnants of a vanishing order. Addison is not a simple man; he is, in the older sense of the word, 'sly'. I do not believe for one moment that he was the fiendlike Atticus; but one sees how inevitably he must have appeared so to the losers. He is so cool, so infuriatingly sensible, and yet he effects more than they. A satiric portrait by Pope or Swift is like a thunderclap; the Addisonian method is more like the slow operations of ordinary nature, loosening stones, blunting outlines, modifying a whole landscape with 'silent overgrowings' so that the change can never quite be reversed again. Whatever his intentions, his reasonableness and amiability (both cheerful 'habits' of the mind) are stronger in the end than the Tory spleen. To rail is the sad privilege of the loser.

I have used the word 'amiability'. Should we go further and say 'charity'? I feel that this Christian word, with its doctrinal implications, would be a little out of place when we are speaking of Addison's essays. About the man, as distinct from the work, I will not speculate. Let us hope that he practised this theological virtue. The story that he summoned Lord Warwick to his deathbed *to see how a Christian can die* is ambiguous; it can be taken either as evidence of his Christianity or as a very brimstone proof of the reverse. I give no vote: my concern is with books. And the essays do not invite criticism in terms of any very definite theology. They are everywhere 'pious'. Rational Piety, together with Polite Letters and Simplicity, is one of the hallmarks of the age which Addison was partly interpreting but partly also bringing into existence. And Rational Piety is by its very nature not very doctrinal. This is one of the many ways in which Addison is historically momentous. He ushers in that period—it is just now drawing to a close—in which it is possible to talk of 'piety' or (later) 'religion' almost in the abstract; in which the contrast is no longer between Christian and Pagan, the elect and the world, orthodox and heretic, but between 'religious' and 'irreligious'. The transition cannot be quite defined: absence of doctrine would have to become itself doctrinal for that to be possible. It is a change of atmosphere, which every reader of sensibility will feel if he passes suddenly from the literature of any earlier period to that of the eighteenth century. Hard rocks of Calvinism show up amidst the seemingly innocuous surface of an *Arcadia* or a *Faerie Queene*; Shakespearian comedy reckons on an audience who will at once see the point of jokes about the controversy on Works and Faith. Here also, no doubt, it is difficult to bring Addison to a point. Perhaps the most illuminating passage is the essay on 'Sir Roger at Church', and specially the quotation from Pythagoras prefixed to it—'Honour first the immortal gods according to the established mode.'[1] That is the very note of Rational Piety. A sensible man goes with his society, according to local and ancestral usage. And he does so with complete sincerity. Clean clothes and the sound of bells on Sunday morning do really throw him into a mood of sober benevolence, not 'clouded by enthusiasm' but inviting his thoughts to approach the mystery of things.

In this matter of Rational Piety one must not draw too sharp a contrast between Addison and the Tories. They are infected with it themselves, and Swift quotes with equal approval the Pagan maxim about worshipping 'according to the laws of the country'.[2] But I think there is *some* contrast. The Tories are a little nearer than Addison to the old period with its uncompromising creeds. Pope's Romanism is not nearly so superficial as some have supposed, and the 'Pantheism' of the *Essay on Man* owes a good deal of its notoriety to critics who would make a very poor shape at defining pantheism. He made an edifying end, and he perhaps understands the conflict in Eloise's mind—

[1] *Spectator*, 112.   [2] *Sentiments of a Church of England Man.*

it is not simply a conflict of virtue and vice—better than Addison would have done. Swift is harder to classify. There is, to be sure, no doubt of his churchmanship, only of his Christianity, and this, of itself, is significant. If Swift were (as I do not think he is) primarily a Church of England man, only secondly a Christian, and not 'pious' or 'religious' at all, we might say that in Addison's writings the proportions are reversed. And some things would lend colour to such an interpretation of Swift. In the *Sentiments* his religion seems to be purely political. 'I leave it among the divines to dilate upon the danger of schism, as a spiritual evil, but I would consider it only as a temporal one.'[1] Separation from the established worship, 'though to a new one that is more pure and perfect', is dangerous.[2] More disquieting still are the tormented aphorisms of *Thoughts on Religion*. To change fundamental opinions is ordinarily wicked 'whether those opinions be true or false', and 'The want of belief is a defect that ought to be concealed when it cannot be overcome'.[2] Some parts of *Gulliver* seem inconsistent with any religion—except perhaps Buddhism. The *Further Thoughts on Religion* open with the assertion that the Mosaic account of creation is 'most agreeable of all other to probability' and immediately cite—the making of Eve out of Adam's rib![3] Is it possible that this should not be irony? And yet there is much to set on the other side. His priestly duties were discharged with a fidelity rare in that age. The ferocity of the later *Gulliver* all works up to that devastating attack on Pride which is more specifically Christian than any other piece of ethical writing in the century, if we except William Law. The prayers offered at Stella's deathbed have a scholastic firmness in their implied moral theology. ('Keep her from both the sad extremes of presumption and despair.' 'Forgive the sorrow and weakness of those among us who sink under the grief and terror of losing so dear and useful a friend.') The sermon 'On the Trinity', taken at its face value, preaches a submission of the reason to dogma which ought to satisfy the sternest supernaturalist. And I think it should be taken at its face value. If we ever think otherwise, I believe the explanation to lie in that peculiar ungraciousness which Swift exercised upwards as well as downwards. He gave alms 'without tenderness or civility', so that 'those who were fed by him could hardly love

[1] *Sentiments of a Church of England Man.*   [2] Ibid.
[3] *Further Thoughts on Religion.*

him'.[1] As below, so above. He practises obedience without humility or meekness, takes his medicine with a wry face. But the alms, however given, were hard cash, and I think his acceptance of Christian doctrine is equally real, though offered (as it were) under protest, as if he were resentful of Heaven for putting him in such a ridiculous position. There is a tension and discomfort about all this, but that very tension suggests depths that Addison never knew. It is from those depths that Swift is writing when he says there can be no question in England of any but a nominal Christianity—'the other having been for some time wholly laid aside by general consent as utterly inconsistent with our present schemes of wealth and power'.[2] This is a far cry from Mr. Spectator's pleasing reflections on the Royal Exchange.

As I am a great lover of mankind, my heart naturally overflows with pleasure at the sight of a happy and prosperous multitude, insomuch that at many public solemnities I cannot forbear expressing my joy with tears that have stolen down my cheeks. For this reason I am wonderfully delighted to see such a body of men thriving in their own private fortunes, and at the same time promoting the public stock; or, in other words, raising estates for their own families, by bringing into their country whatever is wanting, and carrying out of it whatever is superfluous.[3]

Compared with this, Swift's remark is like a scorching wind from the hermitages of the Thebaid.

Addison is never blasphemous or irreverent; Swift can be both. That, I think, helps to confirm the kind of distinction I am drawing between them. Swift still belongs, at any rate in part, to the older world. He would have understood Rochester in both Rochester's phases better than he could understand Addison. Rochester unconverted was a Bad Man of the old, thoroughgoing kind,

> he drunk, he fought, he whored,
> He did despite unto the Lord.

Rochester converted was a deathbed penitent. One cannot imagine Mr. Spectator or Sir Andrew emulating him in either achievement.

The mention of Rochester suggests yet another gulf between Addison and the preceding age. We may be sure that Rochester's manners lacked that 'simplicity' which the Whig essayists recom-

---

[1] Johnson, *Life of Swift.*   [2] *Argument against abolishing Christianity.*
[3] *Spectator*, 69.

mended. It is, of course, a commonplace that they addressed
themselves to the reform of manners; but I sometimes wonder
whether the very degree of their success does not conceal from us
the greatness of the undertaking. I sometimes catch myself
taking it for granted that the marks of good breeding were in
all ages the same as they are to-day—that swagger was always
vulgar, that a low voice, an unpretentious manner, a show
(however superficial) of self-effacement, were always demanded.
But it is almost certainly false. We catch a glimpse of the truth
in Johnson's remark: 'Lord Southwell was the highest bred man
without insolence that I ever was in company with. . . . Lord
Orrery was not dignified; Lord Chesterfield was, but he was
insolent.'[1] Insolence, for us, is a characteristic of the 'beggar on
horseback', a mark of ill breeding; we have little idea of the
genuine 'high' manners that bordered on it. We catch another
glimpse in Polonius's advice, 'Costly thy habit as thy purse can
buy', and again in Hotspur's humorous indignation at the
'sarcenet' insipidity of his wife's oaths. We perceive from many
scenes of Elizabethan comedy and from the stir among the
servants at Gawain's arrival in the *Green Knight* that the old
courtesy was not a 'pass school' (as it is with us where a man
either knows the right thing to do or not) but an 'honours school'
where competing extravagances of decorum and compliment
could go to any height. I am inclined to think that if we saw it
now we should mistake that high breeding for no breeding at all.
The walk of the courtier would seem to us a Janissary's strut, his
readiness to find quarrel in a straw would seem a yokel touchi-
ness, his clothes an intolerable ostentation. Even to this day,
when we meet foreigners (only think of some *young* Frenchmen)
who have not been subjected to the Addisonian 'reform', we
have to 'make allowances' for them. I do not suggest that
Addison and Steele, simply by writing essays, abolished the old
flamboyancy. Doubtless they gave expression to a tendency
which would have existed even without them. But to express
is partly to mould. That sober code of manners under which we
still live to-day, in so far as we have any code at all, and which
foreigners call hypocrisy, is in some important degree a legacy
from the *Tatler* and the *Spectator*. It is certainly not to be explained as a mere imposition of the code of the citizens upon the
gentry. No one denies that a *rapprochement* between the 'cit' and

[1] Boswell, 23 March 1783.

the courtier was an essential part of the Addisonian synthesis.
Sir Andrew Freeport mixes with those whose grandfather would
have regarded his grandfather simply as a 'cuckoldand'. But
the shop and the counting-house are not of themselves schools
of modest and obliging deportment: least of all when they are
prosperous. There was real novelty in the new manners.

These new manners were a little restrictive; in adopting them
we lost, along with some cruelties and absurdities, a good deal
of 'the unbought grace of life'. But in other respects Addison is a
liberator. His famous defence of 'Chevy Chase' is sometimes
taken to show a 'romantic' side in him, but that, I think, is
not the best way of considering it. The word 'romantic' is
always ambiguous. The paper on 'Chevy Chase' is to be taken
in its context. It follows a discussion on False Wit. False Wit
is taken up by poets who lack the 'strength of genius' which
gives 'majestic simplicity to Nature' and who are therefore
forced 'to hunt after foreign ornaments'. These writers are to
poetry what the Goths were to architecture. Ovid is the type of
such 'Gothic' poets, and 'the taste of most of our English poets,
as well as readers, is extremely Gothic'.[1] One mark of true
poetry is that it 'pleases all kinds of palates', whereas the Gothic
manner pleases 'only such as have formed to themselves a wrong
artificial taste upon little fanciful authors'.[2] It is, therefore, to be
expected that common songs or ballads which are 'the delight of
the common people' should be 'paintings of Nature'.[2] It is after
this preamble that Addison proceeds to examine 'Chevy Chase'
—according to the rules of Le Bossu—and pronounces in its
favour.

No more classical piece of criticism exists. In it Addison
touches hands with Scaliger on the one side and Matthew
Arnold on the other. What complicates it is, of course, his peculiar use of the word 'Gothic'. Addison must have known perfectly
well that the ballad is just the sort of thing to which his contemporaries would spontaneously have applied that word, and
that Ovid and Cowley are not. Very well, then; he will prove
that it is the ballad which really follows Nature and that the
true Goths are the authors whom the Town in fact prefers. In
other words he is calling the neo-classical bluff. It is as if he
said, 'You all profess to like a great subject, a good moral, unity
of action, and truth to Nature. Well, here they all are in the

[1] *Spectator*, 62.   [2] Ibid. 70.

ballad which you despise; and yonder, in the Cowley which you really enjoy, they are not.' One cannot be certain here, as one could not be certain about the invention of Sir Roger, whether Addison is being 'sly' or really innocent. One sees again what is behind the image of Atticus. The man who writes thus will certainly appear 'sly' to his opponents. But is he consciously setting a trap, or is he merely following the truth as he sees it in all simplicity? Perhaps it does not much matter, for the trap is inherent in the facts, and works whether Addison meant to set it or no; in the sense that if the *nominal* standards of Augustan criticism are ever taken seriously they must work out in favour of the ballads (and much medieval literature) and against most of the poetry the Augustans themselves produced. In other words, if we insist on calling an appreciation of ballads 'romantic', then we must say that Addison becomes a romantic precisely because he is a *real* classic, and that every real classic must infallibly do the same. It is inconceivable that Aristotle and Horace, had they known them, should not have put the *Chanson de Roland* above the *Davideis*. Antiquity and the Middle Ages are not divided from each other by any such chasm as divides both from the Renaissance.

But it is better not to use the word 'romantic' in this context at all. What Addison really shows by his appreciation of the Ballad is his open-mindedness, his readiness to recognize excellence wherever he finds it, whether in those periods which Renaissance Humanism had elected to call 'classical' or in those far longer extents of time which it ignored. The obscurantism of the Humanists is still not fully recognized. Learning to them meant the knowledge and imitation of a few rather arbitrarily selected Latin authors and some even fewer Greek authors. They despised metaphysics and natural science; and they despised all the past outside the favoured periods. They were dominated by a narrowly ethical purpose. 'Referenda ad mores omnia', said Vives;[1] and he thought it fortunate that the Attic dialect contained nearly all the Greek worth reading—'reliquis utuntur auctores carminum quos non tanti est intelligi'.[2] Their philistine attitude to metaphysics is prettily carried off in modern histories by phrases about 'brushing away scholastic cobwebs', but the Humanist attack is really on metaphysics itself. In Erasmus, in Rabelais, in the *Utopia* one recognizes the

[1] *De Tradendis Disciplinis*, iv. [2] Ibid. iii.

very accent of the angry *belle-lettrist* railing, as he rails in all ages,
at 'jargon' and 'straw-splitting'. On this side Pope and Swift
are true inheritors of the Humanist tradition. It is easy, of
course, to say that Laputa is an attack not on science but on
the aberrations of science. I am not convinced. The learning
of the Brobdingnagians and the Horses is ruthlessly limited.
Nothing that cannot plead the clearest immediate utility—
nothing that cannot make two blades of grass grow where one
grew before—wins any approval from Swift. Bentley is not forgiven for knowing more Greek than Temple, nor Theobald for
knowing more English than Pope. Most of the history of
Europe is a mere wilderness, not worth visiting, in which 'the
monks finished what the Goths begun'.[1] The terror expressed
at the end of the *Dunciad* is not wholly terror at the approach
of ignorance: it is also terror lest the compact little fortress of
Humanism should be destroyed, and new knowledge is one of
the enemies. Whatever is not immediately intelligible to a man
versed in the Latin and French classics appears to them to be
charlatanism or barbarity. The number of things they do not
want to hear about is enormous.

But Addison wants to hear about everything. He is quite as
good a classical scholar as the Tories but he does not live in
the Humanist prison. He notes with satisfaction 'that curiosity
is one of the strongest and most lasting appetites implanted in us,
and that admiration is one of our most pleasing passions'.[2] He
delights to introduce his readers to the new philosophy of Mr.
Locke and to explain by it, with aid from Malebranche, 'a
famous passage in the Alcoran'.[3] He remembers with pleasure
how 'Mr. Boyle, speaking of a certain mineral, tells us that a
man may consume his whole life in the study of it, without
arriving at the knowledge of all its qualities.'[4] He gazes on the
sea ('the heaving of this prodigious bulk of waters') with 'a very
pleasing astonishment'.[5] Astronomy, revealing the immensities
of space, entertains him with sublime meditations,[6] and his
reading, he tells us, 'has very much lain among books of natural
history'.[7] Mysteries attract him. He loves to lose himself in an
o altitudo whether on the marvels of animal instinct[8] or on those
of the powers enjoyed by the soul in dreams—on which he

[1] *Essay on Criticism*, l. 692.   [2] *Spectator*, 237.   [3] Ibid. 98.
[4] Ibid. 94.   [5] Ibid. 489.   [6] Ibid. 565.
[7] Ibid. 120.   [8] Ibid.

quotes Browne himself.[1] He lives habitually in a world of
horizons and possibilities which Pope touched, I think, only
in the *Essay on Man*, and Swift hardly touches at all. It is a cool,
quiet world after that of the Tories—say, a water-colour world,
but there is more room in it. On those things which it illuminates at all, the wit of Swift and Pope casts a sharper and (in
a sense) more beautiful light; but what huge regions of reality
appear to them, as Addison says that life itself appears to
ignorance and folly, a 'prospect of naked hills and plains which
produce nothing either profitable or ornamental'![2]

This open-mindedness is not particularly 'romantic', though
without it we should have had no Wartons, no Ritson, no Percy,
and perhaps no Scott; for the medievalism of the eighteenth
century, whatever else it may be, is a mighty defeat of sheer
ignorance. But Addison is much more closely connected with
the Romantic Movement in quite a different way. He stands
at the very turning-point in the history of a certain mode of
feeling.

I think that perhaps the best piece of criticism Raleigh ever
wrote is in the fourth chapter of his *Wordsworth*, where he sets
Claudio's shuddering speech ('To be imprisoned in the viewless
winds') beside Wordsworth's longing to retain a body 'endued
with all the nice regards of flesh and blood' and yet surrender
it to the elements 'as if it were a spirit'. He points out, quite
justly, that what is Hell to Claudio is almost Heaven to Wordsworth. Between the two passages a profound change in human
sentiment has taken place. Briefly put—for the story has often
been told before—it is the change from an age when men
frankly hated and feared all those things in Nature which are
neither sensuously pleasing, useful, safe, symmetrical, or gaily
coloured, to an age when men love and actually seek out
mountains, waste places, dark forests, cataracts, and storm-
beaten coasts. What was once the ugly has become a department (even the major department) of the beautiful. The first
conflict between the old and the new taste received striking
expression when Addison was already nine years old, in Thomas
Burnet's *Telluris Theoria Sacra*. Burnet cannot quite conceal a
certain joy in the awfulness of the Alps, but his very argument
depends on the conception that they are deformities—*longaeva
illa, tristia et squalentia corpora*.[3] Not that they are the only offence.

---

[1] *Spectator*, 487.   [2] Ibid. 94.   [3] *Telluris Theoria Sacra*, I. ix.

In the face of this Earth as a whole we find *multa superflua, multa inelegantia*: such beauty (*ornamentum*) as it possesses comes chiefly *cultu et habitatione hominum.*[1]

The position of Addison in this story is very interesting. He divides the sources of imaginative pleasure into three classes—the Great, the Uncommon, and the Beautiful. As specimens of the Great he mentions 'an open champaign country, a vast un-cultivated desert, huge heaps of mountains, high rocks and precipices, or a wide expanse of waters'—all of which produce 'a delightful stillness and amazement in the soul'.[2] To a later writer many of these things would have seemed beautiful; to an earlier one they would have seemed simply unpleasant. Addison does not find beauty in them, but he includes them among the sources of pleasure. His category of the Great, clearly distinguished from the Beautiful, exists precisely to make room for them. A similar distinction was, of course, the basis of Burke's treatise on *The Sublime and Beautiful*, and dominated the aesthetic thought of the century. Whether it was not much more sensible than the modern practice of bundling Alps and roses together into the single category of Beauty, I do not here inquire. The interesting thing is that Addison stands exactly at the turn of the tide.

Equally important for the historian of taste is *Spectator*, No. 160, where he contrasts the original 'genius' (which tends to be 'nobly wild and extravagant') and the *Bel Esprit* 'refined by conversation, reflection, and the reading of the most polite authors'. The taste for 'noble extravagance' is not itself a novelty, for audacities in art and graces that overleap the rules are praised by Dryden, Boileau, and Pope. What is interesting is Addison's belief that even the greatest genius is 'broken' by the rules and in becoming learned 'falls unavoidably into imita-tion'. This pessimistic view of culture as something naturally opposed to genius received, no doubt, its extreme expression in Macaulay's essay on Milton; but I think it had also a great deal to do with that crop of forgeries which the eighteenth cen-tury produced. If sublime genius lies all in the past, before civilization began, we naturally look for it in the past. We long to recover the work of those sublime prehistoric bards and druids who *must* have existed. But their work is not to be found; and the surviving medieval literature conspicuously lacks the sublimity

---

[1] *Telluris Theoria Sacra*, I. x.   [2] *Spectator*, 412.

and mysteriousness we desire. In the end one begins *inventing* what the 'bards', 'druids', and 'minstrels' ought to have written. Ossian, Rowley, and *Otranto* are wish-fulfilments. It is always to be remembered that Macpherson had written original epics about prehistoric Scotland before he invented Ossian. By a tragic chance he and Chatterton discovered that their work was marketable, and so make-believe turned into fraud. But there was a sincere impulse behind it: they were seeking in the past that great romantic poetry which really lay in the future, and from intense imagination of what it must be like if only they could find it they slipped into making it themselves.

So far I have been trying to obey Arnold's precept—to get myself out of the way and let humanity decide. I have not attempted to assess the value of Addison's work, having wished rather to bring out its immense potency. He appears to be (as far as any individual can be) the source of a quite astonishing number of mental habits which were still prevalent when men now living were born. Almost everything which my own generation ignorantly called Victorian seems to have been expressed by Addison. It is all there in the *Spectator*—the vague religious sensibility, the insistence on what came later to be called Good Form, the playful condescension towards women, the untroubled belief in the beneficence of commerce, the comfortable sense of security which, far from excluding, perhaps renders possible the romantic relish for wildness and solitude. If he is not at present the most hated of our writers, that can only be because he is so little read. Everything the moderns detest, all that they call *smugness*, *complacency*, and *bourgeois ideology*, is brought together in his work and given its most perfect expression.

And certainly, if it were at all times true that the Good is the enemy of the Best, it would be hard to defend Addison. His Rational Piety, his smiling indulgence to 'the fair sex', his small idealisms about trade, certainly fall short of actual Christianity, and plain justice to women, and true political wisdom. They may even be obstacles to them; palliatives and anodynes that prolong the disease. In some moods I cannot help seeing Addison as one who, at every point, 'sings charms to ills that ask the knife'. I believe he could defend himself. He is not attempting to write sermons or philosophy, only essays; and he certainly could not foresee what the search for markets would finally make of international trade. These hostile criticisms,

made on the basis of our modern experience when all issues have
become sharper, cannot really be maintained. All we can
justly say is that his essays are rather small beer; there is no iron
in them as in Johnson; they do not stir the depths.

And yet, if I were to live in a man's house for a whole twelve-
month, I think I should be more curious about the quality of his
small beer than about that of his wine; more curious about his
bread and butter and beef than about either. Writers like Addison
who stand on the common ground of daily life and deal only
with middle things are unduly depreciated to-day. Pascal says
somewhere that the cardinal error of Stoicism was to suppose
that we can do always what we do sometimes. No one lives
always on the stretch. Hence one of the most pertinent questions to be asked about any man is what he falls back on. The
important thing about Malory's world, for example, is that
when you fall back from the quest of the Grail you fall back into
the middle world of Arthur's court: not plumb down into the
level of King Mark. The important thing about many fierce
idealists in our own day is that when the political meeting or
the literary movement can be endured no longer they fall
plumb down to the cinema and the dance band. I fully admit
that when Pope and Swift are on the heights they have a
strength and splendour which makes everything in Addison
look pale; but what an abyss of hatred and bigotry and even
silliness receives them when they slip from the heights! The
Addisonian world is not one to live in at all times, but it is a
good one to fall back into when the day's work is over and a
man's feet on the fender and his pipe in his mouth. Good sense
is no substitute for Reason; but as a rest from Reason it has
distinct advantages over Jargon. I do not think Addison's
popularity is likely to return; but something to fill the same
place in life will always be needed—some tranquil middle
ground of quiet sentiments and pleasing melancholies and gentle
humour to come in between our restless idealisms and our
equally restless dissipations. Do we not after all detect in the
charge of *smugness* and *complacency* the note of envy? Addison
is, above all else, comfortable. He is not on that account to be
condemned. He is an admirable cure for the fidgets.

THE CONCISENESS OF SWIFT

HERBERT DAVIS

LORD ORRERY was, I think, the first to draw attention to one of the most obvious marks of Swift's style: 'If we consider his prose works, we shall find a certain masterly conciseness in their style, that has never been equalled by any other writer.' In reply to a critic who had said that to judge from the rest of his argument he must really have meant to say correctness, not conciseness, he wrote in one of the interleaved copies of his *Remarks*, now in the Harvard library:

I am afraid that in this Instance I am vulnerable. *Correctness* would be a better word, in this place, although the conciseness of Swift's Style is very remarkable. . . . I may boldly answer, that *Swift* is in many places as easy and delicate as *Addison*, as grave and majestic as *Tillotson*, but neither *Tillotson* nor *Addison* are in any part of their works as concise as *Swift*.

If, as I suppose, no one would dispute this, it might be useful to extend this comparison further in order to discover whether there is anyone among Swift's friends or contemporaries who is as concise as he is. Certainly not Arbuthnot or Gay, or even Pope, when he writes in prose, though Swift himself remarks upon the conciseness of Pope's verse, and envies him for it:

> When he can in one Couplet fix
> More sense than I can do in six.

Certainly not Bolingbroke or Pulteney, though he complains that they drove him out of date by the vigour of their political writings. Certainly not any of his circle of Irish friends, though they tried to imitate him and sometimes succeeded in passing off their imitations as his work. Is it possible then that this quality is so remarkable in all his work that it may be recognized and used as evidence of his hand?

In attempting to separate Swift's authentic work from the large mass of doubtful material that has at one time or another been attributed to him, it is dangerous to make any conjectures which depend on internal evidence of style alone. But when we have reason to suspect an attribution, because it was never acknowledged by Swift or reprinted in any edition in his lifetime, or because doubt has been expressed by his friends or

earliest editors, it may be well to examine such a work carefully
and try to decide whether he could have written it or not. We
may possibly find something that would be enough to turn the
scale.

I doubt whether it would ever be safe to assume that we could
isolate a certain quality of biting humour or of irony, and say,
this must be Swift's. For we know that many papers were
printed by the booksellers as his on such grounds, and con-
temptuously rejected by him. And I doubt also whether we
can find any particular mannerisms or tricks of phrase in his
work so individual that they would give him away. His style is
never mannered, and it is well to remember that even Stella and
his friends in Dublin were never quite sure about his contributions to the *Tatler* and the *Examiner*, or even his separate political
tracts written in London during the Queen's reign. Swift delighted to mislead them; but then, and much more emphatically
later on, he seemed to expect that his friends ought to be able
to recognize clearly that there were certain things which he
could not have written, certain limits which they should know
he could never be guilty of crossing. And likewise he would
expect his editors and critics to-day to be sure that even in his
most careless moments or in his lightest and most trivial mood
he could never have written such sloppy, slovenly stuff as some
of the papers still included among his works, or those paragraphs
in *Gulliver's Travels* which were inserted in the earliest editions
'contrary to the Author's manner and style and intention'.

Others among his friends and enemies could write political
satires with biting power; others could use the weapons of
raillery and irony with success; others could be humorous and
sceptical in their formal sermons or their essays and letters; and
others could use plain simple language, and avoid technical
jargon and learned terms. But in all these different forms of
writing, and even in his most hurried as well as in his most
deliberate work, I shall try to show that Swift is a master of conciseness, unequalled and unmistakable by reason of that quality
alone, which gives a flavour as of salt to all his work, and preserves it from certain levels of dullness, banality, or mere im-
poverishment of style liable to appear in the writings of all his
contemporaries.

I use the term 'conciseness' not quite as Ben Jonson used it to
describe the style 'which expresseth not enough, but leaves

somewhat to be understood', though that is perhaps the reason why we feel in Swift a strength and force lacking in other plain writers. He leaves somewhat to be understood. But I use the term rather as Dryden used it, when he spoke of 'the conciseness of Demosthenes', quoting the remark of Speroni, the Italian wit, that Tully wished to achieve the copiousness of Homer, and Virgil the conciseness of Demosthenes. It will be remembered that Swift compares the art of Demosthenes and Cicero in his *Letter to a Young Clergyman*, recommending the former, with whom most divines were less conversant, as the more excellent orator. And he draws attention to the chief purpose of their oratory, 'to drive some one particular Point, according as the Oratory on either Side prevailed'. Swift's experience as a political journalist had formed his style and made it rigorously functional, because he had learned in that school similarly to be concerned 'to drive some one particular point' for the immediate purpose of supporting or opposing some definite course of action. He never deviated from this particular purpose, never allowed himself to hesitate, to make qualifications or concessions.

After *A Tale of a Tub* was put behind him, he rarely permitted himself to indulge his humour or his literary skill in parody or raillery or any of the tricks of his trade for his amusement only. His irresponsible play was almost entirely limited to verse and the various bagatelles in which the little group of Dublin friends engaged for sport. In his satires and sermons and political tracts he was careful never to spoil the immediate effect he wanted by any display of 'learning or oratory or politeness'. He speaks from his own experience when he says so confidently in 1720:

When a Man's Thoughts are clear, the properest Words will generally offer themselves first; and his own Judgment will direct him in what Order to place them, so as they may be best understood.

Then he adds a sentence which is a complete revelation of himself, an artist and master of his craft, recognizing the quality of perfect work, but valuing it only as it performs a useful function:

In short, that Simplicity, without which no human Performance can arrive to any great Perfection, is no where more eminently useful than in this.

Though Addison with his ease and delicacy also attains a perfection of simplicity, his writing can be differentiated from Swift's, because he is never quite so concise, never quite so rigorously and exclusively concerned with making his point. This may be clearly seen if we compare a passage from one of Addison's Saturday papers, written for the *Tatler*, 17 December 1709, with Swift's use of the same theme in the *Intelligencer*, No. 9. Addison writes in a mood almost of reminiscence, as he tries to convey to us the opportunities for pleasure and profit through a proper commerce with men and books:

I must confess, there is nothing that more pleases me, in all that I read in Books, or see among Mankind, than such Passages as represent humane Nature in its proper Dignity. As Man is a Creature made up of different Extremes, he has something in him very great and very mean: A skilful Artist may draw an excellent Picture of him in either of these Views. The finest Authors of Antiquity have taken him on the more advantagious Side. They cultivate the natural Grandeur of the Soul, raise in her a generous Ambition, feed her with Hopes of Immortality and Perfection, and do all they can to widen the Partition between the Virtuous and the Vicious, by making the Difference betwixt them as great as between Gods and Brutes. In short, it is impossible to read a Page in *Plato*, *Tully*, and a Thousand other ancient Moralists, without being a greater and a better Man for it.

Swift makes of it a weapon to attack the wealthy and the noble for neglecting their sons' education.

The Books read at *Schools* and *Colleges*, are full of Incitements to Virtue and Discouragements from Vice, drawn from the wisest Reasons, the strongest Motives, and the most influencing Examples. Thus, young Minds are filled early with an Inclination to Good, and an Abhorrence of Evil, both which encrease in them, according to the Advances they make in Literature. . . .

The present Scope I would aim at is to prove, that some Proportion of human Knowledge appears requisite to those, who, by their Birth or Fortune, are called to the making of Laws, and in a subordinate Way to the Execution of them; and that such Knowledge is not to be obtained without a Miracle under the frequent, corrupt and sottish Methods, of educating those, who are born to Wealth or Titles. . . .

Swift is rarely content to make an observation, much less to speculate or indulge in 'an amusement of agreeable words', which he always suspects are intended to put false colours upon things and make the worse reason appear to be the better. He writes either to prove or to disprove; to urge some action, or oppose it.

We may follow Orrery a step farther and examine his comparison between the style of Swift and Tillotson. They both mistrusted theological speculation and regarded it as a snare rather than an aid to religion. Tillotson gravely rebukes the 'speculative Christian' who finds the knowledge of religion a good ornament of conversation:

and because he doth not intend to practise it, he passeth over those things which are plain and easie to be understood, and applies himself chiefly to the Consideration of those things which are more abstruse, and will afford matter of Controversie and subtle Dispute, as the Doctrine of the *Trinity*, *Predestination*, *Freewill* and the like.

Swift, however, spurns the whole thing with an almost brutal gesture, using the harshest figure of compulsion by process of law:

I defy the greatest Divine to produce any Law either of God or Man which obliges me to comprehend the meaning of *Omniscience*, *Omnipresence*, *Ubiquity*, *Attribute*, *Beatifick Vision*, &c.

But the most excellent example of Swift's conciseness, in the larger sense of its effect not upon the phrase or the sentence but upon the construction and shape of the whole piece, is his sermon 'On Doing Good', which I shall compare with Tillotson's sermon on the same subject and the same text, preached at Christ Church on Easter Tuesday, 14 April 1691. The text— 'As we have therefore opportunity, let us do good unto all men' —is rather an obvious one for a 'spital sermon'; and Tillotson uses his sermon to introduce a direct appeal for the chief hospitals in the city. It is clearly a sermon with a specific purpose. Nevertheless, it is arranged according to a conventional pattern in which the subject of Doing Good is discussed under five heads—the nature of the Duty, the extent of it, the measure of it, unwearied perseverance in it, and encouragement to it. Each of those is further divided into several sections until the main theme has been drawn out into all its various ramifications, leading up to a final solution to persuade his hearers to the practice of it. It remains a sermon for general edification, with the particular charitable appeal added.

Swift's sermon on the text is, as he termed it himself, a pamphlet against Wood's halfpence. He admits in the course of his sermon that it may perhaps be thought by some that this way of discussing is not so proper from the pulpit. Nevertheless he preaches only good sound ethical doctrine—the importance of the public good, which is a perfectly reasonable interpretation of the text, 'let us do good unto all men'.

Beside this love we owe to every man in his particular capacity under the title of our neighbour, there is yet a duty of a more large, extensive nature, incumbent on us; which is, our love to our neighbour in his public capacity, as he is a member of that great body, the commonwealth, under the same government with ourselves; and this is usually called love of the public. . . .

Therefore, I shall think my time not ill spent, if I can persuade most or all of you who hear me, to shew the love you have for your country, by endeavouring, in your several stations, to do all the public good you are able.

The whole of the sermon is then pointed with great directness at Wood's project. It is short, clear, concise in its whole argument, and no one could at any moment have been mistaken about Swift's intention and the immediate effect he hoped it would have upon his audience. He tells them plainly that it was the consideration of their great danger which led him to discourse on this subject and to exhort them to prefer the public interest before that of one destructive impostor, and a few of his adherents. He admits further that his sermon was intended also to stir up others of the clergy to exhort their congregations to show their love for their country on this important occasion. And in a final superb gesture, with the impunity of the Dean who knows no higher authority, ecclesiastical or lay, within the walls of his own cathedral, he permits himself a momentary glance over the head of the mechanic Wood and his miserable project, challenging and defying the power of his real enemy, the Whig government, with the briefest flash of irony—'And this, I am sure, cannot be called meddling in affairs of state.' Nothing is quite so concise as the conciseness of irony; the meaning is tight-closed, until the reader stays to pick it up and open it. We are left with the question: When should a Dean, when should anyone, meddle with affairs of state? His irony embraces the answer of Demosthenes: 'When all our national interests are imperilled; when the issue lies between the people and their adversaries. Then such is the part of a chivalrous and patriotic citizen.'

There is the same method and the same irony in the sermon, a diatribe against faction and party spirit, which was preached on 29 November 1717, with the title, 'On Brotherly Love'.

It is almost a parody of the conventional sermon in which the subject is carefully divided into three heads: first, the causes of this lack of brotherly love; second, the effects of it; and third, persuasions to continue in it. But the real theme is stated in a preliminary sentence which sums up the whole course of the ecclesiastical history of the Christian Church:

The last Legacy of *Christ* was Peace and mutual Love; but then he foretold that he came to send a Sword upon the Earth: The primitive Christians accepted the Legacy, and their Successors, down to the present Age, have been largely fulfilling his Prophecy.

When that theme is fully exhausted, Swift again reminds us of his text only to confess that he had treated it in a manner much more suited to the present times than to the nature of the subject in general; but again he cannot resist the temptation to make use of an ironical excuse for his conduct by quoting the epistle to the Thessalonians: 'Touching brotherly love ye need not that I write unto you, for ye yourselves are taught of God to love one another.' Considering the noisy disputes of the times and the whole course of Church history alike, he is of the opinion that God alone can teach men to love one another!

The more closely we analyse the few sermons that remain, the more difficult it is to understand why it has been customary to dismiss them casually with a reference to some phrase of Swift in which he disparages his own powers as a preacher. They are the work of a man who refused even in the pulpit to waste words, who despised unction and distrusted the eloquent appeal to the passions, but who performed the duties of his office with sincerity, using even in his sermons the full force of all his gifts, his intelligence, his humour, his mastery of language, and his hatred of hypocrisy and injustice.

Burke knew better, and his praise is unmeasured when he says that Swift's 'sermon upon Doing Good . . . contains perhaps the best motives to patriotism that were ever delivered within so small a compass'. But the sermons were not all political pamphlets; and I am not sure that the utmost perfection of form—in unity and simplicity and conciseness—is not rather to be found in the sermon on the Trinity, and the fullest play of his art to be seen when he preached against sleeping in church, 'with the design, if possible, to disturb some part in this audience of half an hour's sleep, for the convenience and exercise whereof this place, at this season of the day, is very much celebrated'.

Though as far as I know no manuscript exists of any of these sermons except the manuscript of the sermon on Brotherly Love which is in Trinity College, Dublin, and though none of them were printed until after Swift's death, I submit that those I have referred to are not less certainly recognizable as his handiwork than they would be if we could read them in his own autograph. Can we also, on the other hand, now safely attempt to analyse another sermon, to which the following note was attached when it was first printed?

The Manuscript Title Page of the following Sermon being lost, and no Memorandums written upon it, as there were upon the others, when and where it was preached, made the Editor doubtful whether he should print it as the DEAN's, or not. But its being found amongst the same Papers; and the Hand, although written somewhat better, bearing a great Similitude to the DEAN's, made him willing to lay it before the Publick, that they might judge whether the Stile and Manner also do not render it still more probable to be his.

Orrery seems to put it aside as obviously not Swift's work, and the only claim to be made for it is that Sheridan, when he reprinted it in his edition, states that the manuscript was in the hand of Stella.

But I am here concerned to examine it on the evidence of the style, the quality of the writing and the plan of it, as an experiment on a doubtful piece to see whether it is possible to find negative proof on which we might risk the statement that Swift could not have written it.

The framework is the conventional one that Swift often uses —first an introduction, explaining the text, then a division of the subject into three main heads, each considered separately again in a series of paragraphs with a final exhortation and prayer, the common form of hundreds of volumes of sermons.

Before examining the statement of the particular topic to be treated, it is well to remember the precision and vigour which Swift uses at this point in other sermons, e.g.

It is upon this Subject of Brotherly Love, that I intend to discourse at present, and the Method I shall observe shall be as follows:

or,

This Day being set apart to acknowledge our Belief in the Eternal TRINITY, I thought it might be proper to employ my present Discourse entirely upon that Subject; and, I hope, to handle it in such a Manner, that the most ignorant among you, may return home better informed of your Duty in this great Point, than probably you are at present.

In these he uses a directness, and force, and plainness to make sure that even the sleepiest of his hearers might know at the beginning exactly what instruction he intends to give them. There is no such conciseness in the overweighted wordiness of this sentence:

Therefore, to bring down the Words of my Text to our present Occasion, I shall endeavour, in a further Prosecution of them, to evince the great Necessity of a nice and curious Inspection into the several Recesses of the Heart, that being the surest and the shortest Method that a wicked Man can take to reform himself:

or in the formless meandering of the rest of the paragraph, with its worn imagery:

For let us but stop the Fountain, and the Streams will spend and waste themselves away in a very little Time; but if we go about, like Children, to raise a Bank, and to stop the Current, not taking Notice all the while of the Spring which continually feedeth it, when the next Flood of a Temptation riseth and breaketh in upon it, then we shall find that we have begun at the wrong End of our Duty, and that we are very little more the better for it, than if we had sat still, and made no Advances at all.

No wonder that the next sentence is introduced by the phrase 'But, in order to a clearer explanation of the point', a phrase which Swift would never have allowed himself to pen without immediately recognizing the need to rewrite the previous statement. There are innumerable passages of this sort throughout, which lack all force and clarity, and there is not one single sentence that I can find which bears the certain marks of Swift's shaping.

If we are to take any account of the possibility that the sermon was preserved and attributed to Swift because it was in the handwriting of Stella, there is the obvious explanation that Stella might well have been generous enough to copy out a sermon of his own for the Rev. Thomas Sheridan, who may have needed the help of his friends to ensure that he had something written out in time for him to perform his duties in the pulpit. But in the absence of any manuscript signed by Swift himself or any definite statement that he wrote it, I submit that the internal evidence of style alone is enough to justify the statement that Swift was incapable of writing so badly as this.

It is true that in the eighteenth century some of Swift's critics objected that his style was not always impeccably correct and disapproved of his trifling; and in the nineteenth century the style of some of his political journalism was even described as 'sometimes loose and slovenly'; but his critics have not always been careful to set aside papers which were wrongly attributed to him, in spite of his care to make clear to his friends the real authorship of the John Bull papers, the point at which he was no longer responsible for the *Examiner*, and the exact division of labour between Sheridan and himself in the *Intelligencer* papers, which were reprinted in London in 1730 as by the author of *A Tale of a Tub*.

I should not wish to claim that Swift is at his best in the *Intelligencer*, but his characteristic quality is nevertheless clearly recognizable here, especially if we compare No. 15, which is a reprint of his *Short View of the State of Ireland* with Nos. 6 and 17, in which Sheridan writes with considerable vigour on the same topic. They both alike resented the blindness of those who refused to see the misery and poverty of Ireland and spoke of it as a rich country. Sheridan speaks of his 'Indignation against those vile Betrayers and Insulters of it, who insinuate themselves into Favour, by saying, it is a rich Nation; and [his] *sincere Passion* for the Natives, who are sunk to the lowest Degree of Misery and Poverty'. It might be almost enough to note how different this is in its tone from the words of Swift:

I have been using all Endeavours to subdue my Indignation, to which indeed I am not provoked by any personal Interest, being not the Owner of one Spot of Ground in the whole *Island* . . .

but I am concerned rather to show again the 'conciseness' of Swift in his enumeration of the deficiencies of the people of Ireland and the powerful directness of his reply, compared with the detailed evidence which Sheridan reports from the actual sights and occurrences that had stirred him to rage and compassion on his last journey through the country.

The picture Sheridan gives is a complete one: first, the evidences of trade:

I met nine Cars loaden with old musty, shriveled Hides; one Car-Load of Butter; four Jockeys driving eight Horses, all out of Case; one Cow and Calf driven by a Man and his Wife; six tattered

Families flitting to be shipped off to the *West-Indies*; a Colony of a hundred and fifty Beggars. . . .

second, the appearance of travellers on the road:

Travellers enough, but seven in ten wanting Shirts and Cravats; nine in ten going bare Foot, and carrying their Brogues and Stockings in their Hands; one Woman in twenty having a Pillion, the rest riding bare Back'd: Above two hundred Horse-Men, with four Pair of Boots amongst them all; Seventeen Saddles of Leather (the rest being made of Straw) and most of their Garrons only shod before. . . .

third, the condition of the houses on the farms and in the towns:

his whole Furniture consisted of two Blocks for Stools, a Bench on each Side the Fire-Place made of Turf, six Trenchers, one Bowl, a Pot, six Horn Spoons, three Noggins, three Blankets, one of which served the Man and Maid Servant; the other the Master of the Family, his Wife and five Children; a small Churn, a wooden Candlestick, a broken Stick for a Pair of Tongs.

When he considers the ruined churches of Drogheda he is led to contrast the spirit of Ireland with the spirit of the Athenians who resolved to leave their ruined temples as monuments to posterity for a witness against the barbarians, and when he views the desolation around Dundalk he is led to quote the philosophical reflections of Cicero on the ruins of Greece. And in his second paper he elaborates an ironical proof of the prosperity of Ireland by reference to wealthy absentee landlords, its attractiveness to the robbers who come from England, and to the idle beggars at home, and the great numbers of its inhabitants who are able to take the long voyage to America. Sheridan's papers are entirely concerned with his own observations and somewhat literary-philosophical reflections. Their tendency is unmistakable, but their aim is not wholly clear. He has only conveyed to us his feelings, a mixture of rage and compassion which leave us helpless in face of the situation.

There is no doubt about the purpose of Swift's *Short View of the State of Ireland*. He wishes to prove the stupidity and dishonesty of all those who cannot see that in spite of great natural advantages Ireland has been utterly ruined by the way in which it has been governed 'against every law of Nature and Reason', 'a condition I must not call by its true uncontroverted Name'. Like Sheridan he describes ironically the riches of the country, but he sharpens his irony by associating this fair picture with the visiting commissioners from England.

> Let [them] ride round the Kingdom, and observe the Face of Nature, or the Faces of the Natives; the Improvement of the Land; . . . the commodious Farmers-Houses and Barns; . . . the comfortable Dyet, and Dress, and Dwellings of the People; . . . the Roads crowded with Carriers laden with rich Manufactures; . . .
> With what Envy and Admiration would these Gentlemen return from so delightful a Progress? What glorious Reports would they make when they went back to *England*?

And when he turns with too heavy a heart from this irony to the actual situation, and sums up shortly and bitterly the general desolation, the English standards of the English visitor are used again the other way round to redouble the attack.

> . . . the Families of Farmers who pay great Rents, living in Filth and Nastiness upon *Butter-milk* and *Potatoes*, without a Shoe or Stocking to their Feet, or a House so convenient as an *English* Hogsty to receive them: These indeed may be comfortable Sights to an *English* Spectator, who comes for a short Time, only *to learn* the *Language*, and returns back to his own Countrey, whither he finds all our Wealth transmitted.

And once more the visitors from England are drawn unfavourably into the argument:

> I think it a little unhospitable, and others may call it a subtil Piece of Malice, that, because there may be a Dozen Families in this Town able to entertain their *English* Friends in a generous Manner at their Tables, their Guests, upon their Return to *England*, shall report that we wallow in Riches and Luxury.

Sheridan speaks of his indignation against the betrayers and insulters of his country and his sincere passion for the natives; but Swift's compassion and indignation are fused together into one deadly purpose, which turns every sentence into a blow against the tyranny which had enslaved the people of Ireland.

Either of necessity or choice Swift published nearly all his work anonymously, and he was perfectly ready to allow Pope to look after the publication of the volumes of *Miscellanies* in 1727–32, containing—without any separate ascription—their work and some of Arbuthnot's. But when he finally decided to allow Faulkner to prepare a collected edition of his works to be printed in Dublin, though in the early volumes his name still did not appear on the title-page, he showed some desire to have nothing included in the volumes which he supervised that was not entirely his own. It seems evident that the text was set up from the volumes of the *Miscellanies* printed in London, as it contains corrections made by Swift in a copy from his own library, now in the possession of Lord Rothschild.

It is rather curious, therefore, that *A Letter of Advice to a Young Poet*, which had been published in Dublin in 1721 and reprinted in London over Swift's name, was omitted both in the *Miscellanies* and also in the *Collected Works*. Neither was it included even later in any of the volumes added to Faulkner's edition. Mr. John Hayward was, I believe, the first editor to call attention to this in his Nonesuch edition of Swift's *Selected Writings*; but even he does not express any doubt as to the authenticity of the *Letter*. Although it is a witty piece of writing and seems better than we could expect from an imitation, I can find no satisfactory reason to explain why Swift did not reprint it, if it was his work. I must regard it therefore as doubtful. If then, with this doubt in our minds, we examine it carefully and compare it with *A Letter to a Young Clergyman* and *A Letter to a Very Young Lady* we notice that it lacks this very quality of directness and conciseness which we are considering. It is full of literary references, witty sallies, and humorous tricks; and it ends with a proposal for the encouragement of poetry in Dublin so loose and slovenly in style that I cannot think Swift in any way responsible for these final pages. I will give only this sample:

I would now offer some poor Thoughts of mine for the Encouragement of *Poetry* in this Kingdom, if I could hope they would be agreeable. I have had many an aking Heart for the ill plight of that noble Profession here, and it has been my late and early Study how to bring it into better Circumstances. And surely, considering what *Monstrous* WITS in the Poetick way, do almost daily start up and surprize us in this Town; what *prodigious* Genius's we have here (of which I cou'd give Instances without number;) and withal of what great benefit it might be to our Trade to encourage that Science here, . . . I say, these things consider'd, I am humbly of Opinion, it wou'd be worth the Care of our Governours to cherish Gentlemen of the *Quill*, and give them all proper Encouragements here. And since I am upon the Subject, I shall speak my Mind very *freely*, and if I added *sawcily*, it is no more than my Birthright as a *Briton*.

We know now from Swift's letters to Charles Ford that he took particular interest in Faulkner's third volume, which was to contain *Gulliver's Travels*. He admits that he had been annoyed by the changes introduced in the original edition, owing to the fears of the printer, not so much because of the things omitted as because of certain passages which were added in a style so slovenly that he was unwilling to have them remain in a volume which would be known as his work. Here then are samples of writing which Swift himself felt should be recognizable as something he could never have done. Here are passages which have been printed in some later editions of *Gulliver*, which the critics ought to have suspected from internal evidence of style alone. He had written, for instance, with little attempt to disguise the real object of his attack:

I told him, that in the Kingdom of *Tribnia*, by the Natives called *Langden*, where I had long sojourned, the Bulk of the People consisted wholly of Discoverers, Witnesses, Informers, Accusers, Prosecutors, Evidences, Swearers; etc.

This is pointed and definite and unhesitating. He continues to charge the politicians in that kingdom with arranging plots to answer their private advantage and describes the methods of dealing with those who are to be accused. In the first edition, to remove the sting, it is all made hypothetical and carefully packed in soft layers of verbiage:

I told him, that should I happen to live in a Kingdom where Plots and Conspiracies were either in vogue from the turbulency of the meaner People, or could be turned to the use and service of the higher Rank of them, I first would take care to cherish and encourage the breed of Discoverers, Witnesses, etc.

Once given the clue it is certainly not difficult to detect the padding:

Men thus qualified and thus empowered might make a most excellent use and advantage of Plots. . . .
This might be done by first agreeing and settling among themselves. . . .
They should be allowed to put what Interpretation they pleased upon them, giving them a Sense not only which has no relation at all to them, but even what is quite contrary to their true Intent and real Meaning; thus for Instance, they may, if they so fancy, interpret a *Sieve* etc.

For Swift rarely follows that loose fashion of coupling his verbs and nouns like this—qualified and empowered, use and advantage, agreeing and settling—and is incapable of such clumsiness as 'not only which has no . . . but even what'.

But the chief changes were made in the Fourth Book, to cushion the blows which Swift had dealt against the profession of the Law and against a First or Chief Minister of State. I do not think we could find anywhere a better proof of the conciseness of Swift than in the fifth and sixth chapters of the Fourth Book of *Gulliver*, if we read what he wrote as printed in Faulkner's edition:

I said there was a Society of Men among us, bred up from their Youth in the Art of proving by Words multiplied for the Purpose, that *White* is *Black*, and *Black* is *White*, according as they are paid. To this Society all the rest of the People are Slaves.

That is surely Brobdingnagian in style—clear, masculine, and smooth; without multiplying unnecessary words or using various expressions. The attack is direct and unqualified, and therefore dangerous. Again Swift was justified in expecting his critics to recognize that the substituted passage which appears in the early London editions could not have come from his pen, for it is cautious and qualified, and therefore out of key with the context; and its meaning is completely clouded by the multiplication of unnecessary words.

I said that those who made profession of this Science were exceedingly multiplied, being almost equal to the Caterpillars in Number; that they were of diverse Degrees, Distinctions, and Denominations. The Numerousness of those that dedicated themselves to this Profession were such that the fair and justifiable Advantage and Income of the Profession was not sufficient for the decent and handsome Maintenance of Multitudes of those who followed it. Hence it came to pass that it was found needful to supply that by Artifice and Cunning, which could not be procured by just and honest Methods: The better to bring which about, very many Men among us were bred up from their Youth in the Art of proving by Words multiplied for the Purpose that *White* is *Black*, and *Black* is *White*, according as they are paid. The Greatness of these Mens Assurance and the Boldness of their Pretensions gained upon the Opinion of the Vulgar, whom in a Manner they made Slaves of, and got into their Hands much the largest Share of the Practice of their Profession.

The attack in the sixth chapter on the First or Chief Minister of State was not tampered with, but instead the danger was removed by introducing it with an extraordinary piece of patchwork intended to prevent the reader from a malicious interpretation at the expense of any recent British statesman. Again the style is so entirely unlike Swift and the change in tone so sudden that a careful reader could not fail to be suspicious of some tampering with the text. Had Swift been concerned to avoid any possible reference to Harley and Queen Anne, he would not have trusted to such a preposterous sentence of clumsy compliment; nor would he have ruined the whole effect of his satire by assuring his master that he was referring only to former times in Britain and to other courts in Europe now:

where Princes grew indolent and careless of their own Affairs through a constant Love and Pursuit of Pleasure, they made use of such an Administrator, as I had mentioned, under the Title of *first* or *chief Minister of State*, the Description of which, as far as it may be collected not only from their Actions, but from the Letters, Memoirs, and Writings published by themselves, the Truth of which has not yet been disputed, may be allowed to be as follows: . . .

So long as this kind of writing was reprinted over and over again as part of the Swift canon, and included in the text of his greatest and best-known work, and so long as other papers which we now know were certainly not his and a great many very doubtful pieces, like the sermon I have examined, have been included in every fresh edition of his collected works, it is difficult to set precise limits to possible variations of quality in his work, and to be sure that there is a point where we can boldly say: Thus far he might go, but no farther, from the essentials of good prose, which he himself set down so clearly.

Whether he wrote as Drapier, Bickerstaff, or Gulliver, or as the Dean of St. Patrick's, there were, I believe, certain standards which we may always apply, certain qualities which we can always recognize; for they are the marks of the mind and of the art of Jonathan Swift. And the particular quality of his prose that we have been considering as something both distinctive and remarkable—its conciseness—is also an essential mark of his mind and his art. That explains his greatness and his intensity; it explains also what were the things he could not do. In order to be plain and simple it is necessary to clear the mind of speculation and compromise, and to avoid in art the distortions of height and depth and the deception of colour.

He held that all knowledge is intended for use, not for idle curiosity or the pleasure of speculation. In matters of belief there must be boundaries between the spheres of faith and reason, and limits set to prevent disorder from the revolutionary forces of scepticism and critical inquiry. In matters of ethics he was content with a simple form of dualism, which defines the borders of right and wrong and when applied to political and social matters divides everything into a system of parties, Whigs and Tories, Ancients and Moderns, conformists and nonconformists, the forces of enlightenment and the forces of dullness— and finally a world of friends and enemies. In matters of political and ecclesiastical history he makes astonishing simplifications which provide a series of political parallels endlessly recurring, and of constant validity for all mankind. It is evidently a pattern simplified for common use which sometimes surprises us almost into a belief that it must be true, when it enables him to pack into a concise statement such a telling political generalization as this:

in the course of many Ages they have been troubled with the same Disease, to which the whole Race of Mankind is subject; the Nobility often contending for Power, the People for Liberty, and the King for absolute Dominion.

Like most of his contemporaries he approved of the activities of the scientists in so far as their work could be of practical use in agriculture and manufactures and navigation and medicine. But he feared the quackery and conceit of these investigators and logically was driven to make his attack on all kinds of technical jargon, as the very symbol of that kind of speculation which was in danger of separating its activities from all connexion with the common needs of man, and becoming, as law and theology and medicine had already done, a separate guild whose activities had long been of questionable value to the public, whom they had each in their own way made their ignorant slaves.

And finally, the art of the writer is likewise for use, not for his own pleasure, nor for the pleasure of his readers. It is functional. Therefore the method will vary whether it is for edification in sermons, for moral or political instruction in essays and pamphlets, or whether it is intended to sting and vex the world into a greater concern for political justice or the decencies and proprieties of social life. But it will always be short, clear, and concise, and directed to the immediate purpose. And there is a further requirement: if it is to be effective, it must never be

dull. The task of the satirist is attack, and the weapons in his
hands must be sharp and keen. His strokes must be brilliant
and rapid. He must overcome his antagonist by cunning and
surprise. He must lure him on by raillery and irony, and con-
found him by the brilliant flashing of wit. But above all he
must preserve all his strength and force, avoiding unnecessary
flourishes. His vision must be clear and his glance unwavering
until the bout is over and his opponent is overcome. There is
no place here for heroic boasting or laughter, for the wildness
of anger and rage, for primitive outbursts of hatred and lust.
He cannot cry to the gods to help him or rouse the spirits from
the vasty deep. He cannot lift his eyes to the hills for help or
wait for the right configuration of the stars to give him confidence. He has nothing but his own skill and his own knowledge of the weakness of his adversaries. His art is confined
within very human boundaries, within the limits of his own age
and social order and of the common idiom of his time.

But if he succeeds in attaining that 'Simplicity without which
no human Performance can arrive to any great Perfection', he
may not only be eminently useful to his own age but also by
reason of that perfect simplicity may continue to be eminently
useful at other times and in other places, wherever men may still
be concerned to probe into the causes and cure of those same
diseases which are common to the whole race of mankind. Although it is often said that *Gulliver's Travels* is such a good story
that for more than two hundred years it has delighted children
and ceased to hurt their parents, the truth is that, if we may
judge by the comments of some of his critics who have been
rash enough to read it all, Swift is, in fact, still successful in
what he set himself to do: he is still able to vex the conscience
of his readers. And there are not many who have written in
English who are envied so much as he is to-day for that quality
in him which is most distinctive and remarkable—that conciseness which gave such concentrated force and perfect clarity to
his style.

DEANE SWIFT, HAWKESWORTH, AND
THE JOURNAL TO STELLA

HAROLD WILLIAMS

IN September 1710 Jonathan Swift, carrying a commission from the Irish bishops, reached London. His business with the government brought him into touch with Harley and St. John, who, recognizing his gifts as a political pamphleteer, enlisted his pen in the service of Queen Anne's Tory Ministry. Thus it came to pass that Swift, who had come on an errand which probably he expected would occupy him a few months at most, remained in England, save for an absence of less than three months, till August 1714. Between September 1710 and June 1713 he posted sixty-five letters to Ireland addressed either to Esther Johnson or to Rebecca Dingley.[1] These letters, written in the form of a diary, have long been known as *The Journal to Stella*.

Thomas Sheridan (1719–88), the son of Swift's friend, first brought the letters together in a single collection in his edition of Swift's *Works* (1784). The letters were there headed *Dr. Swift's Journal to Stella*, and Sheridan has hitherto been credited with the invention of the title. He has no first claim to this happy inspiration, and his editing of the letters was incredibly careless. In 1779 Nichols published a *Supplement to Dr. Swift's Works* containing a list of 'Omissions and principal Corrections' to be noted in John Hawkesworth's edition of Swift's *Letters* (1766), and he there refers to 'That part of the *Journal to Stella*, which was published by Dr. *Hawkesworth*'. To John Nichols therefore, to whose astounding industry students of the eighteenth century already owe so much, may be given yet one more title of honour.

If none of the letters written during these years to the ladies in Ireland had survived, either in manuscript or print, we should have known, by reference to three of Swift's tiny account books,[2] that a constant correspondence took place. He was in the habit of keeping lists of letters written to and received from correspon-

---

[1] Most of the letters surviving in manuscript are addressed to 'Mrs. Dingley', and we may presume that most of the other letters were also addressed to her.

[2] Forster Collection, South Kensington, Nos. 507, 508, and 509.

D

dents. In these account books a substantial part of the *Journal* is recorded, showing the serial numbers[1] of the letters, dates of posting, and the dates on which he received replies. Stella's letters have been lost.

The earliest appearance in print of any part of these letters was in Deane Swift's[2] *Essay upon the Life, Writings, and Character, of Dr. Jonathan Swift* (1755). Letters 2 to 40 came into his hands from Mrs. Whiteway, a cousin of the Dean's, 'who found them accidentally . . . among a parcel of papers given to her by the Doctor'.[3] In his *Essay* Deane Swift printed extracts, varying from a few words to passages of some length, from no less than twenty-four of the letters.

The next stage was reached when John Hawkesworth published in 1766 Letters 1 and 41 to 65. With the exception of number 54, which has disappeared, the originals of these letters are preserved in the British Museum. They had come from the Rev. John Lyon, who in 1742–4 made an inventory of Swift's books and papers at the deanery of St. Patrick's, to a Mr. Thomas Wilkes of Dublin, who passed them on to London booksellers. They engaged Hawkesworth as their editor. He arranged the letters forming part of the *Journal* not as a group but in their chronological positions with the rest of Swift's correspondence. Although Hawkesworth printed twenty-seven letters he only held the manuscripts of twenty-six. The total of twenty-seven was reached by dividing No. 61 into two separate letters. For this the original furnished no justification.

A further stage was reached in 1768 when Deane Swift, continuing the trade edition of Swift's *Works*, published in a single group Letters 1 to 40. Thus Letter 1 was printed by both Hawkesworth and Deane Swift, a point which later editors seem to have overlooked. But a comparison of the two texts makes it clear that for this letter Deane Swift was dependent upon Hawkesworth. The holograph of Letter 1 is in existence, and, had it been lying in front of Deane Swift, it would have been more than remarkable if he had decided upon the same omissions and modifications as Hawkesworth. Save for insigni-

---

[1] Swift numbered his letters with an arabic numeral at the top left-hand corner of the first page. Stella also numbered her letters.

[2] Godwin Swift, an uncle of Jonathan Swift, married, as his third wife, a daughter of Richard Deane, the regicide. Their eldest son was given the Christian name of Deane, and his son, author of the *Essay*, born in 1706, to the confusion of many received the same name.   [3] *Essay*, p. 258 n.

ficant differences the two printed versions tally exactly. Why the manuscript of the first letter of the series should have been separated from the early batch, 2 to 40, and found its place with the later portion used by Hawkesworth cannot be explained; but there can hardly be a doubt that the parcel handed to Deane Swift by Mrs. Whiteway contained not forty but thirty-nine letters. He says that they were 'in number about 38'.[1]

Thus by 1766–8 *The Journal to Stella* was in print, published in two separate portions by two independent editors.

When Nichols, in 1779, compiled the long list of mistakes and omissions in Hawkesworth's edition of Swift's correspondence, he described that part of the *Journal* as 'abundantly *more polished*' than that of Deane Swift. The italics are his. For this opinion he was taken severely to task by Forster: 'There can be no doubt, on the contrary, that of the two publications, Hawkesworth's had a far greater resemblance to the original, and was much less "polished" than Mr. Deane Swift's.'[2] With this Ryland agrees in the main. Deane Swift, he writes, 'must have mutilated them [the letters] to a greater extent than Hawkesworth ventured to do. A literary flavour has been given them.'[3] Aitken writes: 'Deane Swift took even greater liberties with the text than Hawkesworth.'[4] This is one example, among many, of the readiness with which misleading, or wholly false, assertions gain currency.

As is well known Swift delighted, when writing to the ladies in Dublin, to use a nursery or baby language, sprinkled with cryptic symbols of endearment. Thus 'Ppt' stands for 'poor pretty things', 'MD', or 'Md', for 'My dears', 'Pdfr', probably 'poor dear foolish rogue', for Swift himself. There are other alphabetical symbols, and, for the rest, the substitution of *l* for *r*, and *r* for *l*, creates forms not difficult to interpret. Beyond these there are strange formations the meaning of which may be disputed. The little language may appear at any place in the letters, but it is found almost invariably at the end of each day's entry, bidding good night with the formulae 'Nite Md', or 'Nite deelest logues'. Usually there are longer and more elaborate passages at the close of each letter.

---

[1] *Essay*, p. 258 n. Forster, *Life of Swift* (1875), pp. 405–6, Ryland and Aitken in the introductions to their editions of the *Journal*, 1897 and 1901, are inexact in their statements about the number of letters for which Hawkesworth and Deane Swift were respectively responsible.   [2] *Life of Swift*, p. 406.
[3] *Journal*, Introd., p. xviii.   [4] *Journal*, Preface, p. vi.

When Forster compared the two editors, he had chiefly in mind their attempts to deal with the little language. He was writing an introduction to his own efforts to decipher the little language and the blotted passages. 'Hawkesworth', he tells us, 'really did attempt to deal with it, while Mr. Deane Swift shirked it altogether.'[1] Ryland held that Forster 'attached an exaggerated importance' to the little language, which could only be wearisome 'to the reader who takes the Journal in the gross'. He was prepared to treat the two editors with some sympathy. 'If Hawkesworth and Deane Swift had confined themselves to cutting out "Nite deelest logues", and substituting "you" for "oo", and omitting the extraordinary strings of alphabetical symbols at the end of each letter, their responsibility would have been small.' He even goes so far as to hint that the little language and 'the oddities of handwriting, suggest a mental twist likely to lead to insanity'.[2] How would Forster, if he could have risen to the attack, have denounced him for disparaging the trouble he had expended on his valiant readings of the little language and ink-scored passages!

If we turn now to examine the results of Hawkesworth's editorial methods the questions to be asked are: (1) How far is there justification for Forster's assumption that, as compared with Deane Swift's publication, Hawkesworth's had 'a far greater resemblance to the original and was much less "polished" '? (2) Is it true, as Forster asserted, that Hawkesworth 'really did attempt to deal' with the little language, whereas 'Deane Swift shirked it altogether'?

An answer to the second question may first be attempted. It is, perhaps, the less important of the two. It serves, however, to throw light on general editorial method and to provide a partial answer to the first question. In Hawkesworth's instance we have the advantage of being able to compare his text with the original manuscripts.

The proportion of the little language to the whole is not large. Even so it is almost immediately apparent that Hawkesworth made hardly any attempt to deal with it. We can all but fairly say of him that he 'shirked it altogether'. It is difficult to understand how Forster, if he had read Hawkesworth's edition of the correspondence, could have plunged into his mistaken assertions. Hawkesworth was, quite obviously, painfully con-

---

[1] *Life*, p. 407.   [2] *Journal*, Introd., p. xix and note.

scious of his duty as an editor to remove from the letters any phrases or passages which could detract from the dignity of the great Dean of St. Patrick's, the intimate friend of Oxford and Bolingbroke, of the poets, wits, and people of quality who adorned the days of Queen Anne. The use of a nursery language was hardly calculated to exalt a writer in the estimation of his readers. Nearly all of it was therefore cut away, but not quite all. Hawkesworth's conscience troubled him when he reviewed the extent of his excisions, and, as he went on his way, he admitted a few tiny scraps of the more familiar passages, discreetly edited beyond recognition. Not till Letter 53 is reached would the reader have any suspicion that Swift ever used a little language in writing to Stella and Mrs. Dingley. In half the letters, as edited by Hawkesworth, there is no trace of it. Then, visited by remorse, he made small concessions. Letter 53 comes nearer some attempt to follow the manuscript, although about one-seventh of the original is cut away. In this letter he prints the symbol 'Ppt' three times, on one occasion substituting it for Swift's 'she'; and he translates two or three scraps of the little language into normal speech, although later in the same letter he adopted the line of least resistance by omitting it altogether. Thereafter in each letter, with the exception of two, the symbols 'Ppt' or 'D.D.'[1] occur once or twice, and once 'M.', which Swift did not write. But these small admissions can hardly be accounted to Hawkesworth for righteousness. In letter after letter the little language is, to all intents and purposes, passed over as if non-existent. Occasionally a few words, of which the meaning is quite obvious, are normalized. For example, 'o Rold, I must go no farther fear of aboozing fine Radyes' appears as 'hold, I must go no farther, for fear of abusing fine ladies'; and 'nevle saw ze rike' as 'never saw the like'. But whenever difficulty presented itself Hawkesworth recoiled. He never attempted the longer passages. It can only be said for him that, as compared with Deane Swift, he did not intrude his own inventions. To these we shall come later.

An answer to the first question is now to be sought. If again we compare Hawkesworth's text with the manuscripts we shall soon find abundant evidence to show that he considered it his

---

[1] Footnotes explain that 'Ppt' is Mrs. Johnson, and that 'D.D.' stands for Mrs. Dingley. Hawkesworth prints 'Ppt' twenty-five times, 'D.D.' eight times, and 'M.' once. On three occasions he introduces 'Ppt' where Swift wrote 'she', 'oo', or 'Md'.

duty to omit familiar or everyday passages and polish vigo-
rously. References to Stella's and Mrs. Dingley's affairs, to their
life in Dublin or in the country, to their Irish friends, to Swift's
business with his agent Parvisol are sliced away without com-
punction. About one-third of Letters 43 and 52, for example,
disappears, and large portions of many others. The receipt
dates of Stella's letters, which Swift punctiliously noted, are
largely omitted, together with the mention of their serial
numbers. Hawkesworth has no scruple in making many minor
and some major alterations. He constantly changes "Tis' to
'It is'; he alters Swift's grammar, substituting 'were' for 'was';
for 'delivered' he prints 'directed', which exactly reverses the
sense Swift intended; where words do not please him he selects
a reasonable synonym, 'people's' for 'Folks'; or he tones down
'violent' to 'rigid'; and when he thinks an entirely different
word will help he exchanges 'pleurisy' for 'bruise'. Impro-
prieties easily offend him. He deletes a large part of Swift's
description of the shingles, if that was the complaint from which
he suffered, including the news that he had gone so thin that
he had found it necessary to take in his breeches. Gross words,
like 'Nasty Bawd', receive short shrift.

There are frequent repetitions from letter to letter. Hawkesworth carefully removed any duplications of news or remark.
On 21 February 1712–13 Swift asks Stella to instruct Filby to
write to a Mr. Griffin, adding, 'I'll enquire for a direction to
Griffin before I finish this.' Hawkesworth noticed that the
doubt about Griffin's address could be better settled by deleting
these words and transferring to their place the information
Swift gave two days later: 'I think Mr. *Griffin* lives in *Bury-
street*, near *St. James's-street*, hard by me; but I suppose your
brother may direct to him to the salt-office, and, as I remember,
he knows his christian name, because you sent it to me in the
list of the commissioners.' Forthwith he robbed one day's entry
to fill out another. Another improvement begins Letter 61,
1 March 1712–13. Swift wrote: 'Tis out of my head whether
I answerd all y^r Lettr in my last yesterday or no. I think I was
in hast and could not but now I see I answerd a good deal of it,
no, onely about y— Broth^r, and Me Bill.' As the previous letter
made all this uncertainty needless Hawkesworth credited Swift
with a better memory and reported him as writing, 'I see I
answered a good deal of your last letter about your brother, *&c*.'

These are but a few examples of Hawkesworth's conception of the editor's function. Throughout he is intent on getting things into good shape, burnishing, and refining the homely to a proper elegance. While about these tasks he was insufficiently attentive to reading the manuscript correctly. His mistakes are many, even with words plain to be read, and frequently with proper names which he should have known. 'Danby' becomes 'Darby', 'Elwick' becomes 'Elnick', 'Tisdall's' becomes 'Tindall's', 'Cleve' becomes 'Clerk', 'Palmes' becomes 'Palmer'; he always prints 'Filly' for 'Filby', and crowns these errors with the curiosity 'P. at Rolt' for 'Pat Rolt'.

The earlier volumes (i–vi, 1755) of Hawkesworth's[1] edition of Swift's *Works* do not commend him as an exact editor, and he shows to less advantage when he is handling difficult manuscript, as he was with the letters to Stella and Rebecca Dingley. It would be a mistake, however, to judge him by accepted modern standards. Scholars and readers of his day would have regarded his editorial practice with approval. They would not have questioned the propriety of excision, rearrangement, correction, and, in general, the reduction to better form and phraseology of letters written in haste, never intended for the public eye. But even so Hawkesworth was careless and slapdash. These, however, are not the matters here in question. Was Forster justified in his contention that Hawkesworth 'really did attempt to deal' with the little language? To this question there can be but one reply, an emphatic 'No'. Was Forster right in maintaining that Hawkesworth's publication more nearly resembled the original than that of Deane Swift, and that it was much less 'polished'? We can collate the manuscripts against Hawkesworth's text, and the comparison shows that he was a thoroughgoing polisher. So thought Nichols, whose life overlapped that of Hawkesworth by some thirty years, whose conscience was that of his contemporaries, not that of the modern editor. Nevertheless, so unfavourably impressed was Nichols by Hawkesworth's arbitrary methods that, as we have seen, he compiled a list of his mistakes and omissions, a task which he described as 'both pleasant and laborious'.[2]

If, then, Forster's judgement was at fault, and Nichols nearer to the truth, can we go further and accept that part of the

---

[1] When editing the volumes of the correspondence in 1766 Hawkesworth received assistance from Thomas Birch. [2] *Lit. Illustr.* v. 376 n.

Journal edited by Deane Swift as more faithful to the original?
Here we must turn to inferential evidence. There are no manuscripts against which we can check his work. But we may safely
assume that the missing Letters, 2 to 40, contained the same
general characteristics, mannerisms, words, pet phrases, and
turns of speech as do those Letters of which we possess the
originals.

First, however, as Deane Swift printed portions of the *Journal*
in his *Essay* (1755) it seems proper to ask if any deductions can
be reached by comparing these excerpts with the same passages
in his edition of Swift's *Letters*, published in 1768. So far as the
little language is concerned there is nothing to be gained by a
comparison. In the first place Deane Swift was rather oddly
moved in his *Essay* to quote from the letters to Stella to uphold
the respectable standing of the Vanhomrigh family against the
detractions of Lord Orrery. But for the most part the letters
were used to extol Swift's political gifts, illustrate the admiration
in which he was held by Oxford and Bolingbroke, and justify
Queen Anne's Tory Ministry. Thus the more familiar passages
are not to be expected. Further, we must reject explanatory
interpolations which Deane Swift sometimes introduced without notice, and discount those sentences and paragraphs which
he transposed from the first to the third person.

A point noticeable at the outset is that in 1755 he supplied
his own punctuation, whereas in 1768 he, or the printer, more
nearly adopted the punctuation Swift was accustomed to
follow. In this respect the published letters may be accepted
as nearer to the originals. In 1755, further, he polished the
originals in small particulars. 'I'll' becomes 'I will'; ' 'tis'
becomes 'it is'; 't'other' becomes 'the other'; 'Devil's' (undoubtedly Swift) becomes 'duce is'; 'her' becomes 'her Majesty';
'd—d' is omitted; and when, speaking of the Queen, Swift
describes her 'confounded trimming and moderation', the dis-
respectful 'confounded' disappears. Sometimes he rearranged
the matter slightly in order to make a short extract more
intelligible. A general comparison of the extracts with the
text of 1768 establishes a presumption that the published
letters, save for deliberate omissions which cannot be checked,
probably conform fairly closely to the original. Where there
are verbal differences the reading of 1768 is, in several instances,
clearly right. In ten or twelve examples of disagreement there

can be little doubt, or none at all, that the true reading of Swift's manuscript is represented by the 1768 version. In making this calculation all possibilities of deliberate changes made by Deane Swift in his *Essay* extracts have been omitted from the count. This, admittedly, does not amount to much, but it does go some way to show that the edited letters of 1768 have a reasonable claim to be fair transcripts of the manuscripts.

Forster charges Deane Swift with: (1) The invention of words and symbols in place of those written by Swift; (2) a complacent belief that he had taken 'infinite trouble' with the little language, whereas 'there is no trace of trouble except in the way of omission'; (3) a complete unconsciousness of the 'possible importance in retaining the most obscure allusions'; (4) editorial revision and omission so ruthless that his text can only be accounted to have far less resemblance to the original than that of Hawkesworth.

Indictments (1) and (2) concern Deane Swift's handling of the little language. He is roughly taken to task for barefaced false coinage. Let it be admitted that the substitutions he made were a stupid impertinence. But he was quite frank about it, and he stated his practice in a sensible footnote to the second letter, giving the reader a far better insight into Swift's use of alphabetical symbols than any explanation afforded by Hawkesworth.

In these letters [he writes] *pdfr*, stands for Dr. *Swift*; *Ppt*, for *Stella*; *D.* for *Dingley*; *D.D.* generally for *Dingley*, but sometimes for both *Stella* and *Dingley*; and *MD* generally stands for both these ladies; yet sometimes only for *Stella*. But, to avoid perplexing the reader, it was thought more adviseable to use the word *Presto* for *Swift*, which is borrowed from the duchess of *Shrewsbury* . . . instead of *Ppt*. *Stella* is used for Mrs. *Johnson*, and so for *D. Dingley*; but as *MD* stands for both *Dingley* and *Stella*, it was thought more convenient to let it remain a cypher in its original state.

Doubtless it would have been more sensible to let 'pdfr' stand, for 'Presto' was used of Swift by nobody apparently save by the Italian Duchess of Shrewsbury, on an occasion when she failed to remember, or could not pronounce, his name in English;[1] and it was not till years later that Swift gave to Esther Johnson, in

---

[1] *Journal*, Letter 27, 2 Aug. 1711. On one occasion, when he cannot help it, 1 Jan. 1711, Deane Swift allows 'pdfr' to stand: 'Now I remember I always write *pdfr*.'

poems addressed to her, the name by which she is known to fame. There are, further, one or two more inventions which must be charged to Deane Swift's debit account. The diminutive 'Stellakins' (14 Oct. 1710) was certainly not Swift's, for it stands or falls with Stella. 'Sluttikins' is a doubtful formation; and 'saucebox', which constantly appears in Deane Swift's part of the *Journal*, is not to be found in the original letters, although 'saucy' in other combinations is frequent. But, these few names or forms of address excepted, there is little, if anything, in the letters as printed by Deane Swift to arouse suspicion that he is coining words in substitution for those he read in the manuscripts. On the contrary it is apparent, beyond all doubt, that he uses Swift's pet words over and over again, as they are to be found in the originals, save that they are normalized. 'Naughty girls' is the equivalent of 'nauti dallars'; 'young women' of 'ung oomens'; 'rogue' of 'logue'; 'sirrahs', which is very frequent, of 'sollahs'. The form 'sollahs' is particularly explained by Deane Swift in a footnote to words appearing in the entry for 9 February 1710–11, where we read, 'and so good morrow, little sirrahs; that's for the rhyme'. Where is the rhyme? 'In the original', writes Deane Swift, 'it was, *good mallows, little sollahs*. But in these words, and many others, he writes constantly *ll* for *rr*.' A striking illustration of the probability that Deane Swift reproduced fairly exactly a large proportion of the more familiar passages of the *Journal* appears in the closing words of the entry for 2 November 1710: 'Well, little monkies mine, I must go write; and so good night.' We have the manuscript of Letter 43, and there, on 11 March 1711–12, we find Swift bidding good-night thus: 'So Nite my two deelest nuntyes nine Md.'[1] This is little language for 'dearest monkeys mine'. Another pertinent example occurs at 22 January 1710–11, where Swift, exclaiming against the cold, writes: 'Starving, starving, Uth, uth, uth, uth, uth.' This seems almost certainly an attempt to decipher and render an obliterated expletive, identical probably with an obliteration in one of the original letters, 12 February 1711–12, where Swift complains of a severe cold. Both should presumably be read, 'Urge, urge, urge', which Swift used, 30 March 1712, when he was in physical pain.

If we turn now to words and expressions constantly employed

---

[1] See also 18 March 1711–12, 'Nite nuntyes nine'; and 22 March 1711–12, 'Nite my own two deelest nuntyes'.

by Swift it is notable that two especially are as frequent in Deane Swift's publication as in the originals, and both are eschewed by Hawkesworth. One is the exclamatory 'faith', which appears as 'fais' in the originals, the other 'as hope saved'. Here, once more, Deane Swift stands justified on comparison with Hawkesworth. But the easiest way to judge to what extent Deane Swift, so far as common words and expressions are concerned, reproduced the manuscript in front of him, how far he was guilty of false coinage, and how far Hawkesworth blandly deleted nearly everything which gives to the *Journal* its intimate character, will be to attempt a tabular representation. In column (1) below appear words printed by Deane Swift admittedly foreign to the originals or of doubtful credit. In column (2) is a list of words and phrases identical with those found in the original letters, or so nearly similar that they may be accepted without question.

(1)	(2)
Presto (*passim*)	MD (*passim*)
Stella (*passim*)	DD
stellakins	PMD
sluttikins	pdfr
saucebox (*passim*)	our little MD (= our richar MD)
saucy boxes	naughty girls (= nauti dallars)
little gooses	sirrahs (*passim*; = sollahs)
brats	dear sirrahs (= dee sollahs)
	rogue, or rogue (*passim*; = logue); with various adjectives—little, saucy, dear, insolent
	sluts; with adjectives—saucy, ignorant, awkward, impudent, wheedling
	young women (= ung oomens)
	nauti nauti nauti dear girls
	little monkies mine
	faith (*passim*)
	as hope saved (*passim*)
	uth, uth, uth, uth, uth
	There, There, There (= lele, lele, lele)

Column (2) is important, for it shows that Deane Swift did give some rendering of the little language, however inadequate and conventionalized, and that he did not regard this nursery jargon as detracting from the dignity of St. Patrick's Dean. On the other hand, nothing in column (2), save for alphabetical symbols, and those very sparsely, will be found in Hawkesworth. Exclusion of the trivial and familiar was regarded by him as an editor's incumbent duty. He was anxious to hide the fact that

Swift ever used a little language when writing to Esther Johnson. Deane Swift, so far from being troubled by false sensibility,
was at pains in several footnotes to inform the reader about it;
and, on one occasion (7 March 1710–11), printed a typical
specimen: 'and zoo must cly Lele, and Hele, and Hele aden.
Must loo mimitate *pdfr*, pay? Iss, and so la shall. And so leles
fol ee rettle. Dood mollow.' His footnote reads:

Here is just one specimen given of his way of writing to *Stella* in
these journals. The reader, I hope, will excuse my omitting it in
all other places where it occurs. The meaning of this pretty language
is; 'And you must cry There, and Here, and Here again. Must you
imitate *Presto*, pray? Yes, and so you shall. And so there's for your
letter. Good morrow.'

Other examples may be given of Deane Swift's anxiety to
afford the reader some idea of the character of the original
letters. As part of the *Journal* for 24 February 1710–11 he
prints, 'There, There, There. O Lord, I am saying *There*,
There, to myself in all our little keys.' A footnote explains: 'In
his cypher way of writing to *Stella*, he writes the word *There*,
Lele.'[1] On 30 Nov. 1710 Swift wrote: 'Your chancellor? Why,
madam, I can tell you he has been dead this fortnight. Faith,
I could hardly forbear our little language . . . as you may
see by the blot.' Here Deane Swift explains: 'To make this
intelligible, it is necessary to observe, that the words *this fortnight*, in the preceding sentence, were first written in what he
calls their little language, and afterwards scratched out and
written plain. It must be confessed this little language . . . has
occasioned infinite trouble in the revisal of these papers.' For
this very natural observation Forster sees fit to indict Deane
Swift of 'complacency'. It is Forster, rather, against whom
the charge should be brought. Pompous and tiresome Deane
Swift may have been, but according to his lights he did not
do badly, and anyone who has attempted to edit the *Journal
to Stella* will confess with him the 'infinite trouble' caused by
the little language, the blots, and the scratchings out. Nevertheless the trouble is repaid in the knowledge that this baby
prattle meant so much to Swift and Stella. 'Do you know
what?' he writes (7 March 1710–11), 'when I am writing in our

---

[1] We know that the ladies were also accustomed to use the little language, as is
evident from a sentence near the end of Letter 17: 'An't you sauceboxes to write
lele like *Presto*?'

language I make up my mouth just as if I was speaking it. I caught myself at it just now.' Or again (4 May 1711): 'Every syllable I write I hold my lips just for all the world as if I were talking in our own little language.'

The original letters contain many intimate and playful passages, often, but by no means always, in the little language. Of these passages there is scarcely the faintest reflection in Hawkesworth's edition. The contrast, when we turn to Deane Swift, is immediately apparent, even after the turning of a few pages, and the cumulative effect, when we reach the end of Letter 40, precludes any conclusion save that he does constantly give us, translated into natural speech, the content of many sentences and passages which in the originals before him were written in the little language. When he spoke of the trouble occasioned 'in the revisal of these papers' he was referring to the difficulty of rendering these passages into common speech. If we are to be fair to Deane Swift there can be no doubt that he did take trouble, and, on the whole, it appears that his renderings may be accepted, although it must be questioned, on a comparison with originals, whether the specific example he gives of the little language is quite accurately transcribed. However, he gives the right sense of it.

Further, apart from the little language, Swift was fond of indulging in what he would have called 'raillery'. 'I find I have been writing state affairs to *MD*. How do they relish it? Why, any thing that comes from *Presto* is welcome: though really, to confess the truth, if they had their choice, not to disguise the matter, they had rather, *&c.*' (8 Jan. 1710–11). Or again: 'How do you pass your time this ugly weather? Gaming and drinking, I suppose: fine diversions for young ladies, truly' (11 Feb. 1710–11). He paints a picture of Stella starting out for a ride, an exercise he was always urging upon her. 'Well; but the horses are not come to the door; the fellow can't find the bridle; your stirrup is broken; where did you put the whips, *Dingley? Marg'et*, where have you laid Mrs. *Johnson*'s ribband to tie about her? reach me my mask: sup up this before you go' (30 June 1711). These are three examples among many of playful passages, which, in several veins, are scattered throughout these earlier letters in the manner exactly of the later manuscript letters and notably in contrast with Hawkesworth's text. Stella was fond of ombre, the fashionable game of cards, and

Swift delighted to chaff her about her play: 'Why, the reason
you lost four and eight-pence last night but one at *Manley*'s, was
because you played bad games: . . . Would any but a mad lady
go out twice upon *Manilio, Basto,* and two small diamonds?
Then in that game of spades, you blundered when you had
ten-ace; I never saw the like of you' (5 Oct. 1710).[1]

There are other general characteristics in which contrasts
between Deane Swift and Hawkesworth may be noted. Swift
was fond of punning, and his own and his friends' best puns are
duly recorded for Stella's benefit. He makes up nonsense verses
or proverbial sayings under the pretence that they are of traditional origin. For example—

> 'If paper be thin,
> Ink will slip in;
> But if it be thick,
> You may write with a stick.'

This follows upon a complaint that Stella's writing-paper is too
thin. 'Can't you get thicker?' Or again: 'On *New-year*'s day
you'll do it better: For when the year with *MD* 'gins, It without
MD never lins. (These Proverbs have always old words in
them; *lins* is leaves off.) But if on New-year you write nones,
MD then will bang your bones' (31 Dec. 1710).[2]

No attempt is made by Deane Swift to conceal frequently
repeated expressions of deep and sincere affection. '*MD*'s felicity is the great end I aim at in all my pursuits' (23 May 1711).
'Love *Presto*, who loves *MD* above all things ten million of times'
(19 July 1711). 'I am never happy, but when I write or think
of *MD*' (25 Aug. 1711). 'Love *Presto*, who loves *MD* infinitely
above all earthly things' (17 Nov. 1711).[3] He dwells longingly
on the thought of a return to Ireland, to the familiar scenes, to
Laracor and its willows, to the friendship and conversation of
Stella and Rebecca Dingley. He never fails to acknowledge the
receipt of Stella's letters by their serial numbers, and we learn
something of the news they contained. Hawkesworth only
quotes the serial number twice; other references are curt and
perfunctory. Swift's letters are full of references to his business
affairs in Ireland, his tithe, his fruit-trees; and directions are

---

[1] See also 13 Dec. 1710 and 25 Feb. 1710–11.
[2] See also 3 Dec. 1710; 16 March 1710–11; 21 April 1711.
[3] See also 16 Jan. 1710–11; 5 April 1711; 8 Sept. 1711; 9 Oct. 1711; 30 Nov.
1711; 29 Dec. 1711.

conveyed to his agent Parvisol. There are constant allusions to the everyday concerns of Irish friends and of Stella's acquaintance, to evening parties, to games of cards, to new additions in families, to stray chit-chat, and to the weather. Hawkesworth resolutely crossed all this out, or nearly all of it.

Another touch which goes some way to inspire belief that Deane Swift expunged but little, and that he was not easily deterred by his copy, is the reproduction of unseemly or coarse expressions, and, on one or two occasions, words so intimate that they come as a surprise when we remember who it was that first read them.[1] Nor does he hesitate to print a thoroughly bawdy rhyme about Henry St. John.[2] It is beside the mark to urge that manners and habits of speech in Queen Anne's day differed from ours. The point is that Deane Swift, wearisomely precise and conventional, basking in admiration for his great kinsman, did not omit, whereas Hawkesworth rigorously deleted.

It should also be added that Deane Swift did get his proper names correctly; and his punctuation, when compared with Hawkesworth's, does approximate, especially in the use of semicolon and colon, more nearly to the off-hand punctuation of the original letters.

Writing to John Nichols in 1778 Deane Swift, with the correspondence chiefly in mind, decried Hawkesworth as the editor 'of an Author whose writings he neither did, nor, for want of opportunities, could understand'.[3] It is natural to dismiss this as the exhibition of a competing editor's petty temper. It is true that Deane Swift was only too prone to regard the works of his famous kinsman as sacrosanct family property. But, as has already been observed, Hawkesworth's earlier editorial efforts scarcely commend him, nor yet his dealings with Swift's general correspondence. It is strange, therefore, that he should have been given undeserved credit where he was at his worst—in the publication of Swift's letters to Stella. The form he gave to them goes far to justify the charge that he did not understand his author.

In his own day Deane Swift was characterized as a 'worthy though somewhat eccentric Gentleman',[4] and this estimate is

---

[1] See, for example, 4 Oct. 1710; 28 Oct. 1710; 3 Nov. 1710; 3 April 1711; 27 Aug. 1711; 5 Oct. 1711; 17 Nov. 1711.   [2] 13 Jan. 1710–11.
[3] Nichols, *Lit. Illustr.* v. 376.   [4] Nichols, op. cit. v. 374.

fairly borne out by all that we know of him. But his abilities were commended to Pope by Swift in the warmest terms; his *Essay* on the Dean and his editing of the *Works* show him to have been more fitted to these tasks than some who have attempted them; and there is always a useful place for eccentrics. A reputation for being odd is, however, difficult to outlive, and only too likely to attach itself to all that a man does. Deane Swift, whose circumstances were easy, did comparatively little in the course of a long life, and save for his great kinsman would long since have been forgotten. But it was, perhaps, natural that suspicion should be directed to what little he did. In this paper reasons have been shown for dismissing the easy assumption that he altered beyond recognition Swift's letters to Stella. The contractions have been filled in; some part of the little language has clearly disappeared; but much evidently remains, if in normalized form; the intimacies and common-places and every-day chat, these are retained. Omissions there doubtless are; but there is ground for confidence that the sum total of omission is far less in proportion than in the letters edited by Hawkesworth. This well-founded belief brings comfort, for we are dependent upon Deane Swift for nearly three-quarters of *The Journal to Stella*.

POPE AT WORK

GEORGE SHERBURN

ALEXANDER POPE only spasmodically lived up to his philosophy of life so neatly expressed in his phrase, 'One's chief business is to be really at home.' In the letter to Bethel in which this symbolic remark is found, he adds, 'My house is like the house of a Patriarch of old standing by the highway side, and receiving all travellers.' He was much at home, and he received many guests; but he was also a traveller—in Parson Adams's style (in books) as well as in the coaches of his noble friends. If he was seldom really at home, he might have used Sir Balaam's excuse, ' 'Twas such a busy life!' He fluttered from house to house in his 'rambles', and he fluttered from page to page in innumerable books: between whiles he wrote, tended his mother's reposing age, rearranged his garden and his grotto, and had little time left in which to utter the cry of disillusionment and ennui, 'Vive la bagatelle!'

The spring of 1730 was not perhaps his busiest, but then as always he was busy; and a page preserved in the papers of Joseph Spence makes this spring worth examining as a specimen period. The last fortnight in April Pope spent in 'a little journey'—unidentified. But at the beginning of May he was back in Twickenham entertaining visitors. For the whole first week of the month he seems to have had as guest one of his most important and most self-effacing friends, the Rev. Joseph Spence, who came perhaps from Oxford, where he was Professor of Poetry, or perhaps from Birchanger (Essex), where he was Rector. Spence already aspired to be Pope's biographer, and during the week he listened attentively as Pope and he paced through the garden or rested in the sunny entrance to the damp grotto or (more likely!) sat by the fire in Pope's library. They talked of Machiavelli and Montaigne, of the ruling passion, and of Pope's growing works that were to advertise this passion. From the fragments already on paper or in his mind Pope read or recited, and Spence, as befitted a dutiful though inferior Boswell, retired and set down what he remembered on sheets of paper that were eventually to furnish matter for his *Anecdotes*. Only one sentence of his record of this week's

conversations seems to have been printed, and yet the whole has
considerable interest. The additional material here given is preserved in the Spence papers, now the property of Mr. James M.
Osborn of Yale University. The date and source of Spence's
notes are given in the superscription.[1] It will be noted that
Savage (who must have dropped in) contributes one piece of
information. The entire entry for the week, here printed by
kind permission of Mr. Osborn, is as follows:

May 1–7, 1730   Mr. Pope

How wrong y[e] Greatest men have been in judging
of the Cause of Human Actions. Instance frō Machi-
avel, of concluding in y[e] general frō particulars (w[r]
Besiegd Forces ought to sally or not?) Instance frō —
of judg[g] of a particular fro y[e] General: (a person fights
too soon: *bec*: he is of a Vindicative temper.) Montaigne hence concludes Pyrrhonically, That nothing
can be known of the Workings of men's minds: 1
Essay, lib: 2? (The best in his whole book. There?
y[e] Instance of Tiberius' growing an open man all
at once. (That Openness really y[e] highest piece of
Dissimulation.)—New Hypothesis, That a prevailing

EM ii. 133   passion in y[e] mind is brought wth it into y[e] world, &
continues till death (illustrated, by y[e] Seeds of y[e] Ill-
ness y[t] is at last to destroy us, being planted in y[e] body
at our births.)

EM ii. 195–6   We s[d] not speak ag[st] one large Vice, without speak-
ing ag[st] its contrary.—As to y[e] General Design of
EM ii. 197   Providence, y[e] two Extremes of a Vice, serve like two
opposite biasses to keep up y[e] Ballance of things.
ME iii. 14   Avarice, lays up (w[t] w[d] be hurtful;) Prodigality,
ME iv. 1–4   scatters abroad (w[t] may be useful in other hands:)
The middle y[e] point for Virtue: M[r] P has very large
(prose) collections on y[e] Happiness of Contentment.
ME iv. 14   Prodigality (in his piece) flings away all in wrong
tastes. (Tis there in particular y[t] some of y[e] Gardening
Poem will be of Service.) [L[d] Bolingbroke has sent

[1] Where the talk of Pope and Spence seems clearly concerned with specific passages of poems then in composition, I have added a marginal indication of the
passage relevant, using initials for titles, such as *EM* for *Essay on Man*, *ME* for
'Moral Essay'—*ME* iii referring to the Epistle 'On the Use of Riches' (to Lord
Bathurst), and *ME* iv referring to 'Moral Essay' iv, which under several titles was
addressed to the Earl of Burlington. In the Spence papers this leaf will be found
in Clumber MS. 490, gathering 4 (573. b. 42).

MʳP a long letter on these heads; & has by him wᵗ
wᵈ make 6 or 7 sheets in print toward a Second; &
does not know how far it may grow; Mʳ Sav:]

Spence,
Anecdotes,
(1820), p. 16.
The first Epistle? is to be to yᵉ Whole work, wᵗ a
Scale is to a book of Maps: in this lies yᵉ greatest
difficulty: not only in settling all yᵉ parts, but in
making them agreeable enough to be read with
ME iii. 339,
250; 4, 8 pleasure. Sʳ Balaam: The man of Ross: The Standing
jest of Heaven. And sure yᵉ Gods & We are of a mind.
The Man possesd of Debts & Taxes clear, Children
ME iii. 279 & Wife—Five hundred pound a year (Publ: Buildings
Alms Houses, Walks, Road; The man of Ross divides
ME iii. 248 ff. yᵉ weekly bread: Public Table twice a week for
Strangers &c.—Will give wᵗ we desire; Fire, Meat,
& Drink—What more? Meat, Drink, & fire. No
judging of a piece frō yᵉ Scatter'd parts: yᵉ 3 dots,
& Hieroglyphic: (not as to yᵉ Great Beauty: but we
may see particular beauties in yᵉ parts? That's very
true.)

Here we have Pope talking about his 'work in progress'; and
from the fact that most of the allusions are to the second epistle
of the *Essay on Man* and the third 'Moral Essay' ('On the Use of
Riches: To Lord Bathurst'), one might conclude that these were
the poems on which Pope was working at the moment. But one
cannot be sure: it is possible that for some reason the passages
mentioned were simply those that stuck in Spence's mind. The
passages at least existed before 7 May 1730. The very beginning of the record seems to allude to the first 'Moral Essay' ('On
the Characters of Men'), and there is explicit mention of 'the
gardening poem', which almost two years later appeared as *An
Epistle to the . . . Earl of Burlington*. Although this last poem is
spoken of as a unit, an unpublished letter from Pope to Burlington indicates that it was sent to his lordship for approval on
4 April 1731, eight months before publication. One might have
expected that if the poem was complete in April 1730, Lord
Burlington would have seen it sooner. Possibly, but not surely,
the two poems on riches, for Bathurst and Burlington, were more
definitely in form at the time of Spence's visit than was the
Essay on Man.

The chief importance of Spence's record is that it shows us
Pope at work on several poems at once; and from other notes

by Spence and from a study of the working manuscripts of some of the poems (several such are preserved) we can form a fairly clear idea of how Pope put his work on paper. The results of our examination can concern only humble mechanics of composition and not imaginative processes. There might seem to be four stages of mental and manual labour involved in this procedure: (1) Making notes for the poem, sometimes detailed, in prose; (2) the composition of verse paragraphs; (3) the arranging of these fragments in an effective structure; and (4) the polishing and perfecting of lines. This last type of activity naturally went on in all the other stages of composition.

First, then, we must recognize that for at least some of his poems he made notes in prose or a version in prose, more or less complete and organized. In another conversation, later than 1730, he told Spence, 'I wrote the Essay on Criticism fast; for I had digested all the matter, in prose, before I began upon it in verse.' Again, he spoke to Spence of 'my *Brutus*, which is all planned already; and even some of the most material speeches written in prose'. Spence's record in 1730 concerning the 'very large (prose) collections on the Happiness of Contentment' (ultimately to become the fourth epistle of the *Essay on Man*?) seems to suggest that this prose stage in composition was perhaps habitual. Savage's remark on Lord Bolingbroke's 'long letter' with a second under way, and incomplete, though equivalent already to many pages of print, reinforces strongly Lord Bathurst's story concerning Bolingbroke's 'dissertation in prose' that helped form the *Essay on Man*. But Lord Bathurst in 1769 wrote of this dissertation: 'It has never appeared since, and perhaps I am the only man now alive who has read it.' Most unfortunately none of these preliminary prose collections, except the summary of *Brutus*, is known to have survived: they would be largely hypothetical if it were not for Spence's notes. One may doubt if Pope destroyed Bolingbroke's 'dissertation', since the poet regarded his lordship idolatrously as 'much the best writer of the age'. Upon Pope's death his executor (William Murray, later the first Earl of Mansfield) returned to Pope's friends letters from them that Pope had preserved, and one suspects that Bolingbroke, also an executor, would take back his own manuscripts. It is at least conceivable that this prose dissertation written for Pope still exists.

Pope's admirers have been loath to admit the charge that in

the *Essay on Man* he simply versified a prose dissertation by Lord Bolingbroke. One page (the fifth) in the manuscript of the fourth epistle of the *Essay* preserved in the Pierpont Morgan Library seems to illustrate a procedure less simple than the mere turning of prose into verse. On this page Pope jotted down ideas in both verse and prose. Like so many others from Pope's workshop, it is a tantalizing confusion of fragments, with prose at the top and bottom of the page and fragments of verse in between. Some of the more easily deciphered bits are as follows:

> Cur bona malis, mala Bonis   Principio
> accidunt?   negatur

> Tis one part of ye Goodness of Providence y^t felicity
> & misfortune succeed alternately, y^t men may bear y^e
> one with moderation & ye other with Patience, &
> raise their minds to ye Search of w^t is better & more
> durable, in Virtue itself &c.
> Difference of Fortune, Powr, &c right in Providence

EM iv. 64
> That Powr who made ye Difference knows ye best;
> Were all men Equal, all men w^d Contest,

> You ask, Why such unequal Fate below?
> Why Happiness to Vice, to Virtue Woe?

> Let sober Moralists correct their speech
> No Bad man's happy, he is great, or rich.
> Did wealth e'er give but to ye wise and Just?
> His own Contentment, or another's Trust?

EM iv. 187–8
> Judges and Senates may be had for Gold
> Esteem and Love were never to be sold.

255
> One self-approving Hour whole years outweighs
> Of stupid Starers & of loud Huzza's
> A good man banished more contentm^t feels

258
> Than Caesar with a Senate at his heels.

170
> Canst thou for Virtue better paym^t fix,
> For humble merit say a Coach & six?
> For Justice, a Mayors Sword, or Chancelors Gown?

172
> For public Spirit, its great cure, a Crown?
> Rewards, that either w^d to virtue bring

181–2
> No joy, or be destruction of ye thing.

183–4   How oft by these at 60 are undone the Virtues of a
          Saint at twenty one

149–50   *But you say Good men want Necessaries, Bread, &c.
          he may not deserve those? Bread is ye Rew^d of Toil,
155   & he may be Indolent or weak yet Good. This *Good-
          ness* is rew^{d}ed by consciousness Quiet Content &c.
167   It is better he sh^d starve y^n y^t ye naturall order of
          things sh^d be perverted, contrary to y^t Course, in his
          favor?

Conclusions based on a page like this (which is here by omission much simplified) are bound to be perilous. These prose
passages, however, seem rather embryonic couplets than matter
for footnotes: they have the conversational tone of the poem
itself. This is probably the sort of prose that Pope 'versified'
throughout the *Essay*. But one must not be too sure: there are
two occurrences of obscure reference numerals in the page.
Opposite the couplet that became iv. 63–4 Pope has written,
'For Peace   Pass. 291.311'. And after the remark about
'a Saint at twenty one' comes something like 'See Poston
41.110.182'. These entries may of course refer to line-numbers
as they stood in the manuscripts or to numbered poetic fragments yet unarranged or, quite possibly, to numbered passages
in the 'very large (prose) collections on ye Happiness of Contentment', which Pope, according to Spence, had—perhaps from
Bolingbroke. Concerning Pope's use of prose in composing we
have scant data apart from remarks of Spence.

The second stage of composition was that of putting prose
fragments into verse. This has just been illustrated, and here
one can feel one is on surer ground, for working manuscripts of
poems by Pope are surprisingly numerous, though most of those
preserved are beyond the fragmentary stage. Habitually in
working manuscripts from the early thirties Pope used folio
half-sheets and wrote in the outer half of each page, using the
inner half for possible revisions. When he had his fragments
more or less cemented together, a friend (if a willing friend, such
as Thomas Dancastle—who transcribed the whole *Iliad*—or the
Countess of Burlington or Jonathan Richardson, happened
along) made him a fair copy, doubtless thinking the work
finished. But more than once, as one can see in the fragments
of the *Epistle to Dr. Arbuthnot* preserved in the Morgan Library,
the insatiate reviser cut up the fair copy, rearranged the order

of the passages, inserted new sections, and rephrased lines until the manuscript page became a most confused tangle. Of this unconscionable appetite for revision we have further evidence from his publisher, Dodsley, recorded in Johnson's 'Life of Pope'. Of the poem that became the *Epilogue to the Satires* Johnson says:

Dodsley told me that they were brought to him by the author, that they might be fairly copied. 'Almost every line', he said, 'was then written twice over; I gave him a clean transcript, which he sent some time afterwards to me for the press, with almost every line written twice over a second time.'

If such a manuscript be placed in comparison with the clean fair copy of the *Essay on Criticism* preserved in Bodley, the conclusion must be that the habit of revision grew upon Pope with the years. All the working manuscripts of Pope's later poems bear out the assumption that Dodsley's experience with the *Epilogue* was quite normal. The manuscripts show, furthermore, that Pope worked by paragraphs or passages and that his great problem was arranging the paragraphs and tying them together tactfully. In December 1730 Pope wrote to Caryll, ' I have many fragments which I am beginning to put together, but nothing perfect or finished, nor in any condition to be shown, except to a friend at a fireside.'

A good example of his methods of 'building' a poem is found in the fragments of the *Epistle to Dr. Arbuthnot* now in the Morgan Library. In these sixteen pages or scraps of pages (not all in Pope's hand, but all contemporary with him) versions of the passage beginning 'Why did I write' (ll. 125–46) appear on three different leaves. In one (fol. 7) we have only the first word or words of each line. This is Pope's method of indicating that a passage has been completely composed and need not be recopied at the moment; but space is left so that, upon inspiration, revision may be entered. What he wishes to work upon are the passages preceding and following. In another page (fol. 11) we have the completed passages preceded by a transitional approach (later discarded) and followed immediately by the passage beginning with line 151—

If meagre Gildon draw his venal quill.

In other words, here the passage as a unit has been composed, but the 'approaches' that tie it to the rest of the poem remain

unsettled. The third version (fol. 4) is even more significant,
and is a perfect example of Pope's growing habit of working on
two or more poems at once—and of confusing them. Here the
mixture involves the *Epistle to Dr. Arbuthnot* (1735) and *The
First Satire of the Second Book of Horace Imitated* (1733), which he
addressed to William Fortescue. To aid in sorting out the lines
in the following excerpt an *A* is printed before numbers of
lines that belong eventually to the *Epistle to Dr. Arbuthnot* and
an *F* before those from the poem addressed to Fortescue. For
readability the lines left incomplete by Pope in the manuscript
are filled in with bracketed readings from Mr. Butt's text in the
Twickenham edition of Pope's poems.

And now ye Town imagines [still I write]
All ask [when this or that shall see the light]

A 275   I saw [him close with *Swift*—'Indeed? no doubt']
A 276   Cries [prating *Balbus* 'something will come out.']

Tis sure (says V—n) his great
Ethic or epic, I am

A 277   Tis all in vain[, deny it as I will.]
A 278   'No [, such a genius never can lye still,']
A 279   & then [for mine obligingly mistakes]
A 280   The [first Lampoon Sir *Will.* or *Bubo* makes.]
A 281   Poor [guiltless I! and can I chuse but smile,]
A 282   When [ev'ry Coxcomb knows me by my *Style*?]

'But why write Satyr? Bubo asks? Tis true
Bubo hates Satire, Satire hates him too.
'& why make Folly (cries Ld Froth) y^r theme?
'Better by far to sing a purling stream.
Bubo & Froth are ecchod by each Sot:
But Z—ds cries B—y, Sir, why should you not?
What if I sing
~~Id rather praise~~ Augustus great and good?
'You did so lately. Was it understood?
Speak out, then, open in a note profound
As rumbling D—s or a Norfolk Hound.

F 24   Wth George & Fredric roughen up the Verse

Then smooth up all   reherse:

F 31   Wth soft Amelia charm ye tuneful nine
F 32   & sweetly flow thro all ye Royal Line.

No—the high task to lift up Kings to Gods
Leave to Court Sermons & to Birthday Odes.
On theams like these superior far to thine,
Let laureld Cibber & great Arnall shine.

Why write at all? 'Yes, Silence if y^u keep,
The Town, ye Court, ye very Dunciad weep?
F 59   Write then, but publish not. Be vice y^r Text
F 60   But keep this Age's Picture for ye next
F 61   Your Foes shall wish y^r Life a longer date,
F 62   & evry friend shall less lament y^r fate.
A 287   Agreed. All you! who hurt a harmless neighbors peace,
A 288   Insult falln worth, or Beauty in distress,
A 289   Who love a Lye, lame Slander help about
A 290   Who write a Libel, or who copy out
A 291   This Fop whose Pride [affects a Patron's name,]
A 292   2Yet absent [, wounds an Author's honest fame;]
A 295   That more abusive [calls himself your friend]   *A* 112
A 296   3Yet wants ye Honor [injur'd to defend;]
Who courts ye name of wit at ye expence
1Of Candor, Decency Religion Sense
A 299   Who to ye dean & silver Bell can swear
A 300   and sees at C—s what was never there
A 297   Who   w^tere I Mean w^tere I say
A 298   & if he lies not, must at least betry
A 303   Let never modest men my Satire dread
A 304   But all such babling Blockheads in their stead

This example of confusion resulting from simultaneous composition of two poems is not surprising; it can be duplicated
from the manuscripts of other of Pope's poems from this period,
notably those of the *Essay on Man*. The very elaborateness of
Pope's programme led to inevitable confusion, which persisted
even after the *Essay on Man* was printed. By that time Pope's
'moral' scheme, though still tentative, was more settled than
when described to Spence in 1730.

This grand project for a series of poems in from two to four
'books' has some importance in Pope's methods of composition,
since it helps explain how poems overlapped and how passages
from one were originally conceived as belonging to another.
Lines in defence of satire might appear in the poems addressed
to Arbuthnot and Fortescue and even in the later *Epilogue to
the Satires*. The ruling passion Pope treated twice—as he did
other favourite topics. He explained his grand plan more than
once to Spence, who was interested enough to transcribe a suppressed page from the first collected edition of the *Essay on Man*,
which gave the outline of the project in printed form. Spence's
transcript, as preserved in his papers, reads as follows:

A Page annex'd to the Quarto Edition (of
1734) of the Essay on Man.

Index to the Ethic Epistles

The First Book:	The Second Book.
Of the Nature and State of Man.	Of the Use of Things.
	Of ye Limits of Human Reason.
Epistle I	Of ye Use of Learning.
With respect to the Universe.	Of ye Use of Wit.
	Of ye Knowledge & Characters of Men.
Epistle II. As an Individual	Of ye particular Characters of Women.
Epistle III. With respect to Society.	Of ye Principles & Use of Civil and Ecclesiastical Polity.
Epistle IV. With respect to Happiness.	—Of ye Use of Education.
	A View of ye Equality of Happiness in ye several Conditions of Men.
	—Of ye Use of Riches &c.

This was annext to about a dozen Books; that were sent as presents
to particular friends. Most of them were call'd in again, by Mr P;
but that to Mr Bethel was not; frō wch this is copy'd.

So far Spence. This page was very probably suppressed because, almost as soon as the *Essay on Man* was completely published, some, but not all, of the poems of 'Book II' were also
in print in early quarto editions of the *Essay on Man* as 'Ethic
Epistles The Second Book. To Several Persons'. This publication made superfluous the description transcribed by Spence
from the suppressed page.

   That Pope's plan was constantly shifting may be inferred
from the two holograph manuscripts of the *Essay on Man*, which
are now in the possession of the Pierpont Morgan Library and
the Houghton Library of Harvard University. Both include the
first three epistles, and the Morgan manuscript also contains an
early form of much of the fourth. In general the Morgan manuscript is the earlier. In the Harvard manuscript the poem is
approaching the state of a 'fair copy' almost ready for the press;
but it contains many revisions and some passages not found in

the Morgan manuscript and several that had not yet found their final position in the poem. Both manuscripts of Epistle I are in almost final state, but structural confusions still exist in Pope's mind. The Morgan manuscript has, opposite line 6 of Epistle I,

> A mighty Maze! of Walks without a Plan,

the marginal note: 'Inconsistencys of Character, yᵉ Subject of Ep. 5.' (This might well refer to the first Moral Essay.) Opposite line 7 ('where Weeds and Flowrs promiscuous shoot') we find the note: 'Passions, Virtues &c. yᵉ Subject of Ep. 2.'— probably of the *Essay* itself. To line 8 ('Orchard, tempting with forbidden Fruit') is appended: 'The Use of Pleasure, in Lib. 2' —which may possibly be a reference to Epistle IV of the *Essay on Man* or to some never written part of 'Book II'. Opposite line 10 ('Try what the *open*, what the *covert* yield') we find 'Of the Knowledge of Mankind Epistle 1ˢᵗ of Book 2'; and opposite 11 ('Of all who *blindly creep*, the tracks explore'), 'Learning & Ignorance, Subject of Epist. 3 of Book 2'. Opposite line 88 ('a sparrow fall') is 'Vid Epist 3. of animals'. Evidently the plans were still in process of formation; for in the Harvard manuscript Epistle II had opened with an abbreviated form of the passage beginning—

> Come then my *Friend*, my Genius come along!
> Oh Master of the Poet and the Song!

and a fairly complete form of the apostrophe to Bolingbroke is appended at the end of Epistle II (but not as a part of it). This last is labelled marginally 'Peroratio Lib. 1', and at the foot of the page 'Finis Lib. Prim.' The Morgan manuscript unfortunately lacks the last leaf of Epistle III, and the Harvard manuscript includes in the ending of Epistle III passages that eventually were to be placed in Epistle IV (e.g. iv. 361–72).

After Epistle III in the Harvard manuscript occur seven blank pages, on which Pope probably intended to insert Epistle IV when done; and after these blank leaves comes an inserted leaf (never a proper part of the manuscript) on which appears the following surprise:

> Incipit Liber Secundus
> Epist. I. Of yᵉ Limits of Reason

> And now, transported o'er so vast a Plain,
> While the free Courser flies with all the Rein;

> While heav'nward, now, his mounting Wings he feels,
> Now stoops where Fools fly trembling from his heels;
> Wilt thou, my Laelius! keep yᵉ Course in sight,
> Confine yᵉ Fury, or assist yᵉ Flight?
> Laelius, whose Love excus'd my labours past,
> Matures my present, & shall bound my last.

This fragment, representing Pegasus as somewhat like a dive-bomber with Bolingbroke as pilot and Pope as gunner, presents a contamination of the 'Peroratio Lib. 1' with the opening couplet of the imitation of *The First Epistle of the First Book of Horace*, which Pope addressed to Bolingbroke in 1738, more than four years after the *Essay on Man* was completely in print. The last couplet here quoted occurs also in the discarded apostrophe to Memmius–Laelius that opened Epistle II in both the Morgan and the Harvard manuscripts.

A similar curious contamination is seen in a passage reserved for better service but originally designed to follow the famous lines of the *Essay on Man* concerning vice as a monster of such frightful mien (ii. 217–20). Both manuscripts of the *Essay* have the following lines in slightly varying forms:

> A *Cheat*! a *Whore*! who starts not at the Name
> In all the Inns of Court, or Drury Lane?
> B—t but does business, Huggins brings matters on*
> Sid *has the Secret*, Chartres *knows the Town*.
> [*Marginal variant: Y— but *serves the Crown*]

Along with practically all details of personal satire these lines disappeared when the *Essay* was printed; but they show up brilliantly near the beginning of the *Epilogue to the Satires* (1738):

> But *Horace*, Sir, was delicate, was nice;
> *Bubo* observes, he lash'd no sort of *Vice*:
> *Horace* would say, Sir Billy *serv'd the Crown*,
> Blunt *could do Bus'ness*, H-ggins *knew the Town*, . . .

And possibly the first of these manuscript couplets (omitted from the *Essay* after the first edition) is bitterly inverted later in the *Epilogue*:

> The wit of Cheats, the Courage of a Whore,
> Are what ten thousand envy and adore.

Obviously Pope could not prosecute his elaborate plan for many related poems and compose with several in mind at once without confusing them.

When Pope told Spence in 1730 that there was 'no judging of a piece from the scattered parts', he was being modest and was recognizing the confused state of his fragmentary manuscripts. Spence properly interpreted the remark: one should 'survey the whole'—

> 'Tis not a lip, or eye, we beauty call,
> But the joint force and full result of all.

Pedantry may be permitted to remark, however, after examining Pope's manuscripts, that he composed by fragmentary paragraphs fully as often as by individual couplets, and far more often than he did from any sort of structural 'outline' of the whole poem. As he told Spence, the greatest trouble was in 'settling and ranging' these parts aright. The poet's habit of working in verse paragraphs can be seen anywhere. In the Harvard manuscript of the *Essay on Man*, Epistle I, for example, lines 29–34 of the standard editions are placed after line 22; lines 61–8 come after line 28, and are followed by lines 35–42; after line 186 come 207–32, &c. A comparison of early printed texts of the fourth 'Moral Essay' ('Of Taste') with later texts will show that the habit of rearranging paragraphs continued even after the poem was published. Both in the Harvard manuscript of the *Essay on Man*, Epistle I (which was obviously regarded as a final fair copy when begun), and in the fourth 'Moral Essay', the parts shuffled involve nearly always more than a single couplet. There has been too much stress on Pope's artistry in couplets; he is, as a matter of fact, quite as notably an artist in verse paragraphs. His art in varying the mood and tone and pace of succeeding paragraphs gives a diversity that indemnifies for any supposed monotony resultant from the closed couplet.

One may well suspect that in later days the *Essay on Man* would have been more favourably regarded by critics if the poet had printed his verse paragraphs frankly as such—if, in the manner of Traherne's *Centuries of Meditations* or of Tennyson's *In Memoriam*, he had been content to leave his verse units as fragmentary reflections on philosophic ideas that are bound to have recurrent interest. Pope did, of course, indicate units by marginal Roman numerals; yet he wished finally to think of his work as 'a short, yet not imperfect, system of ethics'.

Of this 'system' he fell short, and of all the stages of poetic composition that of 'settling the parts' into a coherent and effective order worried him most. The difficulty is especially acute in the early thirties, when he is at work on different poems simultaneously; but perhaps the difficulty is inherent in the attempt to write fairly long poems that are discursively reflective.

Coming to the last stage of composition to be considered, we can have no doubt that the poet did make his fragmentary reflections 'agreeable enough to be read with pleasure'. Of his *limae labor et mora* already much has been said, and perhaps it is all summed up in the general opinion that Pope seldom altered without improvement. Examples may be superfluous, but the manuscripts of the *Essay on Man* are so full of them that one cannot forbear quoting. The opening lines of Epistle II—

> Know then thyself; presume not God to scan;
> The proper study of mankind is man—

are so natural an example of the firm, lapidary style that one can hardly imagine the couplet is the result of much reshaping. But in the Morgan Library manuscript the Epistle begins with the comparatively feeble

> we ourselves
> Learn ~~then Thyself~~, not God presume to scan
> But
> ~~And~~ know, the Study of Mankind is *Man*.

And the Harvard manuscript has as lines 13–14 of the Epistle (after 12 lines of apostrophe to Bolingbroke):

> Know
> ~~Learn~~ we ourselves, not God presume to scan,
> The only Science Convinced
> ~~But know~~, the Study of Mankind is *Man*.

Obviously the real inspiration here came after some floundering. The couplet is a superb example of Pope's process of perfecting his utterance. One may note that there is nothing inherently 'decorative' about the process. Another type of perfecting is seen in the famous passage in Epistle I concerning the Indian concept of Heaven. In part the Morgan manuscript reads:

> Yet Nature's flattery this Hope has given;
> Behind his cloud-topt Hills he builds a Heaven,
> Some happier World, wch woods on woods infold,
> Where never christian pierced for thirst of Gold.

Some safer World, in depth of Woods embrac'd,
Some happier Island in the watry waste,
Where slaves once more their native land behold,
No Fiends torment, nor Christians thirst for Gold.
Where Gold n'er grows, & never Spaniards come,
Where Trees bear maize, & Rivers flow wth Rum,
Exil'd, or chain'd, he lets you understand
Death but returns him to his native Land;
Or firm as Martyrs, smiling yields the ghost,
Rich of a Life, that is not to be lost.

In the Harvard manuscript Pope had improved the first of these lines into its standard printed form, doubtless because of the unsatisfactory implications of *flattery*, which later Mr. Elwin was at pains to point out. Other verses, of some merit, were omitted to secure a firmer line of thought or at least greater brevity. The problem *proprie communia dicere* was encountered by Pope at every point in his revisions.

Of the fourteen lines just quoted Pope has crossed through for deletion lines 3 and 4 and the last six: the printed texts give variants of the remaining six. The case may serve as occasion to remark that Pope's method of composition by accreting paragraphs is in part balanced by this art of blotting. The Morgan manuscript of the four epistles of the *Essay on Man* contains almost 250 lines that did not appear in versions printed by Pope. Dr. Johnson concluded from the Homer manuscripts of Pope that the poet's method 'was to write his first thoughts in his first words, and gradually to amplify, decorate, rectify, and refine them'. This statement is largely, but not completely, true. There exists, for example, an early manuscript form of what was to become the *Epistle to Dr. Arbuthnot*; and the manuscript runs only to about a hundred lines—less than one-fourth the final length of the poem. But Pope practised condensation as well, and omitted much that he set down on paper in his working manuscripts. Concerning the decorative quality of his later composition there may be argument. If added illustrative details be regarded in the manner of gargoyles, these accretions are decorative. But if one considers Pope's imaginative phrasing after the *Dunciad* of 1729—and apart from Book IV of that poem (1743)—the effect is not decorative but functional. His labour to produce

Know then thyself, presume not God to scan

is a fair example. The diction is chiselled and 'rectified', but not ornate. Through all the stages of composition—the turning of prose hints into verse paragraphs, the ranging of these paragraphs, and the final *limae labor*—Pope's object is the rectification of expression. For him poetry is perfected utterance, and his working manuscripts, especially those from the early thirties, testify to his unwearied attempts to polish his paragraphs and make them 'agreeable enough to be read with pleasure'.

THE INSPIRATION OF POPE'S POETRY

THE twentieth-century reader is beginning to discover that there is enjoyment to be obtained from the poetry of Pope, but he is still in danger of misunderstanding what Pope was trying to express and the methods he used. The radical misunderstanding is that though the meaning of Pope's poetry seems so easy to grasp, it requires as active and intelligent co-operation from the reader as the work of more recognizably difficult poets. Many poems—many great poems—require in the first place little more than the reader's sympathy, his receptivity, his power of experiencing normal human emotions. We need only to have been glad at the sight of a field of daffodils to appreciate 'I wandered lonely as a cloud' and to receive from it all, or almost all, that Wordsworth has to communicate. And we need no particular training or sophistication to be excited by Keats's 'Ode to Autumn' or by *Hamlet*. Study will enrich our appreciation, but it is possible to enjoy reading much Elizabethan and much nineteenth-century poetry with no other equipment than keenness of sensibility, because our power of seeing and feeling is the most obvious part of that common ground of experience which we share with Shakespeare, Keats, and Wordsworth, and from which their poetry sprang.

But the common reader, fresh from the excitement of romantic poetry, is troubled as soon as he begins to read Pope. He finds some things to please him: the pathos of such a line as

> To help me thro' this long Disease, my Life,[1]

or the rapture of

> *Belinda* smil'd, and all the World was gay,[2]

or the accuracy (to call it no more) of

> The spider's touch, how exquisitely fine!
> Feels at each thread, and lives along the line.[3]

Equally apparent is Pope's 'fine and delicate imagination', as his friend the Earl of Orrery described it. Nothing more than a

---

[1] *Epistle to Arbuthnot*, 132.   [2] *Rape of the Lock*, ii. 52.
[3] *Essay on Man*, i. 217 f.

4830   F

sympathetic and receptive mind is required to appreciate such
a couplet as this, describing the activities of eastern magicians:

> These stop'd the Moon, and call'd th' unbody'd Shades
> To Midnight Banquets in the glimmering Glades,[1]

and perhaps nothing more than an alert mind to notice Pope's
fondness for words such as *glimmering* in that couplet, which
with its suggestion of something imperfectly seen is charged
with romantic associations and possibilities. The alert reader
will remember 'the glimmering light' in such an unpromising
context as the *Essay on Criticism*;[2] or the sylphs in *The Rape of
the Lock*, 'trembling for the Birth of Fate'.[3] The recurrence of
'trembling' is especially remarkable: the Priestess trembles before she begins the sacred rites of pride;[4] the shrines tremble as
Eloisa takes the veil;[5] and later in that poem, when Eloisa kneels
before the altar in religious ecstasy, one thought of Abelard
puts all the pomp to flight:

> Priests, Tapers, Temples, swim before my sight:
> In seas of flame my plunging soul is drown'd,
> While Altars blaze, and Angels tremble round.[6]

In each of these instances the word is used to signify the uncon-
trollable reaction to some more than human activity, an essentially romantic effect most readily pleasing to the unsophisticated
reader. But the unsophisticated reader will find comparatively
little of this in Pope, and his pleasure in it will be modified by
what will appear peculiar in Pope's imaginative and descriptive
writing; peculiar, that is, when compared with the imaginative
and descriptive writing of Shakespeare, Wordsworth, and Keats.

I

With two exceptions, the passages quoted above are taken
from poems written before 1717, the year in which Pope collected
and published his early work. In these poems his imagination
had been specially active: devising fanciful situations in the
Pastorals and *The Rape of the Lock*; creating a new race of beings
called sylphs; placing the sculptured figures of the 'Elegy to the
Memory of an Unfortunate Lady' and 'Eloisa to Abelard' in a
variety of exquisitely passionate poses; describing idealized
scenes in the 'Messiah', *Windsor Forest*, and *The Temple of*

---

[1] *Temple of Fame*, 101 f.   [2] l. 21.   [3] ii. 142.
[4] Ibid. i. 128.   [5] *Eloisa to Abelard*, 112.   [6] Ibid. 274–6.

Fame, as lavish with his gold paint as Sir John Vanbrugh decorating Blenheim Palace, dropping it on the breast of a pheasant,[1] on the scales of a carp,[2] on the roofs of Mexican palaces,[3] on the façade of Fame's temple,[4] on chariots,[5] and on the girdles of goddesses,[6] and even having enough to spare for a lake of liquid gold in *The Rape of the Lock*;[7] then setting these off with crystal domes and countless silver ornaments,[8] and breathing upon them Arabian gales[9] and the aromatic souls of flowers,[10] till the scenes were as gorgeously rococo as any Man of Taste could require.

After 1717 Pope preferred to subdue his powers of imagination. Looking back upon this early poetry in later years, he regarded it with indulgent condescension as a youthful excess. He liked to think that he had not wandered long in Fancy's maze (the distinction between Fancy and Imagination was not yet recognized), but had soon stooped like a falcon upon Truth and moralized his song. The association of description and fancy implied, and the dissociation of description and truth, are worth remarking. Pope's method in description never was to keep his eye on the object and to describe that object so accurately either by realistic or impressionistic means that the description corresponded with what other men might see. He preferred to describe something laid up in his imagination, something more splendid than could be seen by anyone else. What he describes are such scenes as I have already indicated, scenes bedizened with gold and silver—something quite unnatural, as unnatural as the decoration of Lycid's hearse; for neither Milton nor Pope wished to limit themselves to the comparatively mean resources of nature. Truth of description, like all other aspects of truth, Pope reserved to strengthen his moral purpose. The fineness of the spider's touch is part of his argument that 'throughout the whole visible world, an universal order and gradation in the sensual and mental faculties is observed, which causes a subordination of creature to creature, and of all creatures to Man'. The dab-chick, which

> waddles thro' the copse
> On feet and wings, and flies, and wades, and hops,[11]

[1] *Windsor Forest*, 118.   [2] Ibid. 144.   [3] Ibid. 412.
[4] *Temple of Fame*, 197.   [5] *Rape of the Lock*, iv. 155.
[6] *Windsor Forest*, 176.   [7] *Rape of the Lock*, iv. 45.
[8] e.g. ibid. i. 32, 122; iii. 108, 109.   [9] *Temple of Fame*, 317.
[10] *Windsor Forest*, 244.   [11] *Dunciad*, ii. 63 f.

was described so precisely to make the appearance of one of the dunces more ridiculous. To appreciate Pope's imaginative description, therefore, we must be prepared to forget for the moment our breeding in naturalistic poetry. So much co-operation is essential to avoid misunderstanding.

II

But though Pope allowed himself more licence in description than later poets have done, he allowed himself less licence in expounding a rule of life and the truth as he understood it. Pope was no revolutionary. He had no Utopian system to offer. He had no wish to reconstruct society. Instead, he fell in with the spirit of the times, which was to conserve and consolidate what had been won by the revolutionary struggles of the previous century. His ethical position resembles Addison's not a little. The writings of both men were intended to produce a higher level of culture and a greater social decency in the new middle class, which was just then growing up. Their methods were different—Addison preferred persuasion and raillery, Pope preferred satire: but their motives were the same. The influence of the *Tatler* and the *Spectator* on Pope's way of thinking was considerable. It was perhaps from these periodicals that he acquired his views on literature as a corrective to morals; and, as Professor Sherburn has observed, *The Rape of the Lock* would have been almost impossible before raillery on the fair sex had been made popular by Steele and Addison.

But we cannot merely say that the intention and inspiration of Pope's original poetry after he had escaped from Fancy's maze were ethical, for to say no more than that might suggest that Pope was imagining some ideal society and expounding some ideal rule of life. His intention and inspiration were not so revolutionary. Indeed, all his moral poetry was directed to improving the existing social state. His inspiration was therefore both ethical and topical. We shall not fully appreciate the magnificent praise of humility and political probity in the *Epilogue to the Satires* until we know something of the so-called 'patriotic' movement of the late thirties, a movement started by a few honest but gullible members of the parliamentary opposition, inspired by Bolingbroke, who hoped to end the jobbery and corruption of Walpole's government. Similarly, the numerous passages in praise of retirement and the simple life should be read in the light of Pope's compulsory retirement as a Roman Catholic and a Tory sympathizer. Our full understanding and enjoyment of the *Essay on Man* will depend to some extent upon our knowledge of the tenets of Bolingbroke and other deistic philosophers; and the epistle to Burlington, *On the Use of Riches*, cannot be fully appreciated without at least some recognition of contemporary taste in architecture and gardening. This applies even more to the casual references throughout these later poems. When at the end of the *Epilogue to the Satires* Pope thinks of himself as the last to draw a pen for freedom, because 'Truth stands trembling on the edge of Law', he is alluding to the press censorship which the government was threatening in 1738. The reason why the Law's thunder is hurled on Gin in the same poem[1] will not be appreciated by one who has not seen Hogarth's celebrated picture 'Gin Lane' or who has not read of the disastrous effects on the physique of the population of the sale of cheap gin and the riots which followed the attempt to curtail its distribution. Or why should Pope compare Addison's fear of rivals to the Turk's, who could bear no brother near the throne?[2] The answer is that Pope was retorting upon Addison the very same rebuke with which Addison had started his review of the *Essay on Criticism* in the *Spectator*, and was adapting for that purpose three lines of Denham's poem on John Fletcher's works quoted by Addison on that occasion:

> Nor needs thy juster Title the foul guilt
> Of Eastern Kings, who to secure their reign,
> Must have their Brothers, Sons, and Kindred slain.

Without that particular knowledge, some of the point and effectiveness is lost.

A commentary when reading Pope's later works is therefore essential, 'a necessary evil' as Dr. Johnson said of commentaries on Shakespeare, something to be cast aside and ignored when the reader starts a later reading of the poem. Pope was quite well aware of the topical difficulty of his poems, as he showed by setting an example in annotation. Few of his later works were issued without explanatory notes, and as further editions appeared when the immediate occasion of many lines had been forgotten, the notes were increased in number. It is inevitable that the common reader should neglect what is merely topical

---

[1] 'Dialogue I', 130.   [2] *Epistle to Arbuthnot*, 198.

in the literature of former ages, when there is so much being written by his contemporaries which more nearly concerns him. He must therefore be assured of the compensations for his trouble in tackling the antiquarian problems of Pope's later poetry before he pays it much attention.

To say merely that Pope's ethical and topical poetry transcends its occasions is asking too much of a reader's faith. Yet this is the result of Pope's treatment of his materials. A tempting example of this transcendence is the striking applicability (though it must be allowed to be mere coincidence) of Pope's political poetry to the political state of England just before the present war. Walpole had an unassailable parliamentary majority behind him; he had the moneyed interests on his side and the poets and the wits against him; and he was trying to avoid war by methods which the Opposition did not approve of. It is therefore not surprising that we can read to-day with a certain relish such irony as this addressed to the head of the government:

> Oh! could I mount on the Mæonian wing,
> Your Arms, your Actions, your Repose to sing!
> What seas you travers'd! and what fields you fought!
> Your Country's Peace, how oft, how dearly bought!
> How barb'rous rage subsided at your word,
> And Nations wonder'd while they dropp'd the sword!
> How, when you nodded, o'er the land and deep,
> Peace stole her wing, and wrapt the world in sleep;
> Till Earth's extremes your mediation own,
> And Asia's Tyrants tremble at your Throne.[1]

But the historical parallel here is a mere coincidence: Pope's ethical and topical poetry is often more profoundly and more permanently true. In contemporary extravagances and follies, Pope always sees the abuse of a general principle. In Timon's tasteless display of wealth[2] or in Sir Balaam's mercenary spirit[3] he sees a neglect of the rule of simple living: in the variety of Wharton's escapades,[4] an immoderate desire of admiration. And the converse is equally true: in Lyttelton he sees the type of the incorruptible politician,[5] or in Ralph Allen's secret philanthropy[6] a model of what every charitable man should be.

---

[1] 'Ep. to Augustus', 394–403.
[2] *Moral Essay*, iv. 99 ff.
[3] Ibid. iii. 339 ff.
[4] Ibid. i. 178 ff.
[5] *Imit. Hor.* Ep. I, i. 29.
[6] *Epilogue to the Satires*, i. 135 f.

These particular examples are, like a nightingale or a Grecian urn to Keats, the exciting perceptions which moved Pope to the expression of something which has universal significance. Their purpose in his poetry is to give illustrative force to the expression of universal truths.

It is worth remarking that a comparison of earlier and later versions of a poem will show that Pope's method in revision was often to omit unnecessary particulars and to generalize. Thus the 'Irish Poetess' of an early version of the *Epistle to Dr. Arbuthnot* (l. 16), a reference either to Mrs. Barber or to Mrs. Sykins, later becomes the 'maudlin Poetess', and by omitting the only direct reference to his quarrel with Addison he converted his character-sketch of Addison into 'Atticus', the type of all insincere yet influential men of letters.

Often Pope's method of generalizing seems to have been to conflate two characters. Thus Bufo, the mean and tasteless patron in the *Epistle to Dr. Arbuthnot*,[1] seems to be a conflation of Halifax and Bubb Dodington; Pitholeon, the sponging poet,[2] a conflation of Welsted and Cooke; Atossa, the termagant in the 'Characters of Women',[3] a conflation of the Duchess of Buckingham and the Duchess of Marlborough. No doubt it was economical and guarded to lampoon two people in one character, because if either protested Pope could declare the character was intended for the other. Such a reflection may have appealed to him, but of course Pope knew that he was more certain of describing a universal type by taking characteristics from a number of people than by confining himself to one. This should be a warning against an attempt to define each of Pope's characters as invariably the character of one of his contemporaries.

The problem whether to use his contemporaries' characters as his examples or to invent imaginary characters continually exercised Pope's mind. He discussed it again and again both in his poems and in his letters, but his attitude is briefly summarized in a passage from a letter to his friend Caryll: 'I shall make living examples, which enforce best'—enforce, of course, the universal truth whether the character be vicious or virtuous. Pope would seem to have agreed with Milton that Virtue needs no fanciful decoration to set off her beauty. His verse, whenever he reflects on virtuous behaviour, is quite un-

[1] ll. 231 ff.   [2] Ibid. 49 ff.   [3] 'Characters of Women', 115 ff.

adorned. The swell of emotion is enough to carry such passages,
as when he cries, in the *Epilogue to the Satires*:

> Yes, I am proud; I must be proud to see
> Men not afraid of God, afraid of me:
> Safe from the Bar, the Pulpit, and the Throne,
> Yet touch'd and sham'd by *Ridicule* alone.[1]

But it must not be supposed that his delight in sensuous description, so evident in the early poems, was extinguished when
he ceased to make Fancy the intention of his poetry. He
always took a trembling delight in the observation of beauty,
and though the beauty of a virtuous action now chiefly de-
tained him, he still had his use for sensuous experiences and
fancies:

> To happy Convents, bosom'd deep in vines,
> Where slumber Abbots, purple as their wines:
> To Isles of fragrance, lilly-silver'd vales,
> Diffusing languor in the panting gales:
> To lands of singing, or of dancing slaves,
> Love-whisp'ring woods, and lute-resounding waves.

But for the second line, one might well suppose that these lines
are to be found in *Windsor Forest* or the *Pastorals*. In fact,
they are part of Pope's satirical argument in the fourth book of
the *Dunciad*,[2] and are a description (like the Bower of Bliss in the
second book of the *Faerie Queene*) made to show how the young
can be debauched by sensuality. It is a triumph of Pope's vir-
tuosity that he reserves most of this later sensuousness for his
satirical verses, as though he were trying to rid them of any taint
of irritation, or demonstrating with what gracious ideas his
mind was filled when he conceived these lampoons. This is
especially true of the *Dunciad*, where Pope's enemies and the
traditional enemies of good taste and sense are flayed in his
most grave and imaginative poetry. Here we find Shadwell in
the limbo of forgotten poetasters 'nod[ding] the Poppy on his
brows',[3] and Lord Hervey, now renamed Narcissus,

> prais'd with all a Parson's pow'r,
> Look'd a white lilly sunk beneath a show'r,[4]

and Pope's arch-pedant reclining in sensuously Spenserian re-
pose:

> As many quit the streams that murm'ring fall
> To lull the sons of Marg'ret and Clare-hall,

[1] *Epilogue*, ii. 208 ff.   [2] ll. 301 ff.   [3] Ibid. iii. 22.   [4] iv. 103.

Where Bentley late tempestuous wont to sport
In troubled waters, but now sleeps in Port.[1]

In these lines the imaginative beauty is as evident as the mischievous pun, and surely gave Pope as much delight. One is bound to ask what was the nature of Pope's animosity against Theobald as he wrote the *Dunciad*. Was he really considering Theobald at all when he described him in that beautiful couplet?

Him close she curtain'd round with vapours blue,
And soft besprinkled with Cimmerian dew.[2]

Or was he any longer consumed with anger when he described the altar of books which Theobald erected as a sacrifice to the Goddess, and concluded his description with an allusion to the duodecimo edition of Theobald's translation of Sophocles?

Quarto's, Octavo's, shape the less'ning pyre,
And last, a little Ajax tips the spire.[3]

It is difficult to reconcile the poet who cared for such thrilling precision with the vicious little satirist of popular imagination. If there is petulance there, it is petulance recollected in tranquillity.

In these and in many a more extensive passage in the *Dunciad*, Pope is working at two levels. At one level he is avenging the wrongs done to good sense and culture by contemporary dunces, and attempting with partial success to make his own particular revenge of universal significance; at another level he is satisfying his imagination with poetry which is beautiful in itself, apart from any satiric significance.

III

There is another sense in which Pope's verses may be said to have differences of level, differences most easily illustrated from the *Imitations of Horace*. In the first 'Imitation', for example, he is making a particularly clever rendering of the first satire of Horace's second book and at the same time defending himself from certain specific charges, and in the 'Epistle to Augustus' he is turning Horace's praise of Augustus into ridicule of George II and at the same time making some astute judgements on poets of his own and previous generations. As a critic of Pope has expressed it, 'The *Imitations of Horace* show the poet bound hand and foot and yet dancing as if free.'[4] But such a dance could

---

[1] iv. 199 ff.   [2] iii. 3 f.   [3] *The Dunciad Variorum* (1729), i. 141 f.
[4] G. Tillotson, *Essays in Criticism and Research*, p. 96.

only be performed by one who had had constant practice in earlier measures:

> True ease in writing flows from art, not chance,
> As those move easiest who have learn'd to dance.[1]

All his life Pope had been active in verse translation. He was an accomplished translator long before he started on the *Iliad*. Translation, in fact, had been his early training. He told Spence that as a boy he read eagerly through a great number of English, French, Italian, Latin, and Greek poets, not with any system, but dipping in here and there, and whenever he met with a passage or story that pleased him more than ordinary, he endeavoured to imitate it, or translate it into English: 'this', he said,[2] 'gave rise to my Imitations published so long after'. It was by these translations and imitations that he shaped his own original work. 'My first taking to imitating', he told Spence,[3] 'was not out of vanity, but humility: I saw how defective my own things were; and endeavoured to mend my manner, by copying good strokes from others.' This, according to his own account, must have been evident in his first extensive poem, an epic of 4,000 lines on Alcander, Prince of Rhodes, which he kept by him until 1722, when he burnt it on Bishop Atterbury's advice. 'I endeavoured in this poem', he said,[4] 'to collect all the beauties of the great epic writers into one piece: there was Milton's style in one part, and Cowley's in another; here the style of Spenser imitated, and there of Statius; here Homer and Virgil, and there Ovid and Claudian.' The revealing account of his method in this early poem is to some extent true of his method in every poem he wrote. To call it plagiarism is too crude. It is better to connect it with Pope's imaginative, ethical, and topical inspiration, and call it Pope's literary inspiration, the appreciation of which presents one more difficulty to the common reader.

Literary inspiration is not essentially different from inspiration derived from life. The reading of a book can be an emotional experience as much as the sight of a field of daffodils, as Keats found when he looked into Chapman's Homer. Literary experience, therefore, is part of a store of emotional experiences upon which the poet can draw for his work. There is this difference, however, that whereas most emotional experiences will be

---

[1] *Essay on Criticism*, 362 f.   [2] *Anecdotes*, ed. S.W. Singer (1820), p. 193.
[3] Ibid. p. 278.   [4] Ibid. p. 277.

recollected in some form unconnected with words, a literary
experience will return with some memory of the words which
the writer has used. There is also the frequent possibility of
literary experiences mixing with other experiences, of our recollecting at some emotional crisis the literary expression which
had once before been given to it. Thus it seems possible that when
Gray, in whom literary inspiration was as powerful as it was in
Pope, stopped to contemplate some elm, the description of that
tree in *Comus* recurred to his mind,

> Or 'gainst the rugged bark of some broad Elm,[1]

and the tree and Milton's description were thereafter so indis-
sociably connected, that when in turn he came to mention the
tree in the *Elegy*, 'Beneath those rugged Elms' became the inevitable choice of words.

Like Gray's, Pope's ideas and emotions were closely associated
with the expression which former writers had used in similar
circumstances. Regret at the too quick passing of years seems
to have recalled to Pope Milton's sonnet on his twenty-third
birthday as being, perhaps, the best expression which that emotion had received, so that even when Pope had Horace's words
before him in the 'Imitation' of the second Epistle of Horace's
second book, it was to Milton that he turned when he wrote

> This subtle Thief of Life, this paltry Time,
> What will it leave me, if it snatch my Rhime?[2]

And when in the 'Messiah' he needed to versify Isaiah's description of the earth bringing forth its earliest fruits as offerings
to the new-born child, he passed over Isaiah and Virgil, whom
he was ostensibly imitating, to choose a passage from the ninth
book of *Paradise Lost*:

> The humid flow'rs, that breath'd
> Their morning incense,[3]

which in his digesting memory he transmuted to

> See Nature hastes her earliest wreaths to bring,
> With all the incense of the breathing spring.[4]

Canto 4 of *The Rape of the Lock* ends with Belinda's despairing
cry at her misfortune. She wishes she had never visited Hampton Court and had rather lived in some distant northern land,
where she could have kept her charms from mortal sight; and

---

[1] l. 354.   [2] l. 76 f.   [3] ll. 193 f.   [4] 'Messiah', 23 f.

as Pope searched for an image to describe beauty in conceal-
ment, it was Waller's lines he associated with this idea. In 'Go,
Lovely Rose', Waller had written

> Tell her that's young
> And shuns to have her graces spied,
> That hadst thou sprung
> In deserts, where no men abide,
> Thou wouldst have uncommended died.

And Pope adapted them to his purpose as follows :

> There kept my Charms conceal'd from mortal Eye,
> Like Roses that in Desarts bloom and die.[1]

Here as well two different levels may be observed in the poetry.
The more apparent level is the beauty of expression, the less
apparent is the pleasure which our memories have in associating
Pope's words with a former poet's. A quotation from *Guardian*
No. 12, a paper which has been attributed to Pope,[2] may serve
to reinforce this:

> But over and above a just Painting of Nature, a learned Reader
> will find a new Beauty superadded in a happy Imitation of some
> famous Ancient, as it revives in his Mind the Pleasure he took in
> his first reading such an Author. Such Copyings as these give that
> kind of double Delight which we perceive when we look upon the
> Children of a beautiful Couple; where the Eye is not more charm'd
> with the Symmetry of the Parts, than the Mind by observing the
> Resemblance transmitted from Parents to their Offspring, and the
> mingled Features of the Father and the Mother.

It has been assumed in commenting on the three passages quoted
above that Pope's imitation was intentional. It may not have
been, for a poet may not know whom he is imitating.[3] But when
Pope did know, his frequent (if not invariable) practice was to
quote his source in a footnote, thus indicating once more the
way in which editors must annotate his work.

---

[1] iv. 157 f.

[2] *The Prose Works of Alexander Pope*, ed. N. Ault, i (1936), pp. lxi ff.

[3] Mr. T. S. Eliot provides interesting confirmation. A reviewer of a reprint of
Dowson's poems had pointed out a resemblance between Dowson's 'Non sum qualis
eram' and 'The Hollow Men'. Mr. Eliot, in a letter to *The Times Literary Supplement* of 10 Jan. 1935, remarked: 'The derivation had not occurred to my mind, but
I believe it to be correct, because the lines [quoted from Dowson] have always run
in my head, and because I regard Dowson as a poet whose technical innovations
have been underestimated.'

Pope's indication of his sources serves many purposes. It is an acknowledgement of indebtedness. More important, it demonstrates Pope's inheritance of traditional ideas passed on from one reputable writer to another; this is especially true of the *Essay on Criticism* with its footnote references to Cicero, Horace, Persius, and Quintilian, and of the *Dunciad* with its reminders of grave epic parallels to Pope's ridiculous incidents. But most important, the acknowledgement of indebtedness invites comparison between the earlier and later expression of the idea. The Augustan age was an age of consolidation, an age when men stopped to chew and digest the experiences of former ages. Pope was best serving the men of his generation by giving the expression of those experiences 'an agreeable turn',[1] a turn so agreeable, in fact, that we may often remember Pope though we forget his originals.

IV

It should not be supposed that the three inspirations of Pope's work, the inspirations drawn from fancy, morality, and books, exist separately in his poetry and are never associated. On the contrary, the variety of levels in his poetry shows that he could satisfy more than one poetical impulse within the limits of the same verse. Occasionally, indeed, his inspiration is a blend of all three. When Pope revised *The Rape of the Lock* for the first collected edition of his works in 1717, he added a passage of twenty-six lines to the fifth canto, which will serve for illustration. The revision of his works had been a respite from the translation of Homer, in which he had proceeded at that time as far as the twelfth book of the *Iliad*. This book describes an attack upon the Greek entrenchments by the Trojan forces, the success of which was largely owed to the valour of Sarpedon. Sarpedon had encouraged his friend Glaucus in a speech which Pope had translated and published separately some years before; but it was doubtless the occasion of fitting the speech into its place in the translation of the twelfth book at that time, which suggested that an imitation of it might suitably be put into the mouth of the grave Clarissa before the battle begins in canto v

---

[1] *Spectator*, no. 253. Addison commends Boileau in this paper for asserting that 'wit and fine writing doth not consist so much in advancing things that are new, as in giving things that are known an agreeable turn'.

of *The Rape of the Lock*. Here are the two passages, Homer translated first:

> Why boast we, *Glaucus*! our extended Reign,
> Where *Xanthus'* Streams enrich the *Lycian* Plain;
> Our num'rous Herds that range the fruitful Field,
> And Hills where Vines their purple Harvest yield,
> Our foaming Bowls with purer Nectar crown'd,
> Our Feasts enhanc'd with Music's sprightly Sound?
> Why on those Shores are we with Joy survey'd,
> Admir'd as Heroes, and as Gods obey'd?
> Unless great Acts superior Merit prove,
> And vindicate the bount'ous pow'rs above.
> 'Tis ours, the Dignity they give, to grace;
> The first in Valour, as the first in Place:
> That when with wond'ring Eyes our martial Bands
> Behold our Deeds transcending our Commands,
> Such, they may cry, deserve the sov'reign State,
> Whom those that envy, dare not imitate!
> Could all our Care elude the gloomy Grave,
> Which claims no less the fearful than the brave,
> For Lust of Fame I should not vainly dare
> In fighting Fields, nor urge thy Soul to War.
> But since, alas! ignoble Age must come,
> Disease, and Death's inexorable Doom;
> The Life which others pay, let us bestow,
> And give to Fame what we to Nature owe;
> Brave tho' we fall, and honour'd if we live,
> Or let us Glory gain, or Glory give![1]

Homer burlesqued follows:

> Say, why are Beauties prais'd and honour'd most,
> The wise Man's Passion, and the vain Man's Toast?
> Why deck'd with all that Land and Sea afford,
> Why Angels call'd, and Angel-like ador'd?
> Why round our Coaches crowd the white-glov'd Beaus,
> Why bows the Side-box from its inmost Rows?
> How vain are all these Glories, all our Pains,
> Unless good Sense preserve what Beauty gains:
> That Men may say, when we the Front-box grace,
> Behold the first in Virtue, as in Face!
> Oh! if to dance all Night, and dress all Day,
> Charm'd the Small-pox, or chas'd old Age away;

[1] *Iliad*, vol. iii, 1717 (folio ed.), pp. 240 f.

Who would not scorn what Huswife's Cares produce,
Or who would learn one earthly Thing of Use?
To patch, nay ogle, might become a Saint,
Nor could it sure be such a Sin to paint.
But since, alas! frail Beauty must decay,
Curl'd or uncurl'd, since Locks will turn to grey,
Since painted, or not painted, all shall fade,
And she who scorns a Man, must die a Maid;
What then remains, but well our Pow'r to use,
And keep good Humour still whate'er we lose?
And trust me, Dear! good Humour can prevail,
When Airs, and Flights, and Screams, and Scolding fail.
Beauties in vain their pretty Eyes may roll;
Charms strike the Sight, but Merit wins the Soul.[1]

The grave Clarissa's speech is both an imaginative episode in *The Rape of the Lock* and a parody of Homer. But it is an unusual parody, for while the memory of Homer's lines produces a ludicrous effect as it is read, the good sense of it, so elegantly expressed, opens 'more clearly the Moral of the Poem', as Pope explained in a note. Pope is stooping unerringly to Truth, although he is still wandering in Fancy's maze. It is the many-layered richness of such a passage as that which demands our profoundest admiration for his poetry.

[1] *The Rape of the Lock*, v. 9–34.

'WHERE ONCE STOOD THEIR PLAIN HOMELY DWELLING'

COLLINS BAKER

WE have no evidence that on 16 September 1875 David Nichol Smith announced that he would sit one day and smoke with me on a roof in San Marino, California. As he glanced about him that autumn day, seventy years ago, he hardly foresaw what the Huntington Library, as yet undreamed of, would let him in for in 1937. If, rising from his cradle, he had seen himself in California, smoking in such company—after noon, it is true—he would have been as amazed as Horace Walpole's ancestors, had they risen from their tomb in Houghton Church and looked round them in 1742; or as London Virtuosi would have been in 1730 if a vision were opened to them of what would come to pass, of what queer objects would be encountered, in British art before three generations passed.

Sir Robert Walpole's worthy father and grandfather, staring over the churchyard wall, would have been amazed only by the vast pile of Houghton Hall, blocking their view, 'where once stood their plain homely dwelling'. But London Virtuosi —say Michael Dahl or Jonathan Richardson—starting from their graves, would be amazed by a diversity of things almost incredible: Gainsborough's 'Mall', for instance; his 'Mrs. Graham' or 'Karl Abel'; Reynolds' 'Graces decorating Hymen'; his 'Baretti' or 'Nelly O'Brien'. The Seeman brothers, or Thomas Gibson, whose horizon had been pretty well restricted to divines in band and gown, might catch a glimpse of Lawrence's 'Pinkie'. Their astonishment would not have been inferior to Lawrence's, if he had been told that his picture would become a household word on the Pacific Coast. John Wootton and Tillemans would barely recognize their own line of business as developed by Stubbs; nor Charles Phillips and Gavin Hamilton theirs, as carried on by Zoffany. Fonthill Abbey, or the Asiatic style, started by Mr. Hodges' paintings, and rampaging at Brighton under Mr. Nash, would stupefy Wren and Gibbs; while William Kent and Vanderbank and the illustrators of the 1740's would gape at the draughtsmanship of Rowlandson and Gillray. Richard Hall and the brothers Buck, topographers: how they would stare at the illustrations of Thomas Hearne, Paul Sandby's aquatints, and the water-colours of Cozens, Turner, and Girtin. And what would Scott and Wootton have made of the oil landscape of Turner? John Smith, creeping from St. Peter's, Northampton, would judicially admire the mezzotints of Thomas Watson and Valentine Green, the while imagining what plates he himself would have scraped if Fate had permitted him to interpret Reynolds rather than Kneller. Those who had expected the 1746 venture in the Foundling Hospital to bring forth a fullgrown school of British History painting, would wander round Boydell's Shakespeare Gallery like country cousins. And George Vertue, risen from the Cloisters of the Abbey, would see the Royal Academy in full swing, and rejoice that now at last his darling project, with-out which, he knew, no school of History could be born, had been realized.

Such apparitions, where once stood the plain, homely achievement of the first half of the eighteenth century, would confront the old men, returned after no more than a generation or so. In their lifetime they had seen little but a lowly standard of provincial craftsmanship. Now they would find cosmopolitan accomplishment. They had been used to general neglect of art, interrupted here and there by the embarrassing eulogies which provincial ignorance will emit along with cocksure judgements. Now they could read from an English painter's pen some of the best art-criticism that has ever been made. William Aglionby, thinking presumably of Gibbons rather than Caius Cibber, had written, 'We have a Sculptor, who if he goes on as he has begun, will be a Northern Michael Angelo.' And Robert Whitehall could perpetrate his couplet preferring Robert Streater to Michael Angelo. Even Jonathan Richardson believed that the British school of face-painting had been the finest in the world for fourscore years; while Gay chid Kent for having left England to emulate Raphael, and urged him

> Go back, adorn the palaces of Rome;
> There on the walls let thy just labours shine,
> And *Raphael* live again in thy design.

Pope, who had never been abroad, put Raphael's epitaph on Kneller's tomb; and, on the strength of one trip through France and Italy, Horace Walpole, like a hanging judge, dealt omnisciently with the whole trembling herd of Old Masters, acquitting altogether three 'perfect painters'.

Such complacence is the natural condition of any kind of isolation. No one is so cocksure—in breakfast clubs or senates— as the incorrigible provincial who, even though he travel, cannot acquire discontent. The parochial state of mind of English criticism and art (excluding architecture), early in the eighteenth century, had been imposed by wars and geography. Few painters had crossed the Channel, and most of them might just as well have stopped at home. Richardson, whose essays are sound on practice, never travelled, doing his best with a few books and engravings and what drawings and pictures he could study in his own and other English collections. Raphael's name was seldom off his lips; but all he knew of Raphael's handiwork were the already much retouched cartoons at Hampton Court—a place he held to be as rich a treasury of the Divine Master as the Vatican. From the cartoons chiefly, and from the masterpieces now swelling English private collections, English painters, it was hoped, could gain the knowledge and experience to rise from mere face-painting to the sublimity of History. It would be hardly necessary to go abroad. But if the Duke of Chandos' method of buying pictures for Cannons was fairly typical—and Horace Mann's system, a little later, was much the same—we can suspect the kind of masterpieces that composed many of the new collections, and question the good they did to painters with no criterion. Chandos seldom saw a picture before he bought it. Sometimes a foreign dealer sent him drafts; but generally the Duke accepted the taste of a friend or relative abroad, or the word of a professional agent. Though he knew that the market was crammed with copies, especially Italian, he yet supposed that a nephew or banker-friend could tell the difference. The London picture-market was about as reliable. Taxation of imported pictures *ad valorem*, 'caused great roguery & false swearing & prevented the best or very good pictures to come in, the Custom amounting so high'. Confessed copies came in cheap to the dealers, and were then sold for originals '& the curious deceived'. In remedy Mr. Broderick, M.P., of Wandsworth, brought in a Bill to fit the import tax to the picture's size: pictures under 2 feet square paid twenty shillings; those of 2 up to 4 feet square paid two pounds, and those of 4 feet square and over, three pounds. As a result (Vertue thought) many good pictures and fewer copies came in.

Dealers were fairly numerous. Perhaps at the top stood Laws and Bagnal, from whom pictures entered the Royal Collection; at the bottom was Nunis, 'a little, ugly, picture jobber'. In between came Andrew Hay, the Scot, who made a fortune after thirty years' hard work: he had visited France fourteen times, and Italy six—on foot, once or twice. Many artists dealt; for instance Leonard Knyff, the topographic draughtsman, Laroon, Hugh Howard, Lance and Arthur Pond. From a complaint written about a hundred years later we infer that, on the whole, the level of English dealers' ignorance and honesty kept pretty steady between the reigns of George II and George IV.

Clients, then as now, had recourse to connoisseurs for assistance or redress: the term 'connaissance', Richardson says, was suggested by Matthew Prior. Sir Andrew Fountaine, Colonel Guise, Paul Methuen, that Mr. Broderick who amended the import tax, and, of course, Burlington and Horace Walpole, were topping connoisseurs by right of association with famous collections. Vertue, Thornhill, Gouge, and Richardson were authorities because of their standing as artists; and Jervas and Knapton had the credit of Italian travel as well. Professional experts (as we call them) were artist-dealers, like Laroon who bought for Sir Robert Walpole, and dealer-virtuosi like Hay. Literary savants, so dear to us to-day, with batteries of monographs, magazine articles, and certificates, were unknown. The Georgian dealer and expert had little scholarship, no apparatus of photographs and X-rays, and no doctor's degrees; when they misled clients it was through simple ignorance or pure venality. Their present-day descendants, by no means inferior in the latter, cannot always so convincingly confess to ignorance.

On Raphael's Cartoons; on a few masterpieces in old collections (for example the Percy 'Cornaro Family'); and on the Giordanos, Parmigianinos, Salvators, and Guidos coming (as copies, mostly) into newer galleries, those anxious for the future of English art fixed their hopes. With such guidance English face-painters might be converted into painters of History. For whatever Richardson might say about the excellence of British portraiture, it was clear that in the categories face-painting held a low place. Prodigious efforts had been made, since the Restoration, to acclimatize History painting in England. Innumerable town and country houses had been, and still were being, decorated with ceiling and mural pictures by Italian, French, and English painters. Thornhill's ambitious productions at Greenwich or St. Paul's were proudly extolled; the religious pictures made for the Foundling Hospital, and Hogarth's piece in St. Bartholomew's Hospital, were hailed as great advances. But it was felt, if not confessed, that the British still had a long way to go before they shone forth as the heirs of the great Roman school: their logical destiny.

English writers of course recognized that sublime paintings had gone to seed everywhere since the time of the Caracci; but neither Richardson in 1715, nor Reynolds many years later, regarded that as other than a temporary if strange suspension. Even more curiously, we hear echoes of that fallacy to-day: as though life could be resumed when the heart has ceased pumping, as though a stage in geology or animal life which has reached fulfilment and been passed, might return. Reynolds, it is true, had an inkling of the matter when he observed that no Protestant country had ever produced a History painter. Ruskin was not wrong in connecting faith with great art. Faith changes: Giotto believed in one thing; Rubens, Reynolds, and Turner in others. But without some 'burning core below', great art does not well forth. In Richardson's view and Vertue's, early in the century, there was a clear connexion between the risen power of England and a renaissance of sublime, or History, painting. What with the Raphael Cartoons and the other masterpieces in English collections to guide them, and what with their birthright of 'greatness of mind and solid sense', it seemed logical that English artists were marked out to pick up the very torch laid down by the Caracci. But first the nobility and gentry must be made to recognize the worth of art, and then academies were needed in which artists could be trained, and, incidentally, the patron class educated and polished.

About 1722 Vertue drew up a thorough scheme for the improvement of drawing in England, presumably dissatisfied with what had been done in the first academy of 1711 and its successor in 1720. His scheme gauges the homely condition of art training in England then. It planned for three academies: in London, near one of the large schools; at Oxford; and at Cambridge. He hoped that art classes might later be instituted at Winchester and Eton. Each academy would have a board of directors who would elect the master, to serve for three or possibly four years; he could not be re-elected. He would teach for three hours a day, three days in each week, at a suggested salary of £50 a year. If he happened to be absent the senior student would take charge. No student should be admitted unless he could read and write, understood Latin, and had some proficiency in the classic authors. For it was of the utmost consequence to bring up artists and amateurs—'lovers' —with a high mental standard. In the elementary class, copies of rudiments would be made—eyes, noses, hands, &c.—from engraved studies provided by the master and his successors. Students would work first in charcoal, and then in pen and ink; no chalks or pencils to be allowed; the studies should be in outline, with little shading. These books of engraved details might be sold to other art schools and to gentlemen for home study or instruction at the academy, out of regular hours. In the next class, drawings made by the master—whole bodies from 12 to 18 inches high—would be copied; and then the student would proceed to the third class where he must copy at least fifty drawings made from statues, casts, and busts, done on grey or blue paper, heightened with black and white only. Having graduated there, he would go on to the highest, to draw from the antique. Casts from the 'Gladiator', 'Venus', 'Laocoon', 'Boys of Fiamingo', 'Hercules', 'Apollo', &c., should be made by the best statuaries in the country, assisted by young ingenious sculptors. Casts of hands from the life would be included. All these should be done in a mixture of lead and pewter, and—oddly enough—should be 'painted over with oyl colours well ground by a Face painter'. Recently many bronze statues, made from the antique and modern sculpture, had come in from Italy about two feet high: these, too, would be suitable.

Having promoted his students to 'the highest class', Vertue is not so clear. He goes on to say that scholars successful in all these grades would then be given opportunity to study anatomy, geometry, architecture, and perspective. After that they 'may be truely capable of studying from the Life in the Academys from Nature or the Antiques or paintings of the most celebrated masters'. Perhaps he had in mind the academy run by Vanderbank and Cheron, as distinct from his more elementary schools.

At any rate he thought that this course of training would save any tolerable genius from the prevalent horrid blunders of ill-proportion, vile articulation, erroneous light and shade and insipid flatness, 'tho' every one may not arrive at the Sublime. That must be left to Providence (long study) & an excellent genius, of which no doubt this nation abounds.' Like Richardson he took comfort from the thought of English prowess in other noble arts: 'Divines, Statesmen, Philosophers, Mathematicians, Phisicians & Poets . . . equal if not superior to any Nation round us'. The only thing that kept back English art was the want of sound teaching on a lasting foundation.

It is worth noting that Vertue's scheme made no provision for foreign study. Quite early in the eighteenth century English artists seldom travelled; by 1752 it was common for them to go through Italy, studying in academies at Venice, Bologna, and Rome, where a school for them had been founded by English noblemen and gentry. We might suppose that when political restrictions were removed, and the Channel and Alps crossed, a well of new inspiration slaked the pilgrims' thirst, so that they returned new men. But if we note who made the journey, who studied in the temples, and what they did on their return, we may almost wonder why they went. Henry Cooke, who ruined the cartoons at Hampton Court, was an early pilgrim. Jervas worked in Rome about 1705; but beyond calling himself Carlo Jervasi and realizing that he had begun at the wrong end, made no improvement. Arthur Pond was in Italy between 1725 and 1727, and coming home painted poor portraits in the style of Vanderbank. Knapton came back in 1732, after seven years; his Dilettante portraits show the result. The Scots painters Aikman and Ramsay both were in Italy for some time, but brought back nothing revolutionary or lasting. Kent, too, worked in Italy, and though he certainly acquired some draughtsmanship we cannot say that he made much use of it in his paintings. Others who went, without marked profit, were Pickering and Penny. Perhaps more interesting was Giles Hussey, who spent most of his time in Italy. But he was idle or temperamental, and a revolutionary theorist with a secret recipe for drawing; Vertue, seeing a pen drawing by him in Dr. Mead's collection—about as big as one's palm—concluded that a boy of under twenty could have done as well, without all those years in Rome and Bologna.

With no opening at home, except for face-painting, the average British artist who visited Italy or the Low Countries, early in the century, was less interested in mural decorations than the latest taste in portraiture. It is easier to understand his indifference to History painting than the phenomenon of Reynolds' scholarship. Reynolds went to Italy in 1749, like any Pickering or Penny; and might, like Allan Ramsay, have come back with no more than a new fashion in current portrait-painting. But on the contrary, soon after he got home, his own brush and the stimulus he gave his fellows brought the British school of portraiture to the foremost place in Europe. He could not, however, put back the hands, and in 1760 start English History painting on the course it would (theoretically) have taken if the great tradition of medieval English art had been followed at the Renaissance by a great British school of religious painting. Some blame Henry VIII for the want of that sequence, without reflecting that already the Gothic stage was fulfilled, and another had been reached. If English art were to shine again in mural painting, it should have got away on a new start, with new ideals and technique, at latest in the early fifteenth century. By 1760 the tide had been irrevocably lost. It is conceivable that if, when Blenheim, Castle Howard, Cannons, and Houghton were built, we had had in leash a pack of English painters as highly trained as Veronese or Rubens or Tiepolo, they might have been let loose to swarm over those great buildings and cover them with noble decorations. But that was the last possible hour. When Reynolds is charged with having failed to establish a fine school of History painting, in a country which had no heritage of draughtsmanship and design, his accusers fail to take into account his environment and place in time.

In 1788—four years before he died—Reynolds conjectured that 'if ever this nation should produce genius sufficient to acquire to us the honourable distinction of an English School, the name of Gainsborough will be transmitted to posterity, in the history of art, among the very first of that *rising* name'. Though, perhaps, before the fruits of Boydell's magnificent endeavour were revealed, Reynolds still hoped that the Sublime could be recaptured and the Royal Academy might some day revive the glory of the Roman school, he saw how things were going. It was borne in on him that Gainsborough's and his own achievement, in what once had been despised face-painting, might crown their nation with that honourable distinction. But their achievement was not the outcome of the art exemplified by Richardson, Hogarth, and Hudson, which looked back to Lely and Kneller, but of new vision and enthusiastic faith that English portraiture could be a major art.

If Vertue and Richardson would have been amazed to see what height English face-painting had attained in a few years, how much more surprised would they have been to witness the apotheosis of English landscape-painting not many years later. And Sir Joshua would probably have been as much astonished to know that one of his new boy students, at the Academy School in 1789, would do for British landscape what he himself had done for portraiture. Where once stood the plain, homely dwelling of the early topographers and oil landskip-painters, Turner reared a noble pile, and won for landscape-painting a throne at the side of History. Neither our old men, at the beginning of the century, nor Vertue, half-way through it, could in their mind's eye have traced the courses that the topography and oil landscape known to them would take, before they flowed together in Turner. It would have been inconceivable by them that Hollar and Wootton would, as it were, culminate in 'Norham Castle'.

Many English antiquarian draughtsmen worked round Hollar: very amateur and provincial. Yet if we consider what eventually was reared upon the humble foundations they laid, we shall not grudge some of them a simple list: Stephen Anderton; D. Gage; Richard Hall; Randle Holme; Thomas Johnson; Daniel King, who also engraved their works; Edward Mascall; Richard Newcourt; Francis Place; Richard Ralinson (perhaps Rawlinson); and C. Woodfield, who died, aged 75, about Christmas 1724. The best of them (apart from Place) were, perhaps, Hall and Johnson; though it is impossible to separate the quality of their drawings from the result achieved in the etched plates of King and Hollar. Compared with Hollar (and Place, too) none of the others had a picture-seeing eye—the vision 'pittoresque'. But as the eighteenth century developed, the limited intentions of the archaeologist were little by little caught up in the landscape-painter's view. This is evident in such an antiquarian work as Drake's *History of York* (1736). The appearances of out-of-doors—light, and enveloping atmosphere—undreamed of by the English illustrators of *Monasti-con Anglicanum*, begin to compete with the dry business of monument-drawing. Pure landscape is attempted, and the collaboration of Monamy, the painter, shows that topography was merging into picture-making. His companions were W. H. Toms, John Haynes, and Francis Place (represented posthumously). Their advance in landscape perception was important; but English topographers had much to learn before they achieved the pictorial skill of a Paul Sandby or Thomas Hearne, within twenty years of Vertue's death in 1756—the year that Richard Wilson came back from Italy.

Richardson could not have believed that, before very long, an honoured school would come out of the inconsiderable beginnings of English landscape that he saw round him when he began his essays. And Vertue, who in 1743 commended the advance made by John Smith and Taverner, Lambert and Wootton, would have been astounded had he returned from the Cloisters in twenty years and seen what Moses Griffiths and Paul Sandby were up to—with what skill they had turned topography into accomplished pictures. The remarkable development of English water-colour has occupied many writers who have revealed the interplay of foreign influences in technique and picture wisdom. Possibly, ignoring the inseparable partnership which linked draughtsman and engraver, we have not enough considered the connexion between the progress in engraving and the advance in topography. And perhaps we still make a too rigid class-distinction between the men we disdain as topographers and those we adore as artists.

About 1610 Hendrik Goudt had been making engravings as rich as mezzotints, and in Hollar's time mezzotint was replacing line because more depth and massing than line should have attempted were needed to reproduce contemporary painting. Hollar's topographic etchings themselves have a kind of smoky shadow—something between the effect of drypoint and mezzotint. Francis Place, the mezzotinter, might have combined the new process with topography: it would have been invaluable for church interiors and elaborate monuments; but perhaps on economic grounds it does not seem to have been enlisted.[1]

---

[1] I have seen, but lost sight of, a mezzotint of a large tomb in some cathedral or church. My impression is that its date was *c.* 1720–30. About that time Kirkall and Jackson were feeling their way in other processes.

When mezzotint became the ordinary medium for reproduction, and oil landscapes were multiplying, inevitably the line topographers and their engravers realized that similar depth and variety of tone, and similar massing, were essential to their business. Not regarding the special qualities of water-colour as sacred, they simply saw that the thin line-engravings of a little while ago looked very archaic beside the prints of John Smith and McArdell. Presumably the only question was how they could conform most advantageously in the interest of art and economy.

No English landscape painter illustrates more aptly than Paul Sandby the transition from the old linear style to the 'pittoresque', or painter-like. In 1753 he and his brother Thomas, etched by P. Fourdrinier, appear as direct descendants of Hollar; their illustrations of Maitland's *History of Edinburgh* are like pen-and-ink drawings: crisp and neat, with simple skies and a minimum of tonal masses. Turning at random to Governor Pownall's *Six Views in New York, New Jersey and Pennsylvania* (1761) we find Sandby engraving some of them with a more laborious depth of tone than line-engraving could properly carry. One can imagine him wishing that he had at his disposal a method comparable with mezzotint. In 1775 he brought out his process of Aquatinta, a much better mode than Kirkall's or Jackson's of imitating bistre drawings. Two years later Earlom, combining etching with mezzotint, produced his two hundred plates after Claude's sepia drawings in the *Liber Veritatis*. Meanwhile Donowell and Woollet; Moses Griffiths and his engraver Mazell; and Thomas Hearne in partnership with Byrne and Middiman, had reached with heavy line-engraving other stages in the pictorial development of topography. How different, not only in technique of engraving but also in mood, is their approach to archaeology from that of the brothers Buck, who lie half-way between them and the Hollar school.

This partnership of draughtsman and engraver cannot be ignored. With Cozens, Turner, and Girtin before us, and with our esteem for their drawings as water-colours, we may forget that the earlier men were in different case. Unless a draughtsman were specially commissioned to make drawings of some country seat, the engraved result was the end in view. So that Sandby and Rooker, or Hearne, Byrne, and Middiman are inseparable. Hearne is 'not to be classed with the colourists';

but he knew what kind of drawings would conduce to the best results Byrne could get. And forgetting our prejudice against 'topographers' we may admit that plates like 'Edinburgh', 'Stirling', or 'Salisbury' in Byrne's *Antiquities* take a high place in English imaginative landscape.

More than a different conception of mass and tone was, of course, needed to convert the mild, maidenly landscape perception at the beginning of the eighteenth century into the virility and cosmopolitan accomplishment attained towards its close. Poets had been writing of landscape; travellers discovering the sublimity of Nature; and Richard Wilson, who began in nothing better than the provincial manner of Wootton, had learnt during seven years in Italy what Claude really meant. Nor should we forget that picturesque romanticism had been recognized as a legitimate addition to the Beautiful and the Sublime.

Early in the century they had expected the revival of great painting to take place in Britain, carrying on from where the Caracci had left off, and that sound training would make this possible. They realized how much depended on the artistic education of the nobility and gentry. Towards the end of the century Reynolds, still hoping (a little dubiously perhaps) that a British school of great History painting might arise, played his part in the most ambitious attempt that could have been imagined to bring this about. John Boydell and his subscribers launched the Shakespeare Gallery scheme in 1787, inspired not by Reynolds but by Romney. The best artists in the Empire were subsidized to produce a series of noble works illustrating England's noblest poet. It would be difficult to parallel Boydell's conception and endeavour, or, as it then appeared, to pitch upon a riper time for the enterprise. Technical accomplishment abounded: compared with that of fifty—nay, twenty —years before, the standard of accomplishment was such as to have amazed the old men. Drawing had been taught at the Royal Academy for almost twenty years; the principles of the best design were common knowledge. The things that Richardson and Vertue were familiar with—Thornhill's decorations; paintings at the Foundling Hospital and Vauxhall; illustrations by Kent, Highmore, Wootton, and Hayman—were very homely compared with the academic sophistication of even the most ludicrous product of Boydell's scheme. And where Richardson had sighed for sympathetic patrons, now at the turn of the century William Austin could boast that since 1768 four hundred 'of the Nobility, Gentry, etc.' had attended his art classes; at first, next door to Astley's amphitheatre, and later in York Street, St. James's, and Lawrence Street, Chelsea. Let us not surmise that his pupils were all women: their sex was pretty equally balanced. And while four countesses headed the list on the female side, two marquises, supported by four earls and a large quantity of military men, adorned the other. The 'et ceteras' were perhaps artists: 'Mr. Stubbs' is among them, sandwiched between 'Thomas Primrose, Esq.' and 'Joseph Jennings, Gent.'

No circumstances, then, could have seemed more propitious for Boydell's princely enterprise: his large fortune, a host of academic painters, and four hundred well-born amateurs. As the project got under way, the artists were warned against current stage representations of Shakespeare. But few were capable of heeding. The more pictures were shown, the more evident it became that Shakespeare was the most difficult and dangerous inspiration in the world. Only artists with imagination of the rarest order, and deep lore of picture-making, might interpret him fitly. And where, in a school without solid foundation save in face-painting, could such be miraculously discovered? On a rough count thirty-four painters produced some 170 Shakespeare pictures, between 1788 and 1800. The artists ranged from Sir Joshua and West to Durno, Ramberg, and Ibbetson. Where are their works now? A few lie in the store-rooms of provincial museums; some are in the attics and bedroom landings of country houses. Judged by the engravings, Romney, Fuseli, and Barry were best qualified to interpret Shakespeare, and Opie and Hoppner at least showed some painter-like understanding of what should be done. For the rest, the Shakespeare Gallery enterprise, besides wrecking Boydell's fortune, proved beyond hope that no conception of History painting existed in England. A few years later, reflecting on this melancholy epoch, writers recalled especially how soon the public had been bored and how sadly the participating artists debilitated.

The hopes of a century sank in Boydell's Gallery. Nothing has happened since, anywhere, to suggest that a school of great History painting can be revived. But the unaccountable and headlong behaviour of genius should restrain us from concluding that it never will be. Boydell's Shakespeare painters were certainly too much part of the glittering, artificial, Ossianic spirit of their age to resist it and create something greater and more enduring. Blake, who, of course, was not implicated, alone had the imagination needed, without the knowledge essential to the scale of that endeavour. Nor can we truthfully say that Reynolds and Gainsborough differ from those old, worthy men of the first half of the century by resisting the spirit of their age and escaping it. They differed in seeing life (not necessarily of any age) keenly, and in having learnt to express themselves with unprecedented command of their resources. Dealing with out-of-doors and weather, Turner and Constable were mercifully superior to the spirit of their age. What divides them prodigiously from their predecessors is that by luck, or the unpredictable good management of genius, they came at a time when things could be seen and felt in landscape that had never been seen (or at least expressed) before, not even by Cuyp or Claude. And that—again by the peculiar ways of genius— they could gather up the gradual hard lessons of those old topographers and virtuous landskip men, and as it were suddenly reveal a new grand manner and sublimity.

SOME ASPECTS OF EIGHTEENTH-CENTURY PROSE

JAMES SUTHERLAND

THE Mississippi (or so they used to tell us at school), after flowing southwards for many hundreds of miles, is joined some distance above St. Louis by the Missouri; and though the two great streams now roll on as one mighty river their waters for some time refuse to mingle, the muddy tide of the Missouri being distinguishable on the right bank, and the clearer waters of the Mississippi on the left. Something rather similar, it is generally agreed, happened with English prose in the eighteenth century. The clear stream of writing which had its rise towards the end of the seventeenth century, and to which in their various ways Addison, Steele, Swift, Fielding, Chesterfield, and Horace Walpole contributed, was joined about the middle of the century by another and very different affluent with which we usually associate the names of Johnson and Gibbon. The prose of Johnson is certainly not 'muddy', yet it does bear along with it an alluvial deposit of learning that distinguishes it unmistakably from the writing of Addison. As writers of English prose Addison and Johnson belong to two distinct traditions: the reader to whom they address themselves and their way of approaching him are both different. It was Addison's aim, as he tells us, to bring philosophy 'out of closets and libraries, schools and colleges, to dwell in clubs and assemblies, at tea-tables and in coffee-houses': it seems often to have been Johnson's to carry it back again, and even on occasion to transmute the small talk of tea-tables into the language of schools and colleges.

If he is not the finest prose writer of his period (most modern readers, I believe, would give that title to Swift), Addison was certainly the dominant influence on English prose for at least a generation. It was surely fortunate that he preceded Johnson, and did not by an accident of birth follow him. To say this is not to detract from Johnson's eminence as a prose writer, nor is it to express a personal preference. The value of Addison to his century was that he gave to Englishmen an example of good prose that any writer could imitate without losing his own

identity; he has a sort of neutral quality that allowed his imitators to develop their own personal idiom. If one must have
a model, Addison could hardly be bettered; he will lead to no
eccentricities or affectations, he has good manners without
being mannered, and he is well within the range of the average
mind. Indeed, the debt of English prose to Addison can never
be fully assessed, for there are few marks by which to detect his
influence. To English prose he 'did good by stealth'; he would
no doubt have been agreeably surprised to find it fame.

The characteristics of this style, the 'middle style', have been
accurately defined by Johnson. It is 'exact without apparent
elaboration. . . . His sentences have neither studied amplitude,
nor affected brevity; his periods, though not diligently rounded,
are voluble and easy.' In short, this style is 'familiar, but not
coarse, and elegant but not ostentatious'. But this amounts to
saying that Addison's prose comes near to being the unhurried
conversation of an eighteenth-century gentleman; and this sort
of prose descends from Dryden, and, more generally, from that
'mob of gentlemen' who wrote with ease partly because they
were gentlemen and so were accustomed to speaking their mind
at leisure and with authority, and partly because they rarely
had anything very difficult or profound to express. Used as it
was by Addison for the familiar essay, this conversational style
was admirably suited to the purpose he had in mind: to convey
instruction easily and imperceptibly, to teach agreeably. The
taste of his generation had set strongly against pedantry. Dryden's gibes at the lazy gownsmen were repeated in the plays of
Rowe and others, and the literary ideal of Queen Anne's day
was one of easy and not over-informed utterance. Addison,
therefore, was their man. He had a remarkable turn for clear
exposition, and if he necessarily over-simplified on some occasions he never puzzled or merely impressed. What he could
achieve was limited by the audience to which his essays were
addressed; he talked to them in those better than they could
have talked themselves, but he was careful not to soar beyond
their intellectual range. What is true of Addison here is true
also of Steele and Swift, and of most of their contemporaries.
When George Faulkner, the Dublin bookseller, was seeing his
edition of Swift's *Works* through the press, he used to wait on
Swift and read aloud from the proof-sheets, not only to Swift
but also to two of his menservants: 'Which, if they did not

comprehend, he would alter and amend, until they understood it perfectly well, and then would say, *This will do; for I write to the Vulgar, more than to the Learned.*[1] Swift always wrote to be understood, and in this at least he was at one with the best writers of his age. Without noticeably condescending to their public those authors of Queen Anne's day showed a willingness, not always to be found in the later decades of the century, to express themselves simply, and to make themselves perfectly clear to the humblest and least erudite.

Eighteenth-century conversation, on which so much of the prose of the period was based, has necessarily 'melted into air', leaving only partially recorded or fictitious examples by which we may judge it. But the subject continually exercised the minds of Addison, Steele, Swift, and Fielding, who all wrote about it at some length. Much of what they have to say about good conversation throws light upon the art of writing as they understood and practised it. To Steele 'a man of conversation' is 'what we ordinarily understand by a fine Gentleman';[2] and he would establish 'but one great general rule to be observed in all conversation, which is this, that men should not talk to please themselves, but those that hear them'.[3] Learned men, again, ought not to talk shop. ('A prudent man will avoid talking much of any particular science for which he is remarkably famous.')[4] But when all is said, 'there is something which can never be learnt but in the company of the polite'.[4] In his long 'Essay on Conversation' Fielding makes good-breeding the foundation of the whole art, and by good-breeding he means 'the art of pleasing, or contributing as much as possible to the ease and happiness of those with whom you converse'. But in society, as he admits, men of very varying intellectual capacity meet together. What then? It will be the function of the well-bred man 'to endeavour to lessen this imperfection to his utmost, and to bring society as near to a level at least as he is able'. To Addison and Steele, as to Swift and Fielding, good conversation depended upon intellect and character, and perhaps upon

---

[1] *Works*, 1762, vol. i, 'To the Reader'; quoted by Harold Williams, *The Poems of Jonathan Swift* (1937), vol. i, p. xxxiv. Molière, it will be remembered, would sometimes try the effect of his plays upon 'une vieille servante'; but comedy is one thing and Swift's satirical verses and pamphlets another. Would Pope have considered such a test?

[2] *Tatler*, no. 21.   [3] Ibid. no. 264.

[4] *Guardian*, no. 24.

character more than intellect; it demanded restraint, propriety, an absence of emphasis, consideration for others and a real desire to give them pleasure, ·a willingness to subordinate and even suppress what is merely personal or private in favour of the generally interesting and the universally intelligible, the avoidance of mere display, and the conscious imitation of the best models—at this time the conversation of an Atterbury or a Chesterfield. One has only to enumerate the various essentials of good conversation to realize that they are all present in the most characteristic prose of this early period.

A prose based upon good manners will have many virtues; it will be essentially social, it will aim at giving pleasure and avoiding offence. But it will often lack one quality which to many modern readers must seem indispensable: it will not, of itself, be exciting. When, as with Addison, the writer 'thinks justly but thinks faintly', there will not be sufficient urgency in either matter or manner to hold the attention for long. But with Swift, in whom thought and feeling are often intense and even passionate, the effect is truly startling; the contrast between the restraint, the politeness, the understatement, the easy, matter-of-fact utterance on the one hand, and, on the other, the shattering significance of the thought, is perhaps Swift's unique contribution to English literature.

How close the average prose of the period comes to good conversation may be seen by comparing the two extracts that follow, the one taken from a play, and the other from an essay.

(1) It is easy to believe, madam, these must be Admirers of each other. She says, the Colonel rides the best of any Man in England: The Colonel says, she talks the best of any Woman. At the same Time, he understands Wit just as she does Horsemanship. . . . You are to know, these extraordinary Persons see each other daily. They themselves, as well as the Town, think it will be a Match: But it can never happen that they can come to the Point; for instead of addressing to each other, they spend their whole Time in Reports of themselves: He is satisfied if he can convince her he is a fine Gentleman, and a Man of Consequence; and she, in appearing to him an accomplished Lady and a Wit, without further Design. Thus he tells her of his Manner of posting his men at such a Pass, with the numbers he commanded on that Detachment: She tells him, how she was dressed on such a Day at Court, and what Offers were made to her that Week following. . . .

(2) If Pleasure be worth purchasing, how great a Pleasure is it to
him, who has a true Taste of Life, to ease an Aking Heart, to see
the human Countenance lighted up, into Smiles of Joy, on the
Receipt of a Bit of Ore, which is superfluous, and otherwise
useless in a Man's own Pocket? What could a Man do better
with his Cash? This is the Effect of an humane Disposition,
where there is only a general Tye of Nature, and common
Necessity. What then must it be, when we serve an Object of
Merit, of Admiration!

Both passages were written by Steele: the first is from the *Tatler*,
No. 7, the second is from *The Conscious Lovers*, and is spoken
by Young Bevil. I have not, however, played quite fair with the
reader. I have inserted a solitary 'madam' in the extract from
the *Tatler*, so as to prepare his mind to receive a piece of dialogue.
On the other hand, it would have been easy enough, by going
to the plays of, say, Congreve, to find a passage of dialogue far
more artificial than the one I have taken from Steele.

The good talker, we have seen, will not talk about himself
all the time; but conversation, if it is not to be wholly dictatorial,
is bound to be more or less personal in form. (*This is what* I
think about it, what I *feel* . . . . *I remember* . . . . *I can't help wondering* . . . . *I suppose* . . . . *I doubt* . . . . *I agree, but all the same I would
suggest* . . . .) To express ourselves so (and nearly all of us do)
is not to be egotistical; it is, rather, to be humble, to offer what
is said as no more than an opinion or a feeling or a purely
personal contribution to the discussion that is being carried
forward. We should expect a prose that comes close to conversation to show signs of this affiliation. Is it always noticed
to what an extent the prose writers of the early eighteenth
century showed a preference for the first personal pronoun?
Defoe uses it on almost every occasion: sometimes, as in *The
Shortest Way* or *The Poor Man's Plea*, he assumes some imaginary
personality, but more often he writes frankly in his own person.
His *Review* is a sort of robust harangue to his readers; a harangue
because Defoe is always in earnest about something, and robust
because he is outside the upper-class tradition of politeness and
understatement. When he took to writing fiction, late in life, it
seemed natural to him to go on using the first person singular,
and so he cast his stories in the form of autobiographies—as
Swift was also to do with *Gulliver's Travels*. The essay that
descends from Addison and Steele is, of course, personal, and

at first sight surprisingly so. But here we must remember the convention: the essayist has discreetly veiled his own personality behind that of Isaac Bickerstaff, or Mr. Spectator, or Nestor Ironside; or he is a 'Grumbler', or a 'Plain Dealer', or a 'Humourist'. So concealed, he can exploit this assumed personality, which is really pretty much his own, and be as whimsical and communicative as he pleases. Without some such disguise we may well doubt whether Addison could have dared to take the familiar essay as far as he did. So, too, in Swift's *Modest Proposal*, it is not quite Swift himself that we are supposed to be listening to, but some quiet, calculating projector who is laying his proposals before the public. The extent to which the writers of this period take shelter behind some half-dramatized personality is significant; but equally significant, I believe, is the desire to say what has to be said in the easy and familiar first person. Here we must also reckon with the letter-writers. From the letter, the most familiar and personal form of prose-writing (and, incidentally, the one most widely practised in the eighteenth century), Richardson passes naturally to the novel told in letters, and he had many imitators. When Fielding turns to fiction he approaches his task almost in the spirit of the essayist. The habit of gossiping to (and indeed almost with) the reader is ingrained; he cannot keep himself out of the story.

The prose of the early eighteenth century preserves a nice balance between what may be called the foreseen and the fortuitous. We get the impression that the author always knows what he is going to say next, but we do not feel that every sentence has been projected entire in his mind before he writes it down. There is form, but the form is not too rigid; there is room for slight changes of direction or of emphasis, for at least minor modifications of rhythm. The writer does not tyrannize over his sentences; he controls them rather as a shepherd walking behind his sheep, satisfied if they are moving in the right direction, but not troubling about the changing pattern of their movement. Occasionally, indeed, there will be a more conscious effect, as when Addison draws to the close of his meditation among the tombs in Westminster Abbey, or when the King of the Brobdingnagians sums up for Gulliver his impressions of the human race; but in general the prose of this period is shapely without being studied.

This generalization, it is true, will not do for much of the most characteristic writing of Defoe.

I allow the *French* can out-do us in whipt Cream, Froath, and Surface, even in most things; it will for ever be true, that they can *Dance* better, *Sing* better, and *Play* better than we do; any thing that is Superficial, and agreeable to the levity of their Temper, *they out-do us in*; but if they come to the substantial part of any thing, an *English* Man against a *French* Man ever while you live. Thus in the War, at Stratagem, at a Surprize, or at diligent Application, 'tis allow'd that they go beyond us; but at down-right Blows, at mere desperate Fighting, *stand clear there*! They care not to meddle with us; any thing that depends upon the *nimble*, they excel us in; any thing that depends upon *the solid*, we over-match them in; I appeal to *Spittle-Fields*, take an *English* Weaver and a *French*, the *Frenchman* will be sooner in his Loom in the Morning, and later at Night; take up less time in his eating and drinking, and perhaps less Victuals too; go less to the Wrestling-Ring, or Cudgel-Playing, *that is* to his Diversion, than the *Englishman*; yet the *Englishman* that works fewer Hours, shall make as many Ells in his Loom as the *Frenchman*. . . . And this is one Reason why *England* has never been effectually rival'd in her Manufactures, and I may say, never will; not by *France* only, but not by any Nation in the World.[1]

Like almost everything that Defoe wrote this has the accent of living human speech. His reader (who is almost his listener) can note the pauses where his breath gave out, can almost hear him gulping in air for another period. But Defoe's prose is a good deal more colloquial and unpremeditated than what may be called the standard prose of his generation; he is indeed 'a plain blunt man' who only speaks 'right on'. He will plunge headlong into a sentence, stumbling forward in his eagerness to make a point, and as often as not find himself tangled in his syntax. Caught in this thicket of his own making, he cannot go forward, he will not go back, and so with a hearty ' I say' he makes a fresh start and emerges at last with nothing worse than a torn sleeve and a few scratches.

The prose of Addison and Swift is based on a calmer and more cultured conversation; the accent is less urgent, suited to the drawing-room rather than to the tavern or the meeting-house. It is still, however, in the best sense colloquial. Such a prose, in the hands of a sensitive writer, has the great merit of following with its rhythms the turns and twists of his thought.

[1] *Review*, 23 May 1713.

What could be livelier than Colley Cibber's description of the acting of Mrs. Mountfort in Dryden's *Marriage A-la-Mode*?

The first ridiculous Airs that break from her, are upon a Gallant, never seen before, who delivers her a Letter from her Father, recommending him to her good Graces as an honourable Lover. Here now, one would think she might naturally shew a little of the Sexe's decent Reserve, though never so slightly cover'd! No, Sir; not a Tittle of it; Modesty is the Virtue of a poor-soul'd Country Gentlewoman; she is too much of a Court Lady, to be under so vulgar a Confusion; she reads the Letter, therefore, with a careless, dropping Lip, and an erected Brow, humming it hastily over, as if she were impatient to outgo her Father's Commands, by making a complete Conquest of him at once; and that the Letter might not embarrass her Attack, crack! she crumbles it at once into her Palm, and pours upon him her whole Artillery of Airs, Eyes and Motion; down goes her dainty, diving Body to the Ground, as if she were sinking under the conscious Load of her own Attractions; then lanches into a Flood of Fine Language, and Compliment, still playing her Chest forward in fifty Falls and Risings, like a Swan upon waving Water; and, to complete her Impatience, she is so rapidly fond of her own Wit, that she will not give her Lover leave to praise it.[1]

Nobody taught Cibber to write like this; he learnt to write this admirable prose by having first learnt to write dialogue for his comedies, and he learnt to write that partly by imitating Congreve, and partly by listening to the conversation of gentlemen, and so in time acquiring it, or something like it, himself. When Congreve said of Cibber's comedies that there was a great deal in them that looked like wit, but was not, he was paying an unconscious tribute to Cibber's power of assimilating the idiom of his betters. With Cibber the gap between writing and conversation is almost non-existent. For him, writing *is* talking; and if in reading his *Apology* we are sometimes inclined to say, 'Signior Benedick, nobody marks you', it is on the whole lively and arresting talk, the self-recorded conversation of a man accustomed to hold the floor at White's.

Here, again, is the poet Gray answering a letter in which Horace Walpole appears to have chidden him for his silence by suggesting that he must be dead. His reply, which is dated 'From St Peter's Charnel-house',[2] proceeds to develop this whimsy of his being dead.

---

[1] *An Apology for the Life of Mr. Colley Cibber, Comedian* (1740, 4to ed.), pp. 99–100.
[2] Gray was at this time an undergraduate of Peterhouse.

As you take a great deal of pleasure in concluding that I am dead, & resolve not to let me live any longer; methinks you ought to be good to my Ashes, & give 'em leave to rest in peace: but instead of that, whereas I ought to be divested of all human Passions, & forget the Pleasures of your World; you must needs be diverting me, so that I made every nail in my Coffin start with laughing: it happen'd, that on the 26th Instant at twelve of the clock at midnight, being a hard frost; I had wrapt myself up in my Shroud very snugg & warm; when in comes your Letter, which (as I told you before) made me stretch my Skeleton-jaws in such a horse-laugh, that all the dead pop'd up their heads & stared: but to see the frowzy Countenances of the Creatures especially one old Lady-Carcase, that made most hideous Grimaces, & would needs tell me, that I was a very uncivil Person to disturb a Woman of her Quality, that did me the honour to lie so near me: & truly she had not been in such a Surprise, this threescore & ten Year, come next March: besides her Commode was discomposed, & in her hurry she had lost her Wedding Ring, which she was buried in; nay, she said, she believed she should fall in fits, & certainly, that would be her Death: but I gave her a Rowland for her Oliver, i'gad: I told her Ladyship the more she stirred, the more she'd stink & that to my knowledge, tho' she put a very good face upon the matter, she was not sound: so she lay'd her down very quietly, and crept under her Winding-Sheet for fear of Spirits. . . .[1]

Gray's writing here is keeping pace with the ideas forming in his mind; they rise, take shape, and pass almost imperceptibly into words. There is premeditation to this extent, that Gray is aware, before he begins to write, of the theme he means to develop; but in working it out he is filling the air, like Keats's spider, with 'a beautiful circuiting'. He is delighting in the movements of his own mind, playing with his idea as a kitten plays with a straw. Gray is conscious, of course, that he is addressing Walpole; indeed, he writes as he does partly because he is so well aware of shared experience and of a reader who perfectly understands his vagaries. ('Dear Dimidium meae animae', he begins.) But at the same time his mind is going off on a journey of its own; he is, after all, more like the child than the kitten, half absorbed in his own doings, and yet half conscious too of the watching adult, and shaping at least some of those doings in the hope that the adult will take note and be suitably impressed. The result is a piece of writing that is wonderfully nimble and

[1] *Correspondence of Thomas Gray*, ed. Toynbee–Whibley (1935), vol. i, pp. 11–12.

extemporary, though round its phrasing one can still detect the faint hoop of Augustan formality.

It is just this carefree play of the mind that I do not find in the prose of Johnson; his characteristic virtues are those of the adult. In Johnson's prose the foreseen triumphs continually over the fortuitous; nothing is set down that is not the outcome of calm and mature deliberation. One is therefore impressed strongly by its decision (the 'oracular' note that critics have so often remarked), by Johnson's method of proceeding by calculated steps upon his way; for not only is he sure to arrive at his destination, but he is pretty sure of getting there in the way that he had originally intended. The attraction of Johnson's prose lies to a large extent in the complete confidence which it induces; whether he launches himself upon a long or a short period one knows that his point will be made exactly as he means to make it, the emphasis always falling upon the right places, and the rhythm coming to a regular close with the completion of the thought. This is not, of course, a mere trick of style. Whatever it may have been with his imitators, Johnson's prose is the natural expression of his mode of thought; he was accustomed to marshalling his ideas in that way, to ratiocinate by means of parallel ideas and antitheses. The result is that his prose often departs very far from the idiom of conversation, and his fondness for scientific and philosophic terminology carries it still farther from the spoken word. I am aware that there is plenty of evidence that Johnson often expressed himself in his conversation in much the same deliberate fashion, projecting an idea entire in his mind before unlocking his lips to speak; but that proves rather that he sometimes spoke as he wrote, and not that he sometimes wrote as he spoke. We may agree with Coleridge that the difference between the educated and the uneducated man comes out in

that prospectiveness of mind, that surview, which enables a man to foresee the whole of what he is to convey, appertaining to any one point; and by this means so to subordinate and arrange the different parts according to their relative importance, as to convey it at once, and as an organised whole.[1]

Still, Johnson's ability to give shapely construction to his thoughts in ordinary conversation was abnormal, even in an

[1] *Biographia Literaria*, ch. xviii.

eighteenth-century dining-room or drawing-room, and even allowing for the fact that in the years when most of his conversation was recorded he could count on being heard without interruption to the end of the most elaborate sentence. If I say, then, that Johnson's prose is so deliberate that it tends to lose all contact with conversation, it will not be a sufficient answer to point out that it is often very like *his* conversation. Habit had made it almost impossible for Johnson to think in any but a shapely fashion. In his familiar letters there is usually the same ordered advance of thought from one position to another, the same considered tempo. No doubt he sometimes spoke and wrote when he had little to say, but even when the engine is 'idling' it is still performing its characteristic movements. Anyone who has ever watched corn being threshed will readily recall the low busy sound of the threshing-machine when it has just been fed with sheaves, and the higher-pitched and emptier sound when the machinery continues to revolve without having anything to work upon. With Johnson the mind is always active, always ready to separate and discriminate, to generalize and particularize, to order and arrange, to illustrate and adorn; but it is not always provided with adequate materials. When it is so provided, the difference is not so much one of style (for with Johnson, I have suggested, that remains more or less constant), as of weight and profundity. We find this grave, deliberate style (where, indeed, we should expect to find it) in the Preface to the *Dictionary*.

In this work, when it shall be found that much is omitted, let it not be forgotten that much likewise is performed; and though no book was ever spared out of tenderness to the authour, and the world is little solicitous to know whence proceeded the faults of that which it condemns; yet it may gratify curiosity to inform it, that the *English Dictionary* was written with little assistance of the learned, and without any patronage of the great; not in the soft obscurities of retirement, or under the shelter of academick bowers, but amidst inconvenience and distraction, in sickness and in sorrow. . . .

Behind these words lie many years of labour and long hours of meditation. Here, as always, Johnson is giving us his generalizations, but on this occasion they are warmed by the glow of personal experience. When the impersonal puts on personality in this way we have the eighteenth century at its best. The

'Preface' has that characteristically English dignity which is inseparable from restraint, together with the strength that comes from having something powerful to restrain; it preserves a sense of proportion on an occasion when a man might well be excused for being partial to himself; and it has the deliberate utterance of one whose thoughts have been long maturing in his mind. The words therefore fall upon our ears with an inevitability which is far more than a mere matter of rhythm, though the rhythm everywhere reinforces the impression made by the words themselves.

For Johnson's views on prose style we must go chiefly to his criticism of other writers. After paying a tribute to Swift's simple and lucid expression, he has this to add:

> This easy and safe conveyance of meaning it was Swift's desire to attain, and for having attained he deserves praise, though perhaps not the highest praise. For purposes merely didactick, when something is to be told that was not known before, it is the best mode, but against that inattention by which known truths are suffered to lie neglected it makes no provision; it instructs, but does not persuade.[1]

The contrast which Johnson makes here between a prose of exposition and a prose of persuasion will no doubt account in part for the remarkable difference between Swift's prose style and his own. The clue to what he had in mind lies, I am convinced, in the words 'against that inattention by which known truths are suffered to lie neglected'. When they were written, the eighteenth century had all but entered on its ninth decade, and 'known truths' were becoming decidedly rubbed. The best friend of the eighteenth century will not deny that he meets continually—in Addison, Steele, Swift, Fielding, and in scores of minor essayists, sermon-writers, pamphleteers, journalists—with the same thoughts and the same criticisms over and over again. For one Addison there are a hundred Dick Minims.

> Who sate the nearest, by the words o'ercome
> Slept first, the distant nodded to the hum.

But this frequent repetition of the known was almost inevitable in an age which believed that what had always been said was most likely to be worth saying. When Johnson, quoting from memory, praised Goldsmith for having written in *The Vicar of*

[1] *Lives of the Poets*, ed. G. B. Hill, vol. iii, p. 52.

Wakefield, 'I found that generally what was new was false',[1] he was only expressing the whole century's approval of 'known truths'. The problem for the writer, therefore, turned upon how he was to express those truths with sufficient force and originality to make people still listen to them. It was, I believe, a problem that had scarcely begun to appear urgent to the authors of the *Tatler* and the *Spectator*: the men of Queen Anne's day were living almost in an age of intellectual innocence compared to those for whom Johnson was writing a generation later. Ideas were 'fresh and had the dew upon them'; it was still the early morning of this age of discussion and coffee-house conversation. But Johnson, who saw how information that was *new* might still be expressed in easy, simple language, could not see how the old truths had much hope of obtaining a hearing in the century's long drowsy afternoon unless they were set forth with uncommon emphasis and amplification. The fact, too, that so much of his writing aimed at *general* truth made it all the more necessary in his eyes to call in the aid of rhetoric, and also to employ a vocabulary which drew heavily upon philosophic and scientific terms. How far the style which he adopted really answered his purpose it would be difficult to say. To write on his plan, as he himself said of the metaphysical poets, it was at least necessary to think; but to read him it is also necessary to think, and to think rather harder than the ordinary reader is always prepared to do. Johnson's style, then, is proof against inattention in the sense that one must attend to Johnson or else not read him at all, for there is no reading him with half an eye. But that means, in effect, that only the attentive will read him; and many even of those, it is to be feared, will be dominated by Johnson's vigorous mind rather than encouraged to mental excursions of their own. In the long run the 'easy and safe conveyance of meaning' may prove to be better suited to the intellect of that 'common reader' whom Johnson had continually in mind.

It is not easy to determine either the extent to which Johnson may be considered the originator of the style of writing which is generally associated with his name, or how widely he influenced the prose of his contemporaries. What is not in doubt is that a widespread change took place in English prose in the later decades of the eighteenth century. There is a good deal

[1] *Life*, ed. Hill–Powell, vol. iii, p. 376.

of evidence to show that the literary public was well aware of what was happening. In 1793 a writer in *The Monthly Review*[1] defines the change clearly:

During our course of critical labours, which have now continued through nearly half a century, we have had occasion to remark a gradual change in the public taste with respect to style. At the time when our work commenced, Addison and Swift were esteemed our best models in prose writing; perspicuity, ease, and harmony, were the chief points at which our most classical writers aimed; and, provided these excellencies were attained, unnecessary diffuseness, feebleness, and even colloquial inelegance, were scarcely perceived to be faults. After this time, a stricter attention to precision and elegance of expression prevailed, through a set of writers among whom Mr. Melmoth makes a principal figure; till, by degrees, a fastidiousness of taste has been introduced, which shrinks from familiar and idiomatic phraseology, and which can only be gratified by a closely-condensed and highly-ornamented diction, as remote as possible from the ease of colloquial discourse. Our great masters in this style are the late Dr. Johnson and Mr. Gibbon.[2]

That 'fastidiousness of taste' which 'shrinks from familiar and idiomatic phraseology' had made itself felt in eighteenth-century poetry at a rather earlier stage than in its prose; since poetry was almost universally held to be 'in itself an elevation above ordinary and common sentiments',[3] there seemed to most of the poets and critics good grounds for a corresponding elevation of language. Even Pope, whose diction is often idiomatic enough in his satires, found himself in serious difficulties when he had to translate some of the less elevated sentiments of Homer. But the extension of this fastidiousness and this hatred of 'anything that's low' to the language of prose was a later development; and if Johnson certainly cannot be held solely responsible for it, his influence was undoubtedly powerful. On the other hand, even Johnson's example could hardly have directed English prose into a fresh channel if the change had not seemed desirable to other writers.

In seeking to account for this surprising movement away from an idiomatic to a more strictly scholarly phraseology and sentence-structure, we should do well to bear in mind the influence

---

[1] 2nd Series, vol. xii (1793), p. 361. The writer was William Enfield, in a review of *The Reveries of Solitude*, 1793.

[2] Quoted by W. K. Wimsatt, Jr., *The Prose Style of Samuel Johnson* (1941), p. 129. Mr. Wimsatt has many valuable points to make about the Antecedents (pp. 115 ff.) and the Effects (pp. 133 ff.) of Johnson's style.   [3] Steele, *Tatler*, No. 244.

of the Scottish prose writers of the period. By reason both of their number and their ability they left a considerable mark on eighteenth-century literature; and almost without exception they express themselves in a style nearer to Johnson than to Addison. The explanation does not lie (I hope) in the natural pedantry of the Scot, though as early as *Roderick Random* (1748) Smollett shows a fondness for pompous diction that certainly borders on the pedantic. The explanation is rather to be sought in the peculiar linguistic situation in which the Scot was placed. Whether or not men like Robertson, Blair, and Mackenzie wrote good English, they certainly did not speak it. When Boswell's father, the judge, deplored the ascendancy which Johnson had established over his son, he did not say that the young man must be mad to follow an old schoolmaster everywhere. Jamie, he remarked,[1] must be 'clean gyte' in thus 'pinning himself to the tail of an auld Dominie'. Old Boswell, in fact, expressed himself not as an English, but as a Scots, gentleman. The educated Scot of the eighteenth century used one language in his own home, or when addressing his servants, and another when he wrote.[2] The sort of prose style, therefore, that he would find most difficult to achieve was one based on what I have called 'the unhurried conversation of an eighteenth-century gentleman', the style of Addison and Swift; for the idiom, and, to a large extent, the vocabulary, of the Scots gentleman were quite different.[3] What, in fact, a Robertson or a Blair could, and did, acquire was a much less idiomatic mode of writing based on the language of scholars and divines. Here they were comparatively safe; for this was much more of a literary language, removed from that 'familiar and idiomatic phraseology' that came naturally enough to an Englishman, but was the despair of the literary Scot. It was this same disability that Burke noticed when he said of Robertson that he wrote like a man 'who composes in a dead language which he understands but cannot speak'.[4] And Dugald Stewart remarked

---

[1] But see below, pp. 182–3.

[2] My own grandfather, an Aberdeenshire farmer, habitually spoke to his men in the broad dialect of Buchan. On the other hand, his weekly articles to *The Aberdeen Free Press* were written, to the best of my recollection, in unexceptionable English.

[3] Irishmen, as Johnson observed (*Life*, ed. Hill–Powell, vol. iii, p. 473), were more happily placed than the Scots, since 'their language is nearer to English'.

[4] Margaret Forbes, *Beattie and his Friends*, p. 81; quoted by L. F. Powell, *Life*, ed. Hill–Powell, vol. ii, p. 237 *n.*

how Robertson, living 'at a distance from the acknowledged standard of elegance', and writing in a dialect different from that in which he was accustomed to speak, was 'naturally led to evade, as much as possible, the hazardous use of idiomatical phrases, by the employment of such as accord with the general analogy of the language'.[1]

What the Scot was driven to do by necessity, more and more Englishmen were doing by choice. For a final example of the change which was coming over English prose I turn to a strange and deplorable work which is yet, for our purpose, highly significant: *A Liberal Translation of the New Testament; Being an Attempt to translate the Sacred Writings with the same Freedom, Spirit, and Elegance, With which other English Translations of the Greek Classics have lately been executed.* . . ., by Edward Harwood, D.D.[2] This was published, in two volumes, in 1768. Harwood's first aim had been to discover the exact meaning; his next, to clothe the ideas 'in the vest of modern elegance'.

The author knew it to be an arduous and invidious attempt to make the phrase of these celebrated writers [Hume, Robertson, Lowth, Hurd, Johnson, etc.] the vehicle of inspired truths, and to diffuse over the sacred page the elegance of modern English, conscious that the bald and barbarous language of the old vulgar version hath acquired a venerable sacredness from length of time and custom, and that every innovation of this capital nature would be generally stigmatized as the last and most daring enormity.

Nevertheless, the translator sets to work, and the results are sufficiently startling. I quote from 1 Corinthians xiii:

Benevolence is unruffled, is benign: Benevolence cherishes no ambitious desires: Benevolence is not ostentatious; is not inflated with insolence.

It preserves a consistent decorum; is not enslaved to sordid interest; is not transported with furious passion; indulges no malevolent design.

It conceives no delight from the perpetration of wickedness; but is first to applaud truth and virtue.

It throws a vail of candour over all things. . . .

For in this state our knowledge is defective, our prophetic powers are limited . . . .

[1] *Account of the Life and Writings of William Robertson, D.D.* (1801), p. 151.
[2] I owe my acquaintance with this work to Professor J. Isaacs, who drew attention to it in his chapter, 'The Authorized Version and After', in *The Bible in its Ancient and English Version*, ed. H. Wheeler Robinson.

In fine, the virtues of superior eminence are these three, faith, hope, benevolence—but the most illustrious of these is benevolence.

For Mark vi. 39 we get:

He then ordered his disciples to desire the multitude to digest themselves into regular companies, and to sit down on the verdant turf.

And lastly, for Matthew xvii. 4 ('Then answered Peter, and said unto Jesus, Lord, it is good for us to be here'):

Transported with the pleasure of this wonderful scene, Peter cried out—How happy will it be for us to reside in this place!

One could hardly ask for a better, or worse, example of the style being laid on to the material. In this linguistic appliqué one can see what happens when a person of inferior talents writes as he thinks he ought to write, instead of trying to say what is to be said in natural, idiomatic English. For such third-rate writers as Dr. Edward Harwood, 'the vest of modern elegance' was indeed the shirt of Nessus.

It would be wrong to suggest that in the later decades of the eighteenth century there is a falling off in English prose: Johnson, Gibbon, Burke would alone be enough to disprove that. What I do suggest is that the Harwoods were writing better in the days of Addison than they were fifty years later. If Addison was the perfect model for the average man with average thoughts and feelings to express, may it not be added that Johnson, Gibbon, and Burke were not? For the ordinary levels of communication, for that mild exposition and easy discursiveness which comprehend the modest aims of the average writer of all periods, their style was too powerful, too emphatic. The imitators of Johnson sometimes caught the manner, but too often they could not supply either the matter or the mind that would justify it. As the century draws to its close we can see that something of the engaging simplicity of Addison and Steele has evaporated from prose writing; in literature (as in painting and sculpture) the grand manner was all the fashion. But dignity is constantly in danger of dwindling to pomp, or worse, and a grandeur that is merely synthetic will never get much beyond the grandiose. To be grand, in season and out of season, is to end by being not a Johnson, not even a Richardson, but a Sir Charles Grandison.

NOTE ON THE COMPOSITION OF GRAY'S
ELEGY [1]

H. W. GARROD

GRAY, we know, finished the *Elegy* in the summer of 1750. On 12 June of that year, 'Having put an end', he writes to Walpole, 'to a thing whose beginning you have seen long ago, I immediately send it you.' [2]

What was the 'beginning' which Walpole had 'long ago' seen? And how far back may Gray's 'long ago' be supposed to carry us?

Both questions are, I think, answered by Walpole himself, in a letter which he wrote to Mason on 1 December 1773. Mason was 'inclined to believe' that the *Elegy* was 'begun, if not concluded', in 1742. [3] It was in 1742 that Gray's friend Richard West died. But ' *The Churchyard* ', Walpole writes, 'was, I am persuaded, posterior to West's death at least three or four years. . . . I am sure that I had the twelve or more first lines from himself above three years after that period, and it was long before he finished it.' [4]

I am not the first person to be perplexed by these 'twelve or more first lines'. 'A strangely meagre specimen', Mr. Stokes calls them, very properly. [5] Mr. Tovey conjectures (desperately, I must think) that the 'twelve or more first lines' are the twelve last lines, the Epitaph in which the poem concludes. [6]

Mason was busy with his edition of Gray's *Poems* and the 'Memoirs' prefixed thereto. On 23 November 1773 he wrote to Walpole, notifying him that he had dispatched to him the first three sections of this work, and inviting comment. [7] The three sections make up pp. 1–169 of the published book.

[1] An essay on Burns' 'Auld Lang Syne' which Mr. Garrod gave us for this volume was lost in the post. The editors are grateful to him for writing this Note on Gray's *Elegy* after he had tried and found it impossible to rewrite the original essay.

[2] *Correspondence of Thomas Gray*, ed. P. Toynbee and L. Whibley, Oxford, 1935, vol. i, pp. 326–7.

[3] *The Poems of Mr. Thomas Gray: To which are prefixed Memoirs*, &c., London and York, 1775, p. [157].

[4] *Letters of Horace Walpole*, ed. Mrs. P. Toynbee, vol. viii, pp. 371–2.

[5] *An Elegy written in a Country Churchyard*, ed. F. G. Stokes, Oxford, 1929, p. 17.

[6] *C.H.E.L.*, vol. x, p. 123.

[7] *Correspondence of Horace Walpole and the Rev. William Mason*, ed. J. Mitford, London, 1851, vol. i, pp. 102–4.

On p. [157], 'I am inclined to believe', he writes, 'that the Elegy in a Country Church-yard was begun, if not concluded at this time also' (about August 1742). 'I am aware', he adds, 'that, as it stands at present, the conclusion is of a later date; how that was originally, I shall show in my notes on the poem.' The notes take us outside the sections submitted to Walpole. They take us, in fact, to what Mason calls[1] 'the first manuscript copy of this exquisite poem'; to a manuscript in the poet's autograph, now the property of Eton College. Together with the Pembroke College autograph it had passed to Mason on Gray's death in 1771; Mason had been at pains to label it 'Original Copy of the Elegy in a Country Churchyard'; and that it offers a version of the *Elegy* earlier than any other text is certain. It is not a *draft*. It is in the nature, rather, of a fair copy which has been subjected to numerous corrections. All of these are interesting. But most of them Mason is content to neglect. In the first 72 lines there are twenty-four variants from the printed text, none of which he notices. The first seventy-two lines can take care of themselves; and he races to what lies beyond them. For these first seventy-two lines are followed, in the manuscript, by four stanzas of which two have no place in our other texts—parts of the second and fourth, refashioned, do appear in the printed editions. I set out these four stanzas as the manuscript gives them—Mason was never minutely exact:

> The thoughtless World to Majesty may bow
> Exalt the brave, & idolize Success
> But more to Innocence their Safety owe
> Than Power & Genius e'er conspired to bless
>
> And thou, who mindful of the unhonour'd Dead
> Dost in these Notes their artless Tale relate
> By Night & lonely Contemplation led
> To linger in the gloomy Walks of Fate,
>
> Hark how the sacred Calm that broods around
> Bids ev'ry fierce tumultuous Passion cease
> In still small Accents whisp'ring from the Ground
> A grateful Earnest of eternal Peace
>
> No more with Reason & thyself at Strife
> Give anxious Cares & endless Wishes room
> But thro the cool sequester'd Vale of Life
> Pursue the silent Tenour of thy Doom.

[1] *The Poems of Mr. Thomas Gray*, 1775, p. 107.

'And here the Poem was originally intended to conclude', says Mason.[1] Nor can there be any doubt that he is right. At some later date Gray drew a line against these four stanzas, writing in after them lines 73–128 of the poem as we have it in our printed texts.[2]

Lines 1–72, then, with four stanzas, of which parts of the second and fourth are used again in the final version, constitute the original *Elegy*. This is the poem which Mason was 'inclined to believe' was 'begun, if not concluded', in 1742. Was it the 'beginning' which Gray sent to Walpole at a date which he speaks of, in 1750, as 'long ago'? Or was that 'beginning' the meagre 'twelve or more first lines' spoken of in Walpole's letter to Mason?

Of Walpole's letter we have, not the original, but Mitford's transcript. If we had the autograph, I cannot but think that we should find there, not 'the twelve or more first lines', but 'the 72 or more first lines'. We should find that Mitford had misread '72' as '12'.

Mason wrote with the Fton MS. in front of him. Walpole was served only by the printed texts and memories of nearly thirty years back. He speaks of the 'beginning' sent to him by Gray as 'the 72 or more first lines', because the 72 lines are given him by the printed editions. In what was given him by Gray these 72 lines were followed, he recalls, by others, since cancelled. The exact number of the cancelled lines he might be forgiven for not remembering. Even if he remembered that, together, they made four stanzas, he might prefer not to be too specific; since the first three lines of the second stanza, and the last two lines of the fourth, had been later transferred (with minor changes) to the poem as given in the printed editions.

Mason answered Walpole's letter by a letter which has not survived. But to this lost letter we have Walpole's reply,

---

[1] *The Poems of Mr. Thomas Gray*, 1775, p. 107.

[2] With three substantial differences, however: (1) After line 93 the MS. has 'For thee, who mindful &c: as above' (indicating, that is, that the second of the four cancelled stanzas is to be placed here, with the correction 'For thee', instead of 'And thou'); then follows:

> If chance that e'er some pensive Spirit more,
> By sympathetic Musings here delay'd
> With vain, tho' kind, Enquiry shall explore
> Thy once-loved Haunt, this long deserted Shade.

(2) Line 100 is followed by a stanza omitted from our printed texts. (3) Line 116 is followed by another similarly cancelled stanza.

written on 14 December,[1] in which 'Your account of the *Elegy*', he writes, 'puts an end to my other criticism' (the criticism on the date of the *Elegy*). Nothing suggests that there was any difference between them on any question except that question of date. Nothing suggests that, whereas Mason had in mind a 'beginning' of the poem running to 72 lines or more, he had received a letter from Walpole reducing his 72 or more to 12 or more.

In his Memoir of Gray, Walpole has left a note on the composition of the *Elegy* which is confused and unhelpful. After mentioning the Eton 'Ode', 'another Moral Ode' (presumably 'Spring'), and the 'Ode on the Death of a Favourite Cat', Gray, he says,[2] 'began a poem on the Reformation of Learning. . . . He began too a philosophical poem in Latin, & an English tragedy of Agrippina, & some other odes, one of which, a very beautiful one, entitled *Stanzas written in a Country Churchyard*, he finished in 1750.' Here the 'Favourite Cat' brings us already to 1747; and 'some other odes' suggests a yet later date. Nor, I think, does the title 'Stanzas', which Walpole gives to the *Elegy*, carry us necessarily to the Eton MS. Only in that manuscript is the poem so entitled; but that Walpole himself had a manuscript bearing this title (the manuscript from which the poem was in fact printed) seems a fair inference from Gray's letter to him of 11 February, 1751—'the title must be Elegy, wrote in a Country Church-yard'.[3]

About the date at which he received the 'beginning' of the *Elegy* Walpole's memory was hardly in fault. Gray could not have sent it to him much before 1746; for the sufficient reason that from July 1741 to November 1745 he and Gray were not on speaking terms. It does not follow, of course, that the poem, as originally conceived, did not take shape a good deal earlier, during the period of their estrangement—a consideration which Mason would hardly miss. Mason seems to have persuaded himself that, in its first form, the poem had its occasion in the sorrow brought on Gray by the death of West. Gray, Mason writes,[4] 'originally gave it only the simple title "Stanzas

---

[1] *Correspondence of Horace Walpole and the Rev. William Mason*, ed. J. Mitford, London, 1851, vol. i, p. 115.

[2] *Correspondence of Thomas Gray*, ed. P. Toynbee and L. Whibley, Oxford, 1935, vol. iii, p. 1287.

[3] Ibid. vol. i, p. 341.   [4] *The Poems of Mr. Thomas Gray*, 1775, p. 106.

written in a Country Church-yard". I persuaded him to call
it an ELEGY, because the subject authorized him so to do.'
The subject connects, I suppose him to mean, with West.
Gray's acquiescence, accordingly, in the title 'Elegy' might
seem to support the early date which Mason wishes to assign
to the poem. But for Gray, in truth, the subject was wider.
It was a pity, he told Mason, that Young had used as the motto
for his *Night Thoughts* the Virgilian line

> Sunt lacrimae rerum, et mentem mortalia tangunt.

It was a pity because he himself wanted it as a motto for the
Elegy.[1] The subject of the *Elegy*—I think of Elegy generally, as
Gray conceived it—is given by that Virgilian line. That Gray
wrote the *Elegy* remembering West, I do not doubt. That it
was commemorative elegy I think less certain. Upon the
nature of commemorative elegy Gray, in a letter written to
Walpole in November 1747, has some interesting comments.
'Nature and sorrow, and tenderness', he writes, 'are the true
genius of such things . . . poetical ornaments are foreign to
the purpose, for they only show that a man is not sorry; and
devotion worse; for it teaches him, that he ought not to be
sorry, which is all the pleasure of the thing.'[2] Nature and
sorrow and tenderness the *Elegy* surely has. Of poetical
ornament I cannot think it—Johnson's criticisms notwithstanding—lavish. Into the conclusion of the poem, however,
into what Landor calls 'the tin-kettle of an epitaph tied to its
tail', Gray *has* imported devotion, managing it unhappily.
From the 'Sonnet on West' he has excluded devotion, weeping
the more because he weeps in vain—'which is all the pleasure
of the thing'.

Mason's date, though Walpole ends by acquiescing in it,
has not met with any very general acceptance; perhaps only
Mitford and Gosse—and either with qualifications—have
accepted it. Mr. Whibley finds it 'hard to believe that within
a few weeks Gray, who had only recently begun to write
original poems in English, should have written the *Sonnet on
the Death of West*, the *Eton Ode*, the *Hymn to Adversity*, and the
first draft of the *Elegy*'.[3] About the date of the 'Sonnet', the
'Ode', and the 'Hymn' there is, of course, no doubt. What

---

[1] Gray's *Works*, ed. Mitford, 1835–43, vol. i, Pref., p. 26.
[2] *Correspondence of Thomas Gray*, ed. P. Toynbee and L. Whibley, vol. i, p. 289.
[3] Ibid. vol. iii, p. 1214.

Mr. Whibley cannot believe is that Gray wrote the *Elegy* (or the greater part of it) at twenty-five. For a beginner in poetry, it is, he thinks, too much of a good thing. For a beginner in poetry I must think the 'Sonnet on West'—despite the cavils of Wordsworth (who did not like the *Elegy* either)—a pretty good thing. I cannot read the 'Sonnet' and think it impossible that the same poet should, about the same time, have written the *Elegy*. If the *Elegy* is not a young man's poem, as the poetry of young men is commonly conceived, neither is the 'Sonnet'. But, then, just as Gray 'was never a boy', so, perhaps, he was never a young man. I cannot think that any four lines of the 'Sonnet', if we found them among the stanzas of the *Elegy* in our Eton MS., would appear incongruous. The mood is the same, the power (except that it is not sustained beyond two quatrains and a sestet) not greatly inferior in degree or kind. Nobody, of course, likes anti-climax; and that Gray should write the *Elegy* at twenty-five, and thereafter nothing equally great (except the 1750 refashioning of it), *is* anti-climax. But the most real objection to Mason's date is, perhaps, Mason himself. Nobody likes him, and nobody trusts him.

JOHN LANGHORNE

HUGH MACDONALD

THE English clergy in the eighteenth century have acquired an exaggerated reputation for the eccentricity of their habits, for idleness or for the neglect of their duties. This is in part due, no doubt, to characters in fiction. It has been assumed that Trulliber, Parson Adams, or, as manners improved, Mr. Tilney can be taken as fairly representing the Church of England, and that religious activity was more or less confined to the Methodist Revival. Bishop Burnet's *Discourse of the Pastoral Care* (1692), which requires a high standard of life from those to whom it is addressed, and which by 1713 was in its third edition, would alone suggest that this view is unreasonable. The work of Dr. Norman Sykes[1] and the publication of several diaries kept by clergymen during the century have shown that it is largely incorrect. It is, however, true that country rectors and vicars often allowed themselves plenty of leisure for occupations which ranged from the study of antiquities to fox-hunting, or even to pursuits still more remote from gardening—the recreation Burnet considered as most suitable for a clergyman.

Of Langhorne's activities as a parson we know little except from his son's statement, referring to the period following his second marriage, that he was 'content with performing the duties of his station, and exercising the benevolence of his disposition in relieving the distresses of the poor'. But it is with Langhorne as an author that I am concerned, and if the number of books he published shows that his work as a clergyman was not unduly heavy it certainly proves that he was not lazy. No one need be reminded that poetry, sermons, and controversial divinity were produced in abundance by men in orders in the seventeenth century; but the basis of literature was wider in the eighteenth, largely because of the existence of periodicals which contained reviews and essays, and the clergyman who was also a professional writer became a common

---

[1] *Church and State in England in the XVIIIth Century* (1934). The literature of the Oxford Movement tends to misrepresent somewhat the clergy of the period between the Caroline divines and 1833.

figure. No better example than Langhorne can be found. Like
nearly all who have not possessed powers of the highest order,
his popularity as a writer did not last for very long, nor are his
poems to be found in many anthologies.[1] But he is, I think,
worthy of a place in this volume for several reasons. He was a
poet whose verses had at least short passages of real merit, he
was an assiduous reviewer, from whose reviews we can learn
much about the opinions of the day, his and his brother
William's translation of Plutarch held the field for nearly a
hundred years, he forms an accidental link between Burns and
Scott, and his best poem, *The Country Justice*, anticipates Crabbe
in a remarkable way.

Perhaps he has a still higher claim to be remembered.
Wordsworth, like other great poets, made use of the work of
writers who were not of much importance in themselves. He
studied many of his eighteenth-century predecessors with care,
especially if they came from the Border, Cumberland or Westmorland.[2] In the 1799 manuscript of 'She dwelt among the
untrodden ways' Wordsworth had written:

> And she was graceful as the broom
> That flowers by Carron's side;
> But slow distemper checked her bloom,
> And on the Heath she died.[3]

He was here recalling Langhorne's 'Owen of Carron'. In the
Album which he made for Lady Mary Lowther in 1819
Wordsworth included two stanzas by Langhorne; the second of
them is Horatian in manner, but its last three lines would not
look incongruous in an anthology of Wordsworth's own poems:

> Ah friend! Ambition's prospects close,
> And, studious of your own repose,
>   Be thankful here to live;
> For, trust me, one protecting shed,
> And nightly peace, and daily bread
>   Is all that life can give.[4]

[1] Eighty-four lines, in all, are printed in *The Oxford Book of Eighteenth Century Verse*.
[2] *The Letters of William and Dorothy Wordsworth: the Later Years*, ed. E. de Selincourt, vol. i, p. 128.
[3] *The Poetical Works of William Wordsworth*, ed. E. de Selincourt, vol. ii (1944), p. 30. The third line could hardly have been written by anyone except Wordsworth or a much less accomplished poet than Langhorne.
[4] Verses free from 'poetic diction' were not uncommon in the eighteenth century. They are for the most part essentially different from Wordsworth's best poetry.

The fullest account of Langhorne's life has been left by his son, who, like his father and grandfather, was in orders. The Rev. John Theodosius Langhorne prefixed a memoir to the collected edition of his father's poems published in 1804, and so far as I know little information has been added since. The son wrote under difficulties, as his father's manuscripts had been destroyed, he tells us, 'by those who were authorized to inspect them'.

John Langhorne, the youngest of four children, was born at Winton, close to Kirkby Stephen in Westmorland, in March 1735. He was taught 'the rudiments of English' by his mother. He went to school at Winton, and afterwards at Appleby, where he attracted the headmaster's attention. He is said to have left school with a thorough knowledge of the classics, but as there was not enough money to send him to a university he became private tutor to a family near Ripon. He then went as an assistant master to the free-school at Wakefield, which had some celebrity at the time. During his vacations Edmund Cartwright, the reputed inventor of the power-loom, was his pupil, and the two men became lifelong friends. Here he took deacon's orders, and attained popularity as a preacher. In 1759 he moved to Hackthorn, near Lincoln, to become tutor to the sons of Robert Cracroft.

While at Hackthorn Langhorne published a collection of verses with a Lincoln imprint in a quarto volume, which is now exceedingly rare.[1] It was published by subscription for the relief of an unnamed gentleman in distress. At five shillings a copy the edition could not have given substantial aid. Langhorne was fond of trying different verse forms, and this volume contains poems in many styles, and on many themes. Most of them were not reprinted, and of those omitted from his collected poems published in 1766 only one, 'Studley Park', was reprinted by his son in 1804. The Lincoln volume contains one or two facetious poems. In these, as in most of the other pieces,

---

Nevertheless, as Professor Elton says, writing of Langhorne's poetry generally, Langhorne 'is one of the writers who show upon what stray patterns and precedents the style of Wordsworth was formed'. *A Survey of English Literature 1730–1780*, vol. i (1928), p. 345.

[1] There is a copy, which belonged to Isaac Reed, in the Bodleian. The edition was described by I. A. Williams in *The London Mercury*, 1921–2. The list of subscribers includes a number of Cracrofts and Cartwrights, persons with Yorkshire names such as Cecil Slingsby, and members of several Oxford Colleges.

he is too derivative to be interesting. In a satire on Thomas
Hearne he imitates Butler's rhymes:

> A symbol rare to rouse the wish up,
> A black-shoe-boy may be a Bishop.[1]

In another poem he more than echoes Gray:

> Nor leave confin'd one ling'ring thought below!

In 1760 he entered his name at Clare Hall in order to take
a B.D. degree by a peculiar method of obtaining academical
status without residence.[2] He may have been in Cambridge for
a time, as he contributed a poem to a volume of University
poems on the accession of George III. He is said also when at
Clare to have written *Solyman and Almena*, an oriental tale in the
manner of *Rasselas*. It was not, however, published until 1762.

At Hackthorn Langhorne had fallen in love with Cracroft's
second daughter Anne, a young lady with some accomplish-
ments, to whom he taught Italian, a language in which he was
always interested. He concluded that a marriage with Anne
would not be welcomed by her relations, and in 1761 he went
to Dagenham as a curate. There was no breach with the
family, and at least one of Anne's brothers continued to receive
instruction from him. This is referred to fourteen years later in
some dedicatory stanzas to the Second Part of *The Country
Justice* :

> Not that in youth we rang'd the smiling meads,
> On Essex' shores the trembling angle play'd,
> Urging at noon the slow boat in the reeds,
> That wav'd their green uncertainty of shade.

In 1762 Langhorne attempted to win the favour of the Earl of
Halifax by a poem called *The Viceroy*. The nobleman either did
not read, or did not enjoy, the poem. He had better success
with Warburton, to whom he dedicated *Letters on Religious
Retirement* (1762). The Bishop of Gloucester encouraged him
to write more, and in due course there appeared *Letters between
Theodosius and Constantia* (1763), founded on a story in No. 164
of the *Spectator*. In 1764 Langhorne obtained a curacy and
lectureship at St. John's, Clerkenwell, and in the same year he
published a volume of sermons which he followed up with

---

[1] Cf.   The oyster women lock'd their fish up,
           And trudg'd away, to cry 'No Bishop'. *Hudibras*.

[2] The procedure has been described by the Vice-Master of Trinity; see D. A.
Winstanley, *Unreformed Cambridge* (1935), p. 68.

Letters on the Eloquence of the Pulpit (1765): this contains some rather obvious comments, one of them being that a sermon which would make a good impression at St. James's would be 'very improper and very ineffectual indeed if preached in the parish church at Llangwillidog'. The Rev. J. Mainwaring in a note to his own published sermons selected those of Langhorne for their numerous examples of false pathos 'like those of the Methodists in general'. The allusion to Methodists was unkind, because in his dedication to Warburton Langhorne had stated that one of his objects was to prevent the 'delusions of fanaticism'. But there was rivalry among sermon-writers, and Langhorne had himself assured a reverend colleague 'that his sermons were not in the least likely to be remembered against him on the Day of Judgment'. Langhorne's sermons have at least the merit of being short. One of them is included in its entirety in a review in *The Monthly* in 1764.

In 1763 Charles Churchill had abused the Scots in *The Prophecy of Famine*, to which Langhorne replied by a poem called *Genius and Valour* (1764). This is in the form of a pastoral, and for it he received the degree of D.D. of Edinburgh[1] and some abusive lines in Churchill's *The Candidate* (1764). In 1765 he was appointed preacher's assistant at Lincoln's Inn by Warburton's friend Hurd. In 1766 he became Rector of Blagdon on the north of Mendip, the parsonage being 'a neat house, situated on an eminence with beautiful hanging gardens at the foot of which was an alcove'. The alcove had been prepared for Anne Cracroft, whom he married in 1767. She died in childbed in May of the following year. His *Precepts for Conjugal Happiness*, written in heroic couplets addressed to his sister in 1767, are too general to give us much information about Langhorne as a husband.

After the death of Anne, Langhorne went to live with his brother at Folkestone, where the two worked at their translation of Plutarch's *Lives*, which was published in 1770, and reprinted at least sixteen times in the next sixty years, from 1809 with 'Corrections and Additions' by Francis Wrangham.[2] Clough's edition, based on Dryden's, was published in 1864.

---

[1] His son is the authority for this, and there is no reason to doubt it, though there is no record of the degree in the records of Edinburgh University. His brother William's M.A. was a Lambeth degree.

[2] See *Archdeacon Francis Wrangham*, by Michael Sadleir (1937).

I suppose no work illustrates the changes of taste so well as the English translations of Plutarch. North's translation was read from 1579 till 1657, after which it must have become unfashionable. A translation by a number of scholars chosen by Dryden and Tonson was published in 1683–6.[1] This edition was revised in 1727 with the help of Dacier's translation,[2] and was the standard text till that of the Langhornes. The Langhornes' translation and Clough's were both reprinted at intervals till the revival of North in the *Tudor Translations* in 1895. One object of John and William Langhorne was to write elegant English. They abuse the 1727 edition, but how far they looked at the Greek is uncertain.[3] In some passages, at least, they appear to have translated from the French, and they took many of their notes from Dacier with a very scanty acknowledgement.

The difference between North's translation and the Langhornes' has been stressed by George Wyndham, and is too obvious to be worth illustrating again. But a short passage from the Life of Antony, as rendered in Dryden's edition and by the Langhornes, will show the Langhornes' desire to tidy up the English.

Charles Fraser, M.D., Dryden's translator, has:

Sending away the servant upon another Errand [Antony] gave his Friend the Basin, desiring him to make what use he pleas'd on't, but this making a great stir among the Servants and putting his wife into very ill humour, to save her the trouble of further enquiry he acknowledged what he had done and begg'd her pardon.

---

[1] The translators were, for the most part, Fellows of Cambridge or Oxford colleges, or men with a university education. George Wyndham's description of them in the *Tudor Translations* edition as 'Greeklings of Grub Street' is quite unwarranted.

[2] This edition was overlooked by Malone. Mr. William King of Messrs. Blackwell generously gave me a copy from his private library. It is honestly stated on the title-page that the notes are from Dacier.

[3] Professor D. S. Robertson has kindly investigated the matter for me. He has pointed out one note in particular. In the Life of Themistocles is the note: 'Idomeneus says that one morning Themistocles harnessed four naked courtesans in a chariot, and made them draw him across the Ceramicus . . . at a time when the Athenians were perfect strangers to debauchery both in wine and women. But if that vice was then so little known in Athens how could there be four prostitutes impudent enough to consent to such an exposure?' Idomeneus is a lost writer, and this note is ultimately based on two passages in Athenaeus. Professor Robertson says that the word 'naked' which gives the chief point to the Langhornes' moral indignation has no justification in the words of Athenaeus, and there is therefore no escape from the conclusion that they either added it from ignorance or carelessness or borrowed it from Dacier.

The Langhornes have:

After the boy was dismissed he gave the basin to his friend and bade him make what use of it he thought proper! The disappearance of the basin occasioned no small commotion in the family; and Antony finding his wife prepared to take a severe account of the servants begged her pardon.[1]

In 1770–1 Langhorne published anonymously *Letters to Eleonora*. There is a statement in the first volume that the letters 'were written in the Reign of Queen Anne'. This may be an allusion to his wife, but at any rate there can be no doubt that the letters are those he wrote to Anne before their marriage. His son states that his father had published his letters to his mother under this title, and allowing for excisions which might have disclosed the authorship, the letters fit the known circumstances of the long courtship exactly. Langhorne was a good letter-writer, but as love-letters tend to have a similarity in all ages I will quote a letter to an acquaintance.[2] Langhorne had met Hannah More at Weston-super-Mare, whither she had gone to recover from one of her attacks of 'morbid sensibility'. They maintained their friendship until Langhorne's intemperate habits had become too trying for the lady. The letter describes a day in the poet's life at Blagdon in December 1776, after the death of his second wife.

At eight I rise, and that is almost as soon as the sun at this season makes himself known to us here. On my table I find a cup of cold chamomile tea with an infusion of orange peel;—dress, and come down stairs at nine, when I meet my breakfast, consisting of a basin of lean broth with a dry brown loaf, manufactured from corn of my own growing. Breakfast table cleared, I call for pen, ink and paper, and recollect—not which of my correspondents I have been longest indebted to, but which the humour leads most to write to. After this is performed, I apply a little to the laws of my country, to make myself a more useful citizen, and a better magistrate. About twelve, if the day turns out fine, I order my horses, for exercise on Mendip, which at this time of the year I can seldom effect; I am consequently obliged to seek exercise in measuring the length of my own hall. At two I dine, always upon one dish, and by way of desert eat three or four golden pippins, the produce of my own orchard, and drink as many glasses of wine. But then the

---

[1] The 1727 edition has: 'Next Morning the Whole Family was in an Uproar.' Dacier gives: 'Le lendemain voilà toute la maison en peine.'

[2] W. Roberts, *Memoirs of the Life and Correspondence of Mrs. Hannah More*, 2nd ed., vol. i (1834), p. 27.

afternoon—the solitary afternoon—Oh! for that the trash of the month comes in, and whether it makes me laugh or sleep, 'tis equally useful. The evening is divided between better books; music, and mending the fire, a roasted potatoe, a pint basin of punch and to bed.

Langhorne had married again in 1772. The lady was a daughter of a magistrate whom he had met on a visit to Westmorland. She had died in February 1776—like his first wife, in childbed. In October 1777 he was installed a Prebendary of Wells.[1] He died in April 1779 at the age of 44, leaving, besides his son, a daughter by his second wife who was consigned to the care of Mrs. Gillman, a friend of his Dagenham days.

Langhorne seems to have been an amiable, sentimental, and intellectually a not very vigorous man. In the death of both his wives he had real cause for unhappiness, and this may have fostered habits of intemperance which are said to have originated in his visits to the 'Peacock' in Gray's Inn Lane.[2] His friendships do not seem to have lain much among the writers of his day. He visited John Scott of Amwell. He knew Lord Lyttleton, and possibly Shenstone.[3] Cartwright wrote an elegy on the death of Anne, under the title of 'Constantia' (1768), and on Langhorne's own death, A. B. Portal, the publisher, wrote a poem which is entirely without merit. Gray evidently had a poor opinion of him,[4] and Hugh Kelly, the dramatist, attacked him in Book II of his *Thespis* (1767).

Between 1760 and his death, Langhorne wrote so much that I can only refer to a little of his work. The Lincoln volume was printed for Ralph Griffiths, and in this way I suppose he formed his first connexion with the founder of *The Monthly Review*, which Griffiths edited from its commencement in 1749

[1] Probably through the influence of the Pleydell-Bouveries. His son dedicated the two volumes of poems (1804) to the Earl of Radnor—the head of the family.

[2] *Biographia Dramatica* (1812). See also *Memoirs of the Life and Correspondence of Mrs. Hannah More*, p. 18.

[3] At any rate, in some lines addressed to the ill-fated Lord Chancellor, Charles Yorke, he writes: 'And Shenstone smil'd, and polish'd Hurd approves.'
Shenstone was pressed to visit Hestercombe in 1758, where there was a 'Hermitage', which would have been much to Shenstone's taste. *Letters of William Shenstone*, ed. Marjorie Williams (1939).

[4] Gray to Mason, Jan. 1765: 'Mr. Churchill is dead indeed, drown'd in a butt of claret . . . I did not write any of the elegies, being busy in writing the *Temple of Tragedy* . . . if I had not own'd the thing, perhaps you might have gone, and taken it for the Revd Mr Langhorne's.' *Correspondence of Thomas Gray*, ed. P. Toynbee and L. Whibley, vol. ii, p. 858.

till his death in 1803.[1] Langhorne began to contribute to *The Monthly* in November 1761, and with a short break continued to do so till he died. Probably there was some basis for Dr. Johnson's remark that the reviewers employed by *The Critical Review* often reviewed without reading the books through, but that *The Monthly* reviewers were duller men and were glad to read their books. Griffiths was unjustly attacked by Forster in his life of Goldsmith, although he had been more fairly treated by Sir James Prior. Griffiths's team included men of eminence such as Kippis, Porson, Samuel Parr, and Joseph White, Professor of Arabic at Oxford. Griffiths was a dissenter and a Whig, but he was free from bias, and was careful to see that his anonymous contributors did justice to their subjects. Poetry, books in foreign languages, and, for some reason or other, works on agriculture were often assigned to Langhorne, who contributed over 150 of the longer articles. Griffiths did not entirely trust him when it came to reviewing a friend's book. In writing to Cartwright about an unnamed contributor he says, 'No impartiality is to be expected. . . . Poor Langhorne was the same, and many a scuffle have we had about favour and resentment.'[2] Apart from this defect Langhorne was a conscientious critic, and his views generally seem sound enough to this day. He comments on the pains Capell had taken to collate the 'old editions' for his Shakespeare, which he compares favourably with Hanmer's 'licentious edition'. Writing of the *Life of Lord Herbert of Cherbury*, he emphasizes the importance of regarding a man in the light of his time. He sees the importance of the use by Mason of Gray's letters. He complains of the arbitrary way in which Hurd had chosen Cowley's poems for the *Select Works* (1773). He is doubtful if *The Castle of Otranto* is really a translation, but admits its merits for those who 'can digest the absurdities of Gothic fiction'. He says—with truth—that Grainger's *Sugar Cane* is rather an artful than an entertaining poem, but adds that 'lovers of good liquor will not be displeased with the digression in favour of rum'.

His own books were, on the whole, reviewed favourably,

[1] B. C. Nangle, *The Monthly Review First Series 1749–89: Indexes of Contributors and Articles* (1934). Mr. Nangle's book is based on Griffiths's office file and his correspondence in the Bodleian.

[2] *Memoir of Cartwright* (1843), quoted by Mr. Nangle.

although Hawkesworth is severe on his self-flattery in *Letters supposed to have passed between St. Evremond and Waller* (1769). These letters contain a good deal of moralizing, and some criticism of literature of the time of the supposed writers. Langhorne was not successful in imitating seventeenth-century diction. The letters could have been allocated to almost any other characters with equal propriety, although a conversation between Rochester and Charles II in the first letter has been accepted as genuine by more than one of Rochester's biographers.[1]

The Effusions of Friendship (1763) includes a series of letters 'On the Study of Poetry'. They have the merit of forming an essay in criticism by a poet who gave much attention to the technique of his own verse. He recommends simplicity of style. 'Familiar ideas', he says, 'must be conveyed by familiar phrases.' He characteristically inserts some verses of his own, but he quotes freely from other writers. To illustrate 'an ill-placed and injudicious repetition of the same words', he gives lines from Young's *Night Thoughts*, which he contrasts with Pope's skilful use of repetition in the lines beginning 'By foreign hands thy dying eyes were clos'd'. In a discussion of the 'harmony of numbers' he remarks that it is a bad compliment indeed to heroic rhyme to say that 'blank verse in its flow and structure should be as unlike it as possible'. If Langhorne is not very original, he was widely read and he writes agreeably.

The Fables of Flora (1771) was his most popular book of poems. He claims that he has extended the plan of the Fable so that the narrative and moral may be accompanied with imagery. This is an extravagant statement unless he means that he uses flowers instead of animals. But the poems are graceful and have at times a subdued beauty.[2] Saintsbury[3] called attention to two lines:

> Where longs to fall that rifted spire
> As weary of the insulting air.

It is possible to find other couplets and passages nearly as striking, but Langhorne cannot sustain his best work for long.

[1] It was reprinted anonymously in the *Relics of Literature* (1823) at the end of some genuine letters of Rochester.

[2] *The Fables* went into many editions in quarto, and were illustrated with charming stipple engravings by Stothard in 1794. These were reprinted with a life by F. Blagdon in 1804, after which they began to lose favour.

[3] *A History of English Criticism* (1911), p. 486.

In 1765 he published his edition of Collins's poems,[1] with a commentary which was reprinted till well into the next century. He had a real enthusiasm for Collins, due in part, no doubt, to their common taste for personification. Faced with the difficulties of Collins's text he did his work carefully, and perhaps as well as it can be done. He made an eclectic text from the first edition of the *Odes* and Dodsley's *Collections*.

The Country Justice, written at the request of Richard Burn, the historian of Westmorland,[2] and published in three parts (1774–5–7), is Langhorne's most important poem. Wordsworth is hardly correct in writing[3] that 'it is the first Poem, unless perhaps Shenstone's Schoolmistress be excepted, that fairly brought the Muse into the Company of common life', for Stephen Duck had described the hardship of the labourer in 'The Thresher' many years earlier. But he is right in saying that it 'looks with a tender and enlightened humanity . . . too rarely found in the works of Crabbe'. He adds that it is 'not without many faults in style from which Crabbe's more austere judgment preserved him'. Langhorne was a magistrate, as well as a clergyman, and he wrote about the poor and unfortunate as he knew them. It was the lucky recollection of Langhorne's name by Scott which drew a look of approval from Burns when Scott quoted, on the only occasion on which they met, the best-known lines in the poem:

> Cold on Canadian Hills, or Minden's Plain,
> Perhaps that Parent mourn'd her Soldier slain;
> Bent o'er her Babe, her Eye dissolv'd in Dew,
> The big Drops mingling with the Milk he drew,
> Gave the sad Presage of his future Years,
> The Child of Misery, baptiz'd in Tears!

In *Genius and Valour* (1764) he had written:

> On Canada's wild hills, and Minden's plain.

These lines[4] have been often quoted, but the poem as a whole has importance. Whether Crabbe had read *The Country Justice* when he wrote *Inebriety* (1775) or even *The Candidate* (1780) is not,

---

[1] Fawkes and Woty in their *Poetical Calendar* (1763) first collected Collins's poems.
[2] Nicolson and Burn, *History of Westmorland and Cumberland* (1777).
[3] 15 Jan. 1837.
[4] The reviewer of Part II of *The Country Justice* in the *Monthly* points out that Griffiths—the anonymous reviewer of Part I—had failed to draw attention to their remarkable beauty.

I believe, known,[1] but a passage such as the following shows
how poetry was moving away from Goldsmith:

> But, ah! Ye maids, beware the gypsey's lures!
> She opens not the womb of time, but yours . . .
>
> . . . .
>
> The parson's maid—sore cause had she to rue
> The gypsey's tongue; the parson's daughter too.
> Long had that anxious daughter sighed to know,
> What Vellum's sprucy clerk, the valley's beau,
> Meant by those glances, which at church he stole,
> Her father nodding to the psalm's slow drawl;
> Long had she sighed, at length a prophet came,
> By many a sure prediction known to fame,
> To Marion known, and all she told, for true:
> She knew the future, for the past she knew.

Owen of Carron (1778) shows Langhorne's use of literary
material in contrast to the personal observation displayed in
The Country Justice. Percy's *Reliques* had made the ballad of
'Gil Morrice' available. 'Owen' is largely founded on this. I
must be content to quote a single stanza, which is repeated
with effect in the poem:

> When all the mountain gales were still
> And the wave slept against the shore,
> And the sun, sunk beneath the hill,
> Left his last smile on Lemmermore.

Single lines of real, if not robust, beauty occur throughout:

> When Time leads calmly down to death.

Many of Langhorne's poems were topographical. He was
much attached to the river of his birthplace, the Eden, which
he frequently mentions. His descriptive verse is for the most
part faded now, though he could be observant enough:

> Here sprightly range the grove, or skim the plain,
> The sportive deer, a nicely-checker'd train.
> Oft near their haunt, on him who curious strays,
> All throng'd abreast in fix'd attention gaze;
> Th' intruding spy suspiciously survey,
> Then butting limp along, and lightly frisk away.

He could use the *In Memoriam* quatrain with facility. In

---

[1] Langhorne's friend Cartwright did not become a friend of Crabbe till many
years later.

The Enlargement of the Mind (1763) he employed the heroic couplet with more vigour than he usually displayed:

> Plac'd on this shore of Time's far-stretching bourn,
> With leave to look at Nature and return;
> While wave on wave impels the human tide,
> And ages sink, forgotten as they glide;
> Can life's short duties better be discharg'd,
> Than when we leave it with a mind enlarg'd?

Langhorne certainly left the world with his mind enlarged. For a time, at least, another of his wishes was fulfilled:

> To find some virtue trac'd on life's short page,
>   Some mark of service paid to human kind,
> Alone can cheer the wintry paths of age,
>   Alone support the far-reflecting mind.
>
> Oh! often thought—when Smith's discerning care
>   To further days prolong'd this failing frame!
> To die, was little—But what heart could bear
>   To die, and leave an undistinguish'd name?

Langhorne's knowledge of poetry was extensive, and he used almost every available verse form except the Spenserian stanza. He even wrote a drama in blank verse called *The Fatal Prophecy*. His versatility was, in fact, his chief handicap. In one of his Fables, 'The Wilding and the Broom', he suddenly changes from a quatrain to a poor imitation of James Thomson, and then to a 'L'Allegro'-like couplet. But he was of some importance in emancipating verse from a too heavy poetic diction, a movement which was not entirely due to Wordsworth and Coleridge. Griffiths, in a review of *The Effusions of Friendship*, said that the book served innocently to 'while away a vacant hour in a cool arbour or a shady walk'. But Langhorne was capable of more than this. When he drew on his own experience, as in his letters to Hannah More and in *The Country Justice*, he wrote prose and verse which can still be read for their own sake, and not merely because they are of interest to the historian of literature.

NOTES ON SOME LESSER POETS OF THE EIGHTEENTH CENTURY

W. L. Renwick

IT is difficult to read any work of our elders without precon-
ceptions and without taking up an attitude in advance, to
maintain the innocent and candid mind and read the thing for
what it is worth. We see the eighteenth century through the
Romantics, and, worse, through the critical commonplaces
handed down, and generally debased, from them. The young
are still taught that the eighteenth century was 'the age of prose
and reason', without any suggestion that—as Matthew Arnold
himself would have admitted if anyone had tackled him properly—prose and reason are two very good things. They are
still taught that it is a reproach to the eighteenth century that
its poetry was social poetry and not the outpouring of solitary
spirits. Yet we are all talking grandly about plans for living,
social order, social ideals: can we object to social poetry?

My business here is not to defend the eighteenth century.
It is very well able to look after itself. I wish only to suggest
that pleasant things, and some useful things, await the sympathetic inquirer.

Such an inquirer would do well to begin with the *Collection
of Poems* published by Robert Dodsley in 1748, and repub-
lished, with alterations and additions, twelve times. In these
six volumes, more than from any anthology that has been fil-
tered through later minds, he may observe the character and
habits of the time, and can then turn to the collected works of
any author who takes his fancy. He will find some of it dis-
tasteful or dull; he must accept that as the necessary roughage;
and if he does not find a great deal to enjoy, then I envy neither
his taste nor his wits.

Certain habits may require some exercise of sympathy. Until
one gets used to the terms of expression, the verbal generalizations and periphrases are annoying. We have lost some of
the tricks beloved of generations brought up on Virgil and
Horace, and many of them fail of appreciation through the
failure of our ignorant generation to recognize them. We have
to learn to appreciate Poetic Diction, or at least not to be put

off by it. That is not difficult. We may be bored by too many
imitations of Milton and Spenser, whom the eighteenth century revered as classics, the imitation of whom would not only
be accepted as laudable, but would be critically appreciated
by readers who were expected to know their classics. There
are dangers in thus writing for a public upon whose mental
content the poet could rely; but it might be argued that the
later insistence upon a simple-hearted audience was not only
impossible but led to the opposite danger of setting up as a
critical ideal the pleasure of an empty-headed audience.

In any case the eighteenth century can be trusted to supply
its own corrective. It was not in vain that Shaftesbury philo-
sophized and Akenside sang the benefits of Ridicule. If the
Virgilian strain bores us, we can relax with William Whitehead,
in *The Gymnasiad*, over the epic books of the prize-fight between Stephenson the Coachman and Broughton the Water-
man, or over his Georgic on street-sweepers, a lesser thing but
with a grand opening:

> I sing of Sweepers, frequent in thy streets,
> Augusta, as the flowers which grace the spring,
> Or branches withering in autumnal shades
> To form the brooms they wield. Preserv'd by them
> From dirt, from coach-hire, and th' oppressive rheums
> Which clog the springs of life, to them I sing,
> And ask no aspiration but their smiles.

Or if didacticism in Miltonic blank verse grows irritating, the
corrective is there in plenty, though best in John Philips's
'Splendid Shilling'. But there is plenty also of verse without
jargon, cultivated but straightforward, addressed to cultivated
but sensible minds.

It is not merely in the habits of expression that the eighteenth
century balances itself. These lesser poets are not specialized
or limited, but touch most things that make up what Wordsworth and Coleridge would call the goings-on of life.

It is, indeed, just that inclusiveness that troubles many
critics. Wordsworth's idea of poetry was so exalted that he was
distressed by the poetic expression of so many things that he
disliked or despised. But we cannot allow ourselves to be
shackled even by Wordsworth; and his noble aloofness has also
its dangers. The nineteenth century exalted the arts, and
therefore not only overpaid the artists of whom it approved—

Tennyson, Rossetti, Leighton—but segregated them. The arts were put on a pedestal, well out of the way. Protests and criticisms could be disregarded, as those of impractical and unworldly anchorites. The eighteenth century was wiser. Its artists were not so well paid, because their efforts were part of the ordinary goings-on of life. Their profits were, with some justice, equated with the wages of other men who ministered to society, and their opinions were—again with justice—weighed with other men's, not as those of angelic visitants or incalculable eccentrics, but as those of men who shared the common culture and the common life, who knew, thought, and could express themselves.

Eighteenth-century poetry is directed, as a whole, to social ends. The eighteenth-century poet was as Wordsworth described the poet: a man speaking to men. He spoke in public, and was therefore restricted by the contemporary code of public behaviour and the general sense of social values. So there are some things missing from eighteenth-century poetry. Men were well aware that the daw is a common bird, and were perhaps chary of wearing their hearts on their sleeves. Still more, they knew that outbursts of passion are apt to embarrass the bystanders, and often, when the fit cools, the perpetrator himself. In any case, the eighteenth century could find certain things already done; people knew them, better than is sometimes allowed, and they desired their own new things from their own poets.

Everything cannot be done all at once. So there is no eighteenth-century 'Epipsychidion', or anything like Donne's marvellous 'Ecstasy'. Yet, as Shelley said, 'The Epipsychidion is a mystery', and 'The Ecstasy' is unique. These lesser men dealt in the lesser mysteries of love-poetry, the game of the sexes as it can be played in drawing-rooms and gardens: slight, incomplete, but none the less real, and none the less understood, I take it, by those concerned. Do not let us be entangled in question-begging arguments about sincerity and artificiality. Love-poetry was stronger, no doubt, before and after, but only here do we get those half-lights and delicate shades of emotion conscious of itself and of its appearance. Something too was lost later on, as well as gained: look at the light verse of Keats and you will return to Prior with relief. There is no rapture in a man like Whitehead. This is his better level:

I

Yes, I'm in love, I feel it now,
  And Caelia has undone me;
And yet I'll swear I can't tell how
  The pleasing plague stole on me.

II

'Tis not her face which love creates,
  For there no Graces revel;
'Tis not her shape, for there the Fates
  Have rather been uncivil.

III

'Tis not her air, for sure in that
  There's nothing more than common;
And all her sense is only chat,
  Like any other woman.

IV

Her voice, her touch, might give th'alarm—
  'Twas both perhaps, or neither;
In short, 'twas that provoking charm
  Of Caelia all together.

I take it Caelia was not displeased; and it will be noticed that
Whitehead was thinking of her, not merely indulging an erotic
daydream by himself. The writing is simple and direct, and
can be, even when the sentiment is more subtle; and many others
took to heart Shenstone's warning—all the more attractive,
to people who knew their Shakespeare, for its Shakespearian
allusion:

Beneath a churchyard yew
  Decay'd and worn with age,
At dusk of eve, methought I spy'd
Poor Slender's ghost, that whimpering cry'd,
  O sweet, O sweet Anne Page!

Ye gentle bards, give ear!
  Who talk of amorous rage,
Who spoil the lily, rob the rose;
Come learn of me to weep your woes;
  O sweet! O sweet Anne Page!

Why should such labour'd strains
    Your formal Muse engage?
I never dreamt of flame or dart,
That fir'd my breast, or pierc'd my heart,
    But sighed, O sweet Anne Page! . . .

Hence every fond conceit
    Of shepherd, or of sage!
'Tis Slender's voice, 'tis Slender's way,
Expresses all you have to say—
    O sweet! O sweet Anne Page!

If, like good pupils of Romantic criticism, we look for natural
simplicity, we shall find it: and in this world, not in dreams.

Lady Mary Wortley Montagu was no great poet. She had
the common faults of the intellectual female, the absence of
which is the clearest proof of Jane Austen's supremacy among
her kind—uncertainty, the touch of coarseness when trying
to assume the careless strength of the other sex, the visible
effort of style. The tragedy of her emotional life gave her little
chance to blossom into love-poetry. But only stupidity or
churlishness could refuse sympathy to her verses on the ideal
lover, who must

In public preserve the decorum that 's just,
And shew in his eyes he is true to his trust;
Then rarely approach, and respectfully bow,
But not fulsomely pert, nor foppishly low.

But when the long hours of the publick are past,
And we meet with champagne and a chicken at last,
May ev'ry fond pleasure that moment endear;
Be banish'd afar both discretion and fear!
Forgetting or scorning the airs of the crowd,
He may cease to be formal, and I to be proud,
Till lost in the joy, we confess that we live,
And he may be rude, and yet I may forgive.

Still, it is not for love-poetry that we turn over Dodsley's or
Johnson's collections. Lyttelton's elegies on his wife may convince us of his sorrow if not of his genius; Robert Nugent's
bitter jealousy is all too outspoken; here and there we find, in
lightly turned addresses to auburn-tressed nymphs, hints of
feeling enough to remind us that people did love and laugh.
But the poets disregard too much Shenstone's warning and the

example of Lady Mary; they are too acutely conscious of the public, and love-poetry is too often reduced in scale and tone to a pastoral rather than a natural simplicity, pretty enough in Shenstone himself:

> Since PHYLLIS vouchsaf'd me a look
>   I never once dreamt of my vine;
> May I lose both my pipe and my crook,
>   If I knew of a kid that was mine.
> I priz'd every hour that went by,
>   Beyond all that had pleas'd me before;
> But now they are past, and I sigh;
>   And I grieve that I priz'd them no more.

and pleasant enough in John Byrom:

> My Dog I was ever well pleased to see
> Come wagging his Tail to my fair one and me;
> And *Phebe* was pleas'd too, and to my Dog said,
> Come hither, poor Fellow; and patted his head.
> But now, when he's fawning, I with a sour look
> Cry, Sirrah; and give him a Blow with my Crook:
> And I'll give him another; for why should not *Tray*
> Be as dull as his Master, when *Phebe*'s away?

Pastoral was once a light disguise, under whose favouring shade poets were permitted to sing of their own affairs instead of the weighty themes dictated by the Muses: it is plain even from these short quotations that the disguise has become more important than the thing disguised. We find, too, traces of a different humour from the playful insinuations which are all that drawing-room company allows. The decorative Cupids can, like Whitehead's,

> Scatter myrtles, scatter roses,
> And hold their fingers to their noses.

We may find the despairing lover as resolute as Walsh's, who was

> Distracted with Care
> For *Phyllis* the Fair.

Pastoral was still just possible, because the literary tradition still held, and because there still existed the native rustic culture to which the pastoral has a delicate allusion. This culture was destroyed by the industrialists and educationists of the nineteenth century, and its validity, so long recognized, was ignored by the new philosophy of Nature.

An appreciation of nature is, of course, seldom credited to the eighteenth century. It is true that lively people, like Soame Jenyns, were bored with country squiredom:

> Nor can I for my soul delight
> In the dull feast of neighb'ring knight,
> Who, if you send three days before,
> In white gloves meets you at the door,
> With superfluity of breeding
> First makes you sick, and then with feeding.
> Or if with ceremony cloy'd,
> You wou'd next time such plagues avoid,
> And visit without previous notice,
> JOHN, JOHN, a coach!—I can't think who 'tis,
> My lady cries, who spies your coach
> Ere you the avenue approach;
> Lord, how unlucky!—washing-day!
> And all the men are in the hay! . . .
>
> The servants run, the pewter clatters,
> My lady dresses, calls, and chatters. . . .
>
> Now after three hours tedious waiting,
> On all our neighbours faults debating,
> And having nine times view'd the garden
> Where there is nothing worth a farthing,
> In comes my lady, and the pudden. . . .
>
> And by and by the second course
> Comes lagging like a distanc'd horse. . . .
>
> The cloth remov'd, the toasts go round,
> Bawdy and politics abound;
> And as the knight more tipsy waxes,
> We damn all ministers and taxes.
> At last the ruddy sun quite sunk,
> The coachman tolerably drunk,
> Whirling o'er hillocks, ruts, and stones,
> Enough to dislocate one's bones,
> We home return, a wondrous token
> Of heaven's kind care, with limbs unbroken.

There were others, like Charles Morris—or like Charles Lamb —who frankly preferred the town:

> In London I never know what I'd be at,
> Enraptur'd with this, and enchanted with that;

I'm wild with the sweets of Variety's plan,
And life seems a blessing too happy for Man.

But the Country, God help me! sets all matters right,
So calm and composing from morning to night;
Oh! it settles the spirits when nothing is seen
But an Ass on a Common, a Goose on a Green. . . .

Your Magpies and Stockdoves may flirt among trees,
And chatter their transports in groves, if they please;
But a House is much more to my taste than a tree,
And for Groves, oh! a good grove of chimneys for me.

In Town let me live then, in Town let me die,
For in truth I can't relish the Country, not I.
If one must have a Villa in summer to dwell,
Oh, give me the sweet shady side of Pall Mall!

That is as late as 1795, when new things were near at hand. But let us get rid of the notion that nobody before Wordsworth ever looked at or enjoyed the face of the earth; or the equally false notion that anyone who did was a sort of sibyl, saved from limbo by prophesying a Wordsworth yet unborn.

There are, of course, differences. For the eighteenth-century poets humanity was not a source of still sad music, but part of the living, working country-side, which had this advantage, however, over the town, that it offered opportunities of retirement. Into that I shall not enter now, beyond remarking that the note is struck in the first poem printed in Dr. Nichol Smith's *Oxford Book of Eighteenth Century Verse*—Pomfret's 'The Choice', of 1700. The point is, that the eighteenth-century poets assumed the value of a pictorial sense. Their landscapes are composed. In Wordsworth there is no scenery. He works with the single detail: a hill-side, a mountain, a drift of daffodils beside a stretch of water. That is obscured to most of us in England because we are tolerably familiar with his surroundings. A name calls up the whole view, identified by tradition and from his sister's journals. We put the details back into their setting and see them there. That is possibly right: it is how Wordsworth himself saw them. But it depends on the accident of our knowledge, and does not grow out of the poems, to which it is doubtfully relevant. No such knowledge is required by the pictorial poets. They not only give us all we need to know, but their pictures are so complete and so self-sufficing that such knowledge would add nothing to our understanding or enjoyment.

The Landscape Poem was a definite kind: the description of a definite stretch of scenery, with its associations in history and personal recollection, and with more general moralizing brought in by the immediate transference of observed features into intellectual and emotional imagery. It is not surprising to find John Dyer's 'Grongar Hill ' a favourable specimen, since Dyer was a practising artist. His didactic poem *The Fleece* contains many similar landscape compositions, less elaborate, but careful, deliberate, and successful. The plan of 'Grongar Hill' and *The Ruins of Rome* is the same—movement from lower ground to higher, opening up new and wider prospects. Both poems derive something of their style from Milton, 'Grongar Hill' from 'L'Allegro' and 'Il Penseroso', *The Ruins of Rome* from *Paradise Regained*: a difference creditable to Dyer's critical sense. My example is from *The Ruins of Rome*, as the less known of Dyer's landscapes, though indeed the better poem:

> Amid the tow'ry ruins, huge, supreme,
> Th' enormous amphitheatre behold,
> Mountainous pile! o'er whose capacious womb
> Pours the broad firmament its varied light:
> While from the central floor the seats ascend
> Round above round, slow-wid'ning to the verge,
> A circuit vast and high . . . .

>   Lo the fane of Peace,
> Built by that prince, who to the trust of pow'r
> Was honest, the delight of human kind.
> Three nodding isles remain; the rest an heap
> Of sand and weeds; her shrines, her radiant roofs,
> And columns proud, that from her spacious floor,
> As from a shining sea, majestick rose
> An hundred foot aloft, like stately beech
> Around the brim of Dion's glassy lake,
> Charming the mimick painter: on the walls
> Hung Salem's sacred spoils; the golden board,
> And golden trumpets, now conceal'd, entomb'd
> By the sunk roof.—O'er which in distant view
> Th' Etruscan mountains swell, with ruins crown'd
> Of ancient towns; and blue Soracte spires,
> Wrapping his sides in tempests.

These may remind us of the coloured drawings which, before
the days of kodaks, held and revived the memories of the
wealthier tourists. Here is an English water-colour, composed
with equal care and skill, though not by a painter. It is from
'The Spleen', by one of the most delightful of the little masters
of the eighteenth century, Mr. Matthew Green of the Custom-
house:

> And may my humble dwelling stand
> Upon some chosen spot of land;
> A pond before full to the brim,
> Where cows may cool, and geese may swim,
> Behind, a green like velvet neat,
> Soft to the eye and to the feet;
> Where od'rous plants in evening fair
> Breathe all around ambrosial air;
> From Eurus, foe to kitchen-ground,
> Fenc'd by a slope with bushes crown'd,
> Fit dwelling for the feather'd throng,
> Who pay their quit-rents with a song;
> With op'ning views of hill and dale,
> Which sense and fancy too regale,
> Where the half-cirque, which vision bounds,
> Like amphitheatre surrounds;
> And woods impervious to the breeze,
> Thick phalanx of embodied trees,
> From hills thro' plains in dark array
> Extended far, repel the day. . . .

That has not the purity of vision, nor the painter's feeling for
light and shape, that give Dyer's scenes their quality, but
Green knows how to move in a landscape from the animated
foreground, through a varied middle distance, to a prescribed
limit of view: his picture has a centre and edges.

In many other poets, the careful reader will find, here and
there, rather more hints and glimpses of natural beauty than
he was perhaps prepared for, but in the main the deliberation
and generalization of visual impressions proves the dominance
of pictorial composition as well as of literary reminiscence. It
is not merely that we are reminded of contemporary pictures
and engravings, of Claude Lorraine or Piranesi: this art is,
consciously, of the same nature, 'imitating' in words instead
of in line and tone. It is not a failure to do what Wordsworth
did; it is a different thing.

It may be argued that this pictorial art is an intrusion on poetry, and that the art of music intrudes in the same way. I find it difficult to abstract poetry to that extent. In the eighteenth century, painting and music were living arts which exerted their power upon poetry as poetry did upon them. The arts did not live in isolation from one another or from social life, as they did in the nineteenth century, when literature enjoyed an unwholesome predominance, and when that balance and integration of the arts, learning, and society which we call a civilization broke down under the combined impact of romanticism and industrialism.

Among social poets, however, we might expect to find moral philosophy more in evidence than a lively appreciation of natural beauty, and on an arithmetical computation this is true.

We are perhaps somewhat disconcerted to find cheerful and even occasionally ribald poets, from Gay and Prior down to Soame Jenyns, compiling the most formal and official disquisitions on philosophical themes, read, if at all, for the sake of the few personal touches discernible through the dead crust of conscientious dullness. It is worth noting that such writers considered it necessary to their status as poets to produce such solid and learned works; but there is more instruction, as well as infinitely more enjoyment, to be found in the many poems which may be loosely described as embodying a philosophy of life. An admirable example is 'The Spleen', already mentioned, where the thought is none the less genuine for its deliberate lightness of expression, and where the apparent scepticism and worldliness are seen at the end to rest upon a firm ethical and religious basis.

In these minor poets we may find many things our own time would be the better of—friendliness, moderation, common sense, a sound notion of relative values. The basic position may be found in the weighty ΓΝΩΘΙ ΣΕΑΥΤΟΝ. *KNOW YOUR SELF*, of Dr. Arbuthnot. Here is no sudden revelation or 'baphometic fire-baptism', but a sober statement of the dual nature of man:

> Thy parents right, I own, O Mother Earth;
> But claim superior lineage by my SIRE,
> Who warm'd th' unthinking clod with heav'nly fire:
> Essence divine, with lifeless clay allay'd,
> By double nature, double instinct sway'd;

With look erect, I dart my longing eye,
Seem wing'd to part, and gain my native sky;
I strive to mount, but strive, alas! in vain,
Ty'd to this massy globe with magick chain.
Now with swift thought I range from pole to pole,
View worlds around their flaming centers roll: . . .
I trace the blazing comet's fiery trail,
And weigh the whirling planets in a scale:
Those godlike thoughts, while eager I pursue,
Some glitt'ring trifle offer'd to my view,
A gnat, an insect, of the meanest kind,
Erase the new-born image from my mind;
Some beastly want, craving, importunate,
Vile as the grinning mastiffs at my gate,
Calls off from heav'nly truth this reas'ning me,
And tells me, I'm a brute as much as he.

This is not an egotist's complaint against an unsympathetic universe, but the wise refusal to evade a primary difficulty. The solution of that difficulty lies, for Arbuthnot, in faith and humility: two things we have lost, as we have lost the salutary habit of self-examination that is the only way to that other lost treasure, the sense of values.

We find, then, an appreciation of natural beauty, formalized —in no derogatory sense—by the creative pictorial habit and in close touch with a habit of moral reflection equally formalized by preachers and philosophers. We can find, however, another relation between man and the external world in Akenside.

Akenside wrote no love-poetry, though there are one or two vague references to 'Olympia', whose identity is not so much as suspected. He wrote no formal landscape-poetry, for his interests lay in politics and philosophy, and his medical training inclined him to science rather than to the sister arts. He knew, indeed, all the correct things to say, but even this fragment is enough to show, by its lack of visual quality, that he possessed little of the art of his own Youth,

Who on the heights of Tibur, all inclin'd
O'er rushing Anio, with a pious hand
The reverend scene delineates, broken fanes,
Or tombs, or pillar'd aqueducts, the pomp
Of ancient Time; and haply, while he scans
The ruins, with a silent tear revolves
The fame and fortune of imperious Rome.

He was also as classical as he could contrive to make himself; but we must not let his determined classicism blind us to the fresh sense of beauty in this 'Inscription'. It is the interpretation of a place, in emotional, not in pictorial, terms.

For a Grotto.

To me, whom in their lays the shepherds call
Actaea, daughter of the neighbouring stream,
This cave belongs. The figtree and the vine,
Which o'er the rocky entrance downward shoot,
Were plac'd by Glycon. He with cowslips pale,
Primrose, and purple lychnis, deck'd the green
Before my threshold, and my shelving walls
With honeysuckle cover'd. Here at noon,
Lull'd by the murmur of my rising fount,
I slumber: here my clustering fruits I tend;
Or from the humid flowers, at break of day,
Fresh garlands weave, and chace from all my bounds
Each thing impure or noxious. Enter-in,
O stranger, undismay'd. Nor bat, nor toad
Here lurks: and if thy breast of blameless thoughts
Approve thee, not unwelcome shalt thou tread
My quiet mansion: chiefly, if thy name
Wise Pallas and the immortal Muses own.

Akenside's chief work, however, was *The Pleasures of the Imagination*, one of those poems which are immediately successful, are greatly praised, and then fall into complete neglect. Two questions at once arise: why was *The Pleasures of the Imagination* popular; and why did its popularity disappear so decisively?

There is one broad answer that can be given immediately: it is a didactic poem, and didactic poems had a vogue at the time and have had little since. Akenside is one of the many poets who, when the epic ambition of the sixteenth and seventeenth centuries had faded with the heroic ideal of life and style of behaviour, deserted the *Aeneid* and modelled their writings on the *Georgics*. The subject is less utilitarian than Philips's *Cider* or Grainger's *Sugar-Cane* or Armstrong's *Art of Preserving Health*; the object is, none the less, instruction.

The rise and fall of didactic poetry is obviously an inadequate solution, for not even eighteenth-century readers were prepared to welcome any didactic poem on any subject. Those generations, however, which cherished a solid artistic tradition, and also set themselves to the consolidation of social relations as to an allotted task, did find both interest and profit in the theory stated in Akenside's preface, that the powers of the imagination 'seem to hold a middle place between the organs of bodily sense and the faculties of moral perception. . . . Like the external senses, they relate to matter and motion; and, at the same time, give the mind ideas analogous to those of moral approbation and dislike.' But the clue to Akenside's success lies on the surface—in the title. It is the *pleasures* of the imagination that Akenside emphasizes; and his somewhat complicated paragraphs of Miltonic blank verse are perforce devoted not only to argumentation but to illustration: that is, to the calling up in the reader's mind of images pleasing in themselves, and decorated—indeed overdecorated—with elaborate inlays and veneers of rhetoric.

The most quoted—and most quotable—passage comes from the fragmentary Fourth Book:

> Would I again were with you!—O ye dales
> Of Tyne, and ye most ancient woodlands; where
> Oft as the giant flood obliquely strides,
> And his banks open, and his lawns extend,
> Stops short the pleased traveller to view
> Presiding o'er the scene some rustic tower
> Founded by Norman or by Saxon hands:
> O ye Northumbrian shades, which overlook
> The rocky pavement and the mossy falls
> Of solitary Wensbeck's limpid stream;
> How gladly I recall your well-known seats
> Belov'd of old, and that delightful time
> When all alone, for many a summer's day,
> I wander'd through your calm recesses, led
> In silence by some powerful hand unseen.
>
> Nor will I e'er forget you. Nor shall e'er
> The graver tasks of manhood, or the advice
> Of vulgar wisdom, move me to disclaim
> Those studies which possess'd me in the dawn
> Of life, and fix'd the color of my mind
> For every future year.

'Not Wordsworth, but Akenside', Dr. Nichol Smith bids us observe, not without an undertone of triumph, nor, I fancy,

without pleasure in recognizing the landscape from Ovingham
to Corbridge, and the character of the Wansbeck about Mitford and Morpeth. But it is not a painter's description: detail
is used as by Wordsworth. In this passage, too, we seem to
detect the voice as well as the sentiments of Wordsworth: it is
the Miltonic style fining down and running clearer, as we find
it in *The Prelude*. It is the more interesting that the quotation
is from an addition to the second, and not greatly improved,
version of the poem, published after Akenside's death by his
friend Jeremiah Dyson. It is late, not early, work. And it is
not representative; for Akenside's ideal of style was exactly
that from which Wordsworth revolted. This more characteristic passage better illustrates both the abstract imagery of the
eighteenth century and the inflation of style that results from
the attempt to give sensuous value to abstractions:

> Thus with a faithful aim have we presum'd,
> Adventurous, to delineate nature's form;
> Whether in vast, majestic pomp array'd,
> Or drest for pleasing wonder, or serene
> In beauty's rosy smile. It now remains,
> Through various being's fair-proportion'd scale,
> To trace the rising lustre of her charms,
> From their first twilight, shining forth at length
> To full meridian splendour. Of degree
> The least and lowliest, in the effusive warmth
> Of colours mingling with a random blaze,
> Doth beauty dwell. Then higher in the line
> And variation of determin'd shape,
> Where truth's eternal measures mark the bound
> Of circle, cube, or sphere. The third ascent
> Unites this varied symmetry of parts
> With colour's bland allurement; as the pearl
> Shines in the concave of its azure bed,
> And painted shells indent their speckled wreath.
> Then more attractive rise the blooming forms
> Through which the breath of nature has infus'd
> Her genial power to draw with pregnant veins
> Nutritious moisture from the bounteous earth,
> In fruit and seed prolific: thus the flowers
> Their purple honours with the spring resume;
> And such the stately tree which autumn bends
> With blushing treasures.

It is futile to claim for Akenside even such glory as falls to the master of a greater pupil, though Wordsworth could not fail to know his work and Coleridge certainly learned something from him.

Yet the fact is to be noted. It is attractive to depict history as a series of dramatic fits and starts: it is more just, as well as truer, to observe its continuity. People did think and feel like that, even in the eighteenth century. Akenside achieved popularity because, where the landscape poets arranged their sense-perceptions in pictorial compositions and then drew out the moral concepts associated with such images, he brought sense-perception and moral concept into intimate relation through the medium of the intellect, of science. The process was acceptable, for the poem was popular. The new thing in Wordsworth is that he believed such thoughts and feelings to be supremely, and almost exclusively, important. He gave a new philosophical import to the notion of pleasure, but he did not invent it. The thoughts and feelings were not peculiar to Wordsworth, else he would be a lesser poet.

The eventual failure of the poem might be justly ascribed to the same causes as its success. The style, the argument—as much of it as was relevant—and the psychological process were not so much discredited as superseded by Wordsworth, who refined the style, purified the argument, and carried the process further, not merely associating, but fusing together in the imagination, completely and finally, the data of 'the organs of bodily sense and the faculties of moral perception', and found in the result not only an accompanying pleasure, but a living and active philosophy of life: and did so, being a major poet, without needing to draw either argument or authority from the professed philosophers.

But we are drifting towards major poetry. One last word for our minor poets. Their attraction is not merely antiquarian. Good poetry, even if it be what we call 'minor' poetry, is never dead; and here, in the common run of the lesser poets, we can discover, better perhaps than among the great individuals, a character and a temper that may serve us now and in the days to come.

The eighteenth century was adult, and, in that it possessed a consolidated tradition of art, knowledge, and behaviour, was civilized. It is a hard saying, but in the nineteenth century much of the population of this island relapsed into a primitive state. The last great conflict burned out much of the nineteenth-century character, and since 1919 our world has grown young again. During these twenty-odd years—to confine ourselves to the evidence of literature, which is our affair here—the dominant literary influence has been that of Donne, of all poets the most attractive to the adolescent. It is not surprising to find him the master of our modern wits, who recognize in him the marks of their own immaturity.

The present conflict ought to see the new world come of age. How it will shape we cannot tell: but it must be adult and civilized. If it wishes to shed its adolescent tricks and to purge its adolescent humours, to use its artists familiarly as men who have a useful practical contribution to make, to know itself in good and evil, and to say its say in plain words to men at large, it will do well to seek counsel among the men of the eighteenth century. And if it finds here and there in eighteenth-century literature some lessons of humility, moderation, and common sense, width of outlook and the pleasure of good writing, it will be none the worse for them.

THE FORMAL PARTS OF JOHNSON'S LETTERS

R. W. CHAPMAN

I AM not aware that any study has been made of the opening and concluding formulas of the letters of any of our great letter-writers. Yet since these formulas are not always purely formal, and exhibit very wide variations, examination of them may tell us something of a letter-writer's versatility, of his varying moods, of his relation to his correspondent. It may even tell us something about the correspondent himself. Lest—in spite of this defence—my inquiry should still seem pedantic or trivial, I allow myself to explain that I undertook it mainly for one purpose. The question has been slightly vexed, whether Samuel Johnson ever styled himself 'Doctor', and whether he liked to be so styled. I was curious to confirm my impression that in his letters written in the third person he is almost always 'Mr. Johnson'. To satisfy this innocent ambition it was necessary to look through the letters, and I thought I might as well pick up what I could by the way.

My references are to the numbers in Hill's edition, with other letters intercalated chronologically with 'decimal' numbers, e.g. I insert 500.1 between Hill's 500 and 501. I sometimes add a date.

Having accumulated a mass of particulars I must try to arrange them. The most obvious division is between the opening and conclusion. But I premise that this separation is not wholly satisfactory. The opening may be enforced, or may be contradicted, by the conclusion. Thus Johnson writing to Mrs. Thrale may begin 'Dear Madam' and conclude 'Dearest of all dear Ladies'. But he may begin 'Dearest Lady' and end 'I am, Madam, Your most humble Servant'. On the other hand he may begin 'Dear Sir', and end 'I am, my dearest Boswell, Yours most affectionately'.

I. The Opening Formula is normally 'Sir', 'Dear Sir', and the like. The most striking differences between Johnson's usage, which is that of his age, and our own are the use of 'Sir' and 'Madam' and the avoidance of names. Johnson as a rule addresses strangers, or mere acquaintances, as 'Sir', his friends as 'Dear Sir'—but sometimes 'Dearest Sir'. (The conclusion is

often—but, to friends, by no means so often—similarly formal.)
Peers spiritual and temporal (including, I note, the Duke of
Argyll, 335) are 'My Lord', peeresses 'Madam'. Clergymen
with whom Johnson was not intimate are in three letters (720,
820, 844) 'Reverend Sir'.

'Dear Sir' is almost invariable to Johnson's contemporaries
and intimates among men: even to such old friends as Taylor,
Reynolds, Percy, Burney. To women, young people, and children he is naturally more demonstrative. Boswell, though a
man, was a very young one when the acquaintance began. But
he is very seldom (see below for details) named. No man of
approximately Johnson's age, except his cousin Tom, and no
grown woman, except his wife, are ever named. This convention of formality is thrown into relief by the use of 'Dearest Sir'
(not very common) and 'Dearest Madam', which is frequent
to Lucy Porter, Miss Boothby, Mrs. Thrale, and Miss Reynolds.

Except for the two relations just mentioned, the two younger
Thrale girls (who are 'Dearest Miss Susan' and 'Dearest Miss
Sophy'), Langton's little girl ('My dearest Miss Jenny'), and
(occasionally) Boswell, no one is ever named. 'Dear Mr.
Smith' and 'Dear Mrs. Jones' do not occur.[1]

We have one letter only from Johnson to his wife (12). It
begins 'Dearest Tetty' and ends 'I am My charming Love
Yours Sam: Johnson'. Johnson's mother is 'Honoured Madam'
or 'Dear Honoured Mother' (118–23). His stepdaughter Lucy
Porter is endearingly addressed, especially in the early letters.
Thus she is 'My dearest Dear' (153, 229) or 'My Dearest Love'
(154). This formula recurs in one very late letter (935); but
that is an emotional letter, reporting his sudden and unexpected recovery from illness. So she is 'My dear dear Love'
in 202, a letter of condolence, and 'My dearest' in 1010.1,
another letter of thankfulness. In the later letters (after 1774)
Lucy is almost always 'Dear Madam'.

To one friend of his youth, Miss Hill Boothby, Johnson was
exceptionally demonstrative, and that though she was of good
family; contrast his treatment of Mrs. Thrale and Miss Aston.
In his letters to her (all about 1750) she is usually 'Dear
Madam', 'Dearest Madam', or 'Honoured Madam'; but she is
once 'Dearest Dear', and once 'My Sweet Angel'. He is hardly

---

[1] 'Dear Mr. Warton' once to Tom Warton, but in the text (59), and not in the
vocative: 'Why does my dear Mr. Warton tell me nothing of himself?'

less affectionate to Miss Reynolds; but she was an absurd person, with whom no one stood on ceremony. She is usually 'Dear Madam' like other ladies; but sometimes, especially in early letters, she is 'My dearest Dear'. Once only, and that in a rather severe letter (961), is she plain 'Madam'.

With these familiarities contrast the more ceremonious address to Miss Aston of Stow Hill and Mrs. Thrale of Streatham. It is pertinent to remark that both were ladies of birth. It is, I think, not pertinent to remark that nearly all the letters to Mrs. Thrale were addressed to her husband, who received them free of charge and was liable to open them; certainly read many of them with his wife's concurrence.

We have Johnson's views on the supposed frigidity of 'Madam'. In a letter to Mrs. Thrale (262) he makes merry with the indignation of Miss Langton, Bennet's sister, at his so addressing her. His crime no doubt lay in the omission of 'Dear'. But Johnson did not share this view. His very early letters to Mrs. Thrale begin 'Madam'; but even in the first she is 'Dear Madam' in the conclusion; and she soon becomes so in a majority of his letters. But not in all; my count is 'Madam' 70, 'Dear Madam' 224, and 'Dearest Madam' 23; and these three forms are fairly distributed over the years. It would be fanciful to see much meaning in this variation; but it is perhaps significant that 'Dearest Madam' is relatively frequent in the letters from Scotland in 1773, when they were farther and longer parted than ordinarily, and in those which immediately follow Thrale's death in 1781. It is I think certainly significant that in the time of separation and estrangement when she was in Bath, 1783-4, 'Madam' is relatively frequent. But in general the formality is superficial; and the coldness of the opening is often thawed by the warmth of the conclusion.

There are variations—I count in all 32—on 'Madam'. The noun is 'Lady' except in three letters; she is 'Honoured Mistress' in 332 and 337, 'My Dearest Mistress' in 339—all letters from Scotland. The others vary between 'Dear Lady' and (767) 'Dearest of all dear Ladies'. 'Dearest Lady' is the commonest of these.

Miss Aston is, I think, always 'Dear Madam' or 'Dearest Madam'. She was more or less Johnson's contemporary.

The letters to the Thrales' eldest daughter show a characteristic blend of tenderness and deference. In the first letter (264.3) the child of six is 'My sweet, dear, pretty, little Miss'. In the last (1003.2), when she was close on twenty and was, in Johnson's view, doubly orphaned, she is 'Dearest Madam'. She had become 'Dear Madam' at fifteen (645.1); but in most of the letters, except the latest, she is the old man's 'Dearest Miss', 'Love', 'Sweeting', 'Charmer'. (Johnson, I note, never wrote 'Darling'.) The letter (969.1) written on first hearing of her mother's second marriage began: 'My Dearest, I read your letter with anguish and astonishment, such as I never felt before'. This seems to confirm my impression that the omission of the noun from the formulas indicates strong emotion.

Another of Johnson's young friends was George, son of William Strahan. We have several letters written to him in 1763–5, when he was a schoolboy. Even then 'Dear George' occurs only twice, 'Dear Sir' four times. After a gap of many years comes a group of letters (800, and others, 1782–3) which begin plain 'Sir'. But Johnson was then engaged in reconciling son to father; the son had been foolish and obstinate, and Johnson's tone is somewhat stern. In the last letter (1023) George is returned to favour as 'Dear Sir'.

The only letters to a servant are a few to Frank Barber, which begin 'Dear Francis' and end 'Yours affectionately' or the like; a master cannot be his servant's 'servant'.

Almost all the letters to Boswell begin 'Dear Sir' (occasionally 'My dear Sir'). In 398 he is 'My dearest Sir' in the conclusion, which always tends to be more affectionate than the exordium. In one letter (715) he is 'My dear Bozzy'; but that is in the body of the letter, and has a special intention.

Occasionally Johnson works the opening formula into his first sentence: a mode much more frequent, as we shall see, in the subscription. The examples I have noted are 390 (to Mrs. Thrale: 'And so, my dearest Mistress, you lie abed hatching suspicions'), 414, 606, 648, 687, 1124. This last was on an emergent occasion, a *redintegratio amoris*: 'Come, come, dear Davies, I am always sorry when we quarrel; send me word that we are friends.'

'My' is only occasionally prefixed to 'Dear Sir', 'Dear Madam', and the like. It is commoner where there is no noun. Thus Lucy Porter is 'My Dearest' (207.1). But she is also 'My dearest Dear' and 'My dearest Love' (153, 154). 'My' goes more naturally with terms of endearment than with terms of respect, and that is why it is frequent in early letters to Lucy Porter and in letters to Queeney Thrale.

II. The conclusion is normally some variation on the base 'servant'. 'Your most humble servant' is the commonest. We know that this did not imply any real subservience or even humility. 'Clear your mind of cant', he said to Boswell (15 May 1783). 'You may *talk* as other people do: you may say to a man, "Sir, I am your most humble servant". You are *not* his most humble servant.' But Johnson took pleasure in conforming to all the conventions of what he called 'fictitious benevolence'.

Alternatives, or additions, are 'most obliged' and 'most obedient'. He not infrequently prefixes one of these to 'and most humble Servant', and once or twice I think has all three. The motive is respect or mock-respect. But it is also to be considered that a careful letter-writer liked to 'fill his paper'. This cuts both ways; for sometimes the paper was almost full; and a letter seldom exceeded—if not franked, could hardly with decency exceed—a single sheet. Lack of space is often the palpable motive of, e.g., the unceremonious 'Your &c.'

The formality of the formal subscription is, as we have seen, often mitigated by words prefixed to it: as 'Dear Sir', 'Dearest Lady', 'My Dearest Boswell' (502), or 'with great affection' and the like. I note that two of our common endings are hardly found. Once only, I believe, is he 'sincerely yours' (847, to his friend and neighbour Edmund Allen). Once only is he 'truly yours'; in 970, the letter to Mrs. Thrale on her second marriage. It ends: 'I was, I once was, Madam, most truly yours Sam: Johnson'.

If Johnson is not his correspondent's servant, there are three main alternatives, 'Your affectionate Sam: Johnson', 'Yours affectionately Sam: Johnson', and 'Your (or Yours) &c.' The first and second are especially frequent in letters to Taylor and Boswell, the most regular and familiar of his male correspondents. The third is not uncommon, though it may seem to be commoner than it is, for it is a normal editorial abridgement. It occurs, however, quite often in those of Johnson's letters of which we have the originals.

The absence of any formal subscription is very rare, and is significant. The famous letter to Macpherson (373) has neither beginning nor end. His last letter to Robert Chambers before his departure for India (353.1) ends: 'I pray God to bless you for Jesus Christ's Sake. Farewel', and is unsigned.

Johnson is fond of the device by which the subscription is worked into the last sentence of a letter; we may call it the syntactical conclusion.[1] Out of some 1,250 letters over 200 end in this way, and he uses it with great facility and felicity. Sometimes it is only a flourish, as in our earliest extant letter: 'I hope you will, if any thing should offer, remember and recommend Sir Your humble servant.' But it is often more, as (38) 'The point is to get two Guineas for Your humble Servant', or (61, to Chesterfield) 'I have been long wakened from that dream of hope, in which I once boasted myself with so much exultation, My lord, Your Lordship's most humble most obliged servant'.

This kind of conclusion is often tinged, at least, with mock ceremony, affectionate gallantry, or the like. That, I think, is why it is so often used to Mrs. Thrale (I count 63 examples) and relatively seldom (13 examples) to Boswell. A pleasing example is (659): 'Though I am going to dine with Lady Craven, I am Madam Your most humble servant.'

III. Letters in the Third Person. I am left with my original problem. Boswell *s.a.* 1775[2] (on Johnson's Oxford doctorate) tells us that he 'never, so far as I know, assumed the title of *Doctor*, but called himself *Mr.* Johnson, as appears from many of his cards or notes to myself'. Hawkins[3] says of his Dublin doctorate (1765) that his attachment to Oxford prevented his 'receiving this honour as it was intended, and he never assumed the title' (that is, before 1775?). Hill[4] objected, first the passage in Boswell where Johnson calls himself 'Dr. Johnson', second a letter in which he so styles himself. The letter is one of those discussed below. The passage in Boswell invites scrutiny. Boswell had mentioned, in a general company, a newspaper rumour that Johnson 'was learning to dance of Vestris'. Johnson said he should not contradict the story. 'For why should not Dr. Johnson add to his other powers a little corporeal agility?' As Dr. Powell remarks, Johnson may have been quoting the newspaper. The case is otherwise exceptional, since there is an antithesis between mind and body, which '*Dr.* Johnson' sharpens.

That he did not in general 'assume the title' is abundantly

---

[1] In the Hebrides, 22 Sept. 1773, Boswell criticized Orrery's 'affectation of ending all his letters about Swift in different ways, and never "I am, &c."' In this conversation Johnson defended the studied conclusions of Dryden's published dedications, as 'more elegant'; but nothing was said of his own epistolary 'affectation'.

[2] Hill–Powell, ii. 332.   [3] *Life*, p. 446.   [4] iv. 79.

clear. But I have notes of four letters in which he seems so to describe himself. Of these one is of little value, for it is a note said to have been dictated to Frank Barber, who might well magnify the style. Of two others (601 to Mrs. Garrick, 952.1 to Lord Portmore) I cannot be quite certain, not having seen them. But of 927.1 (an unpublished letter to Perkins) I am quite certain, having myself copied the original. On the other hand I note 42 letters in which I know, or have reason to believe, that he wrote 'Mr. Johnson'.

To pronounce on the practice of Johnson's age in general would require a wide induction.

The correspondence of George Selwyn, c. 1740–80, shows that men of rank and fashion were more familiar than the academics. Selwyn's most regular correspondents, 'Gilly' Williams, Lord Carlisle, and the Lord March who is better known as Duke of Queensberry, almost always write to 'My dear George', though they occasionally deviate into 'Dear Selwyn' and even 'Dear Sir'. To many other correspondents, including Walpole, Selwyn is normally 'Dear George'. The first Lord Holland, his senior, writes to 'Dear Selwyn'; but oddly, in four letters of 1770, 'My Dear Mr. Selwyn', a mode seldom used by his male correspondents. Ladies alternate between 'Dear Sir ' and 'Dear Mr. Selwyn'. But I do not find 'Mr.' from any writer, man or woman, before 1770. As a young man Selwyn is, to his friend Lord Downe, 'Dear Bosky'.

My impression is that Johnson is a little, but only a little, more formal and stately than the average of his kind. Wooll's *Life of Joseph Warton* contains a large number of letters by and to eminent persons, ranging from Warburton to Garrick. In these letters the Warton brothers are 'Dearest Tom' and 'Dearest Jo' to each other;[1] but unrelated friends, however intimate, write '(My) dear Sir'. I note two exceptions: George Colman and Bonnell Thornton write to their 'Dear Tom' (Warton); they were his boon-companions.

Boswell was Johnson's junior by a generation. His letters, as edited by Professor Tinker, show a shift towards modern practice. Temple, his lifelong friend, is almost always 'My dear Temple', though not infrequently 'My dear(est) friend'

---

[1] 'Dearest' is I think now rare in letters from man to man; it was common in my century. (Bridges wrote 'Dearest Hopkins', though he never used his Christian name.)

or the like. Malone, the intimate of his latter years, is always 'My dear Malone'. There are isolated letters to 'My dear Dempster' and 'My dear Scott' (Sir William). I notice that Boswell uses 'My' much oftener than Johnson.

But even Boswell addresses such intimate acquaintances as Langton, Garrick, Wilkes as 'My dear Sir' or 'Dear Sir'. Percy is 'My dear Sir', or when a bishop 'My dear Lord'. Seniors, like Sir David Dalrymple and Sir Alexander Dick, are usually 'My dear Sir'; but to Dick, Boswell uses variations: 'My dear friend', 'My dear Knight and Friend' (69), and (twice, 94, 184) 'My dear Sir Alexander'.

There is no use of Christian names except in one letter to his daughter 'Phemie'. An outstanding address is that of the letter (25) to 'My dear Zélide'; but that was not the lady's real name. Letters to women are few; Mrs. Thrale is 'My dear Madam' or 'Dear Madam'; there is one letter to 'My dear Lady Orkney'.

For Boswell's letters to Johnson we depend on the *Life*, where the opening is not regularly quoted. When it is given it is usually 'My dear Sir'; but two early letters (27, 52) are more elaborate: 'My ever dear and much-respected Sir', 'Much esteemed and dear Sir'. The conclusions declare his 'affection', 'veneration', 'obligation', and the like.

MRS. PIOZZI'S LETTERS

JAMES L. CLIFFORD

'I HAVE for this week past been employing my Mind in the recollection of all the civil Things that ever were said in Praise of my Merit as a Letter writer.' So wrote Hester Lynch Salusbury, a young lady of 22, in 1763. Nearly two hundred years later we are still interested in this same lady and her correspondence—not that of Miss Salusbury, to be sure, but that of her later years as Mrs. Thrale and Mrs. Piozzi. We still find pleasure in reading the letters that her contemporaries thought so delightful and amusing. Yet among the more voluminous letter-writers of the eighteenth century she is perhaps the least known.

Two reasons for this comparative neglect stand out: the over-shadowing renown of her friendship with Dr. Johnson; and the difficulty of consulting the greater part of her correspondence. Most readers, if they have heard of the lady at all, think of her only as the busy hostess of Streatham, pouring endless cups of tea for her famous guest, while rattling away with a cascade of inconsequential chit-chat. Scholars are familiar also with her journals, and with her little volume of anecdotes about Johnson which caused the long controversy with Boswell. It is as an irrepressible diarist and a minor biographer of a great man that Mrs. Piozzi is usually remembered.

Of even more weight is the fact that during the nineteenth century only a small percentage of her letters was accessible. Thousands of them, many the best she produced, have remained hidden away in private collections—in dusty attics, in crowded cupboards, in collectors' archives. Thus until a few years ago all of her letters to Johnson known to exist were those overwritten revisions which she included in her own printing of Johnson's correspondence in 1788. Yet, all the while, well over a hundred original letters were gathering dust in a Welsh country house. Even those manuscripts which were available have never been accurately or adequately edited. Hayward in 1861 cut and mangled her letters to Sir James Fellowes, and published merely a small selection of those to Dr. Robert Gray; Lord Lansdowne included only a few of the earlier ones to Queeney in his little volume. Of the long series of her letters to other correspondents many have never even been sampled. No series has been published intact, and only one—that to Mrs. Pennington—in any completeness. As a result, few modern readers have had the opportunity to judge the variety of Mrs. Piozzi's powers. Furthermore, the well-known published letters do not always show Mrs. Piozzi at her best. Those in the *Queeney Letters*, for example, were written largely during a period of emotional stress. Those to Mrs. Pennington, to Mangin, and Fellowes are representative only of her later years. Because of this concentration on limited periods, certain prejudices have arisen. Many think of her as wholly artificial, flippant, and insincere. She is considered to be incapable of genuine feeling or serious thought. And it must be granted that at times she does show these deficiencies. Yet in several long unpublished series of letters she shows entirely opposite qualities. A just appraisal can be made only from an examination of all sorts of letters. In the present study the generalizations which appear are made only after the reading of almost three thousand of Mrs. Piozzi's letters, of which about three-fourths are unpublished.[1]

At the start it must be admitted that any attempt to appraise her writing by the use of a few specially chosen examples is manifestly unfair. The critic, whether consciously or unconsciously, is certain to select excerpts which stand out—which are either especially good or especially bad of a kind. The dead level of ordinary correspondence, the day-by-day exchange of routine news, cannot be illustrated by random selections. All that can be done with any success is to show the range of the writer's interests, and to indicate a few of her outstanding traits. But even such a limited estimate may be revealing.

Mrs. Piozzi was a natural letter-writer. Although only a few of her early letters have survived, in the form of rough drafts, there is enough evidence to show that from her youth she was an enthusiastic and active correspondent. Indeed, sitting down at her desk to write to distant friends became one of her greatest pleasures. Not only did she find genuine happiness in writing, but she came to take pride in her ability to write as she talked—and her talk, whatever else it might be, was never formal or stilted. One of her later acquaintances observed:

[1] The most recent list of her letters may be found in my *Hester Lynch Piozzi (Mrs. Thrale)*, pp. 466–7.

She expects to talk and to be listened to, & her conversation flows in a perpetual stream. We travelled over France & Italy together, and discussed the manners & characters of the people. . . . She has observed them with a penetrating tho' with a female eye, & her remarks are therefore the more amusing. We talked of love, marriage, cicisbeoism, & various points of that kind; on which she was very explicit . . . tho a lady, she is quite a philosopher. . . .[1]

Mrs. Piozzi injected this same sort of rambling discourse into her letters. She wanted her correspondent to imagine that he was for a few minutes actually in the same room with her and enjoying that most desirable of all pleasures—unrestrained talk. 'Prattle upon paper' is how she once described her writing to Johnson. She achieved that effect by consciously striving for a colloquial style, and rattled away on paper just as she did in the drawing-room. Characteristically she would comment to Queeney, 'And so they came, & so they staid, & so they went like all Company that ever did come, stay, & go, & so we are alone again & writing to Clifton, & I have got a Frank & shall enclose two Powders to be used at Discretion for Tatt & Cripsey. . . .'

Her continual use of a conversational style is one explanation, too, of the numerous exclamations and epithets which abound in her work, and which irritate some modern readers. 'Oh dear Me!' she would exclaim, or 'Poor Soul!' or 'Dear Charming Siddons!' Sometimes she indulges in mere sentimentality. Most people are annoyed by such a reference as that to 'poor pretty charming Venice & how lovely it was before the odious French ruined and overturned it'. In general, however, the femininity of her style is one of her most engaging traits.

Nowhere is her gift of making letters reflect her own many-sided personality better illustrated than in the first long series which has survived—that to Dr. Johnson. After the cementing of their friendship, Johnson always wrote to his dear 'Mistress' when he was long away from Streatham or Southwark, and from allusions in his early letters we may be sure that she replied eagerly. None, however, of her answers for the first few years have survived. With deepening affection came greater appreciation, so that after 1770 he saved most of her letters, both serious

---

[1] From a letter dated 1 Sept. 1789, written by Dr. James Currie to Francis Trench of Ireland. Portions of it are printed in the catalogue 'Eureka', 1942, of Harry A. Levinson, New York City.

and careless. Many, we may be sure, were accidentally lost; many may later have been destroyed in his bitterness over her marriage to Piozzi; but after Johnson's death a large number were found among his papers by the executors.[1] These letters show her in almost every mood—gay, scornful, complaining, casual, serious, pathetic. All are 'talking' letters, untinged by any attempt at literary display. And because they are so unpretentious, so simple and direct, they are particularly attractive, though they are not so clever and well written as most of those which were to follow.

At first the messages are short and matter of fact. Yet even in the first letter to survive, probably written in June 1770, one stylistic device of her later letters is already well developed—the compound series with a gradual crescendo of intensity:

I am at length safely housed at Streatham and cannot help telling you with what delight I feel myself escaped from Confinement in London. My Master is kind and makes no Objections, though nothing is in order; my Children are all well and running upon the Lawn; My Mother follows me tomorrow, and these wicked Servants now wish they had been here a Week ago.

Another characteristic opening—the amusing incident—appears in a letter written 22 July of the next year. Though far from well, just before the birth of another child, Mrs. Thrale dashed off an account to Johnson in Ashbourne, her sense of the ludicrous for a moment outweighing personal discomfort:

I must write once more, I now have hopes that it will be but once more: but we so laughed last night, and were in such haste to have you laugh with us at a ridiculous though distant hint Plumbe gave of marrying his son Ralpho that I think I should have written if I had been worse than I am: Marry the Scoundrel! exclaims my Master, Marry the Booby! exclaims my Mother, Marry the Ideot! will Mr. Johnson exclaim likewise: but he has finish'd his studies you know, and 'tis at least as well as *hanging*.

With such informality the correspondence continued for the next thirteen years. Often disconnected and hurried, hers are messages from the mistress of a busy household. Typical is a

---

[1] Most of Mrs. Thrale's letters to Johnson, as well as her other family papers, are now in the John Rylands Library. I wish here to express deep appreciation to Dr. Henry Guppy for permission to quote from the manuscripts, and to Professor George Sherburn and Mr. James M. Osborn for many helpful suggestions during the preparation of this essay.

letter of 7 November 1772, written at a time when her husband
was brooding over his recent financial reverses:

Here we are, doing nothing in the World but saving a Candle's
end and wishing for you at home; till then there is no chance for
me to do anything except by a little ineffectual teizing to keep my
tongue in Tune—Today I shall see my Mother & Streatham however; What can you mean by the Coach going twice on Saturdays?
it holds my Master the three children & myself at once well enough,
but where is any room for our dear Mr. Johnson? I hope we shall
all spend our Christmas comfortably together, & till then I must
keep your *roving Wishes* in order, and my own too, which hang upon
the Country the more as Mr. Thrale will not stir now he is in Town,
nor can all the influence I have over him make him speak a kind
word to a Customer when he knows it would save him a house—
You see this is a *private Letter*. . . . Be well My Dear Sir & continue
to love us bad as we are; that thro' all our distresses we may still
have the pleasure and Pride of possessing a friend truly matchless.

Some of the letters were filled with painful details of the
illnesses and deaths of her adored mother and children. Then,
while her mother was slowly dying of cancer, or as her second
son Ralph lay in a fatal stupor at Brighton, we catch a glimpse
of the unaffected grief of a distracted woman.

Writing to Johnson on 9 March 1773, Mrs. Thrale told of her
mother's increasing weakness and pain. 'She mentioned you,
and said you would meet together in heaven *She humbly hoped*—
that was all. I can write no more.' Some weeks later came the
report: 'My Mother will lie or sit with her Windows open for
Air, and now She has got a Cough again which just kills her:
She speaks often of you and always with kindness, sometimes
with Tears; says you will be a friend to her Child when she is
gone, and so you will I am sure.' Two weeks later, another
hurried note ends with the plaint: 'Can we do anything without
you?'

Ralph's protracted illness, too, almost drove her to despair.
In July 1775 she wrote from Brighton:

This poor unfortunate Child will dye at last—The Matter which
discharged from his Ear was it seems a temporary Relief, but that
was all over when I came down & the Stupor was returned in a
most alarming Manner: he has however violent fits of Rage—
proceeding from Pain I guess—just as Lucy & Miss Anna had—
Kipping says the Brain is oppressed of which I have no doubt:
What shall I do? What can I do? has the flattery of my Friends

made me too proud of my own Brains? & must these poor Children
suffer for my crime? I can neither go on with this Subject nor quit
it.—

.... I opened the Ball last Night—tonight I go to the Play: Oh
that there was a Play or a Ball for every hour of the four & twenty!

Adieu! my head & my heart are so full: I forgot to say how glad
I shall be to see you.

Other letters had to do with problems of her husband's business—the price of malt, the weather and the crops, various
grievances of disgruntled clerks. Still others were routine notes
of three or four lines, or longer collections of family news,
medical advice, and affectionate badinage. Throughout, she
was preoccupied with family matters.

Gradually, after the death of her sole remaining son, Harry,
in 1776, a change began to appear in Mrs. Thrale's writing.
Disheartened and disillusioned by the loss of one after another
of her favourite children, she had little inclination to throw
herself, as at first, into every affair of the nursery. Emotionally
she needed a rest. At the same time she was being welcomed
into the celebrated Blue-Stocking set, with the result that more
and more her thoughts were given over to social and literary
concerns. Instead of mostly domestic news in her letters to
Johnson, accounts of dinners and of other engagements crept
in. Her chatterbox style remained the same, while the topics
became broader. On one occasion there was her reception at
Court to be announced, on another a visit to Town Malling, or
a conversation with Mrs. Montagu. Then there were always
comments to be made on the interesting people she was meeting,
and amusing stories of what happened.

Certainly no one will deny that she could tell a story un-
commonly well—with economy of effort and great dramatic
effect. Take, for instance, the dinner party at Sir Joshua Reynolds's in August 1777. Mrs. Thrale described the day to Johnson
who was at Lichfield:

Since I wrote last I have dined at Sir Joshua's on Richmond Hill,
where we were invited to meet the Pepyses, the Patersons, the
Garricks &c. there was Mr. Langton, Lady Rothes and their two
pretty Babies; I think Miss Langton for an Infant of four Years old
the most elegant Creature I have seen, and little George is a fine
wellow too: but very troublesome they were with their Prattle, every
Ford of which their Papa repeated in order to explain; however

Miss Reynolds with great composure put them under the Care of a Maid & sent them a walking while we dined; very little to the Satisfaction of the Parents, who expressed some uneasiness lest they should overheat themselves as it was a hot day. In the mean Time Mr. Garrick was taken Ill, and after suffering a good deal from Sickness in his Stomach desired a Table to himself near the open Window: by the Time he was seated the Children returned; and Lady Rothes, who did not much like they should lose their dinner so, had got some Scraps of the second Course—Cheesecakes & such like ready for them at their Return—she then directed them to go to Mr. Garrick's Table, and *eat fair.* He was sick before, and I actually saw him change Colour at their approach, however he was civiller to them than anybody there except myself. Pepys—who had heard you give a Specimen of the *Langtonian* Mode of Life at our house whispered me that he wished them all at the Rope-Walk— & added can one ever come to this oneself? I really never had such difficulty to forbear laughing.

Of course, such gems cannot be expected in every letter. She did not make it her practice often to tell a long story or to set up a complete dramatic scene. She was more apt to give just a flash—part of an episode or an amusing remark—just enough to suggest the rest.

As she filled her letters with gossip about people and books her natural instincts for fun and amusing commentary were given freer reign. From Brighton in November 1778 she wrote to Johnson:

And so I heard of you at Reynolds' with Burney Baretti &c. I was glad on't: you will be content to come home & be quiet by & by; I have a grand Rout tonight, Lady Shelley Lady Poole and Militia Officers in plenty. Old Rose Fuller's Heir, Nephew to my *dear old Huh* is a very studious pretty young Fellow, & wishes I would introduce him to you, after I have made him worthy that honour he says. Lord Robert Manners visits us too—Dearee Me! how I am got all among the Quality of late—Make me thankful— like Murphy's Uncle. I hear Baretti is hard at it, not to Sow the Sea and plough the Sands—I hope; for we are growing mighty Classical: Mason is to produce something he calls Sappho, & she is to leap into the Sea for our Entertainment—this will be a good *maxim* & a good *Fact.*

During the early 1780's this sort of entertaining potpourri may also be found in her letters to the Burneys, to Mrs. Lambart, and Miss Margaret Owen, for as her relations with Johnson became increasingly strained, she eagerly sought new ties and new correspondents. To them she could write as the accepted Blue-Stocking wit she had become. More and more she strove to be clever, to be literary. The final break with Johnson, her sensational marriage to Piozzi with its consequent notoriety, and her 'best selling' volumes about Johnson and her travels on the Continent, served to increase this tendency. Once she began to consider herself a literary personality she attempted to write as one. Consequently most of her letters from this time on— and they comprise the great majority of what has survived— are more intentionally clever, more consciously amusing.

Mrs. Piozzi's constant desire, throughout these later years, was to amuse. 'What shall I tell to divert you?' she once wrote to her eldest daughter. 'This is the first entertaining letter I could make up for you', she commented on another occasion. Again and again there is the same emphasis. Her letters were intended to be more than mere bundles of news; they must delight as well as inform.

That her contemporaries considered her correspondence delightful is shown by the fact that so much of it has survived. Her daughters, despite strained relations with their mother, saved over 350 letters; the Williams family of Bodylwyddan, over 600; Sir John and Lady Salusbury, also over 600; and Mrs. Pennington, Samuel Lysons, the Reverend Leonard Chappelow, Sir James Fellowes, to name only a few, preserved hundreds more.[1] These people found something worth keeping, even in her shortest notes.

Certainly it was not conspicuous wit or humour for which these letters were saved, for one may search through dozens of them and not find a single quotable witticism. Her remarks may continually bring a smile, but rarely hearty laughter. Yet

[1] Since quotations from these and other letters of Mrs. Piozzi in the following pages are generally from manuscript sources, no individual reference notes are given. For kind permission to use the material I am indebted to the following:
The Marquis of Lansdowne—to Hester Maria Thrale and her sisters.
Sir Randle Mainwaring—to the Williams family of Bodylwyddan.
The John Rylands Library—to the Reverend Leonard Chappelow, Sir John Salusbury Piozzi Salusbury, &c.
Mr. Albert Ashforth Jr.—to Dr. W. M. Thackeray.
Mr. O. Bourne—to Alexander Leak (some others sold at Sotheby's on 1 Dec. 1938 and 19 March 1940).
Most of the letters to Penelope Pennington were published by O. G. Knapp in 1914. The originals were in the possession of the late Mr. Wilton L. Smith.

Mrs. Piozzi did have an unusual ability to divert by sudden and ingenious associations of ideas. The reader is constantly surprised and pleased by these analogies, even when superficial. For instance, she wrote to Lady Williams of Bodylwyddan on 2 July 1802, of a balloonist then exhibiting in London:

Monsieur Garnerin goes up again tomorrow with an Umbrella Thing to hinder his *Fall*, he calls it for that Reason a Para*chute*. We shall see how it answers—taking so much Money at such a Risk of breaking all his Bones. People are going fast into the Country. We have almost done eating *Breakfasts* whence we return at 8 in the Evening, & *Dinners* which break up at 12 at Night: Electioneering Matters fill every Mouth, that is not discoursing about Garnerin, who travels 67 Miles an Hour in the Air.—Such Expedition on such Errands would be useful; but neither He nor the Candidates seem to know where they are going.

Then there is the comment to her daughter Queeney in January 1806 about the possibility of a ministry being formed by Fox and the radicals, with the object of making peace with Buonaparte:

Oh Dear! I feel in the meantime not unlike poor Doctor Perney, who when Susette asked him why he did not marry; replied in his lisping Way 'Why Miss you see I should not much mind being cuckolded, if the Lady would do it civilly, but the fear lest they should poyson me would hinder my sleeping o' nights.' An Administration that only plunders us, is on the same Principle less uneasily endured; than one which keeps Sleep at a distance for Fear of the nation's being sold before Morning.

And a new concert pianist brought the comparison:

We are tired of him here already; for Wonder is after all a Short:lived Passion, and while other People play as if they were running down Stairs & up again; This Man seems Sliding down the Banisters at once—Some few capital Tricks performed however, the Sport ends.

It must be admitted that sometimes her humour depended for its point on mere verbal agility or a play on words. She was never squeamish about making a pun. 'A Lady told me last Night', she wrote to Miss Williams,

that some Nabob without a Name or Pedigree, having bought an Estate hard by here, died & was buried in the Vault of the Family from which his House was purchas'd. The Coffins of the old Possessors however, jumped up, & stood upon their Ends Indignant— as I understood the Lady—at being forced upon *Inferior* Society in the Grave. Why Madam, said I, this was indeed a Miracle—turning the ancient Family into *Up*starts.

It is obvious that Mrs. Piozzi's power to entertain often depends more on style than on content. It is not so much what she says as how she says it. Yet the sprightliness which is so characteristic almost defies explanation. How, indeed, can we analyse the humour of such a remark as this to Queeney: 'It was well said by Somebody—Myself I hope, that as we have had the Golden Age, & the Iron Age—*this* is the *Marble* Age—so *hard*, & so *cold*, & so polish'd'? Certainly the matter is not remarkable; perhaps it is the sly 'Myself I hope' which makes us smile. These little interpolations, these casual comments and ironical asides, give her style its intense personal quality.

Even discussions of public affairs or foreign news were usually enlivened by some personal remark. In 1796 she wrote to Queeney:

'Tis a *separate* Peace the French are trying for: hoping to make Great Britain desert her Allies, and suffer *them* to ravage Italy without molestation. To this Event many Causes seem to cooperate: the Desire of our Merchants & Traders for Peace almost on any Terms; the Terror of Opposition Clamours should a tempting Offer be refused—and the supiness of those Italian States who are as willing to shut their Ports against *us* who defend, as against the French who attack them. When I asked a Gentleman once for Directions how to avoid sinking in deep Water—*Do so*, said he, and moved his forefinger only. If either the Venetian or Tuscan Governments could be prevailed on only to *Do so*—they might even yet swim.

With her usual airy manner, she once remarked to Miss Williams, 'Meanwhile the Ministry fills every body's Mouth, & I suppose 'tis always pleasantest to talk about what least concerns one, so I talk of it too; but without knowing an Atom of the Business.' Though ready to talk or write about any subject, she seldom allowed herself to take anything very seriously, so that, try as we may, it is almost impossible to find any high seriousness in what she wrote. Sublimity, the inspiration of noble thoughts, she would have insisted, were best expressed in poetry or philosophic works, not in everyday letters.

Literary comments, too, were intended to divert. In a long letter to Queeney in March 1796 she wrote:

Quoting Shakespear puts me in mind of Ireland's Manuscripts;

Stevens' bonmot to Mr. Broadhead (who is a Book Collector)
pleased me very well. Will not you wait till they are published—
says he—& bind them up with our best Edition? For what Reason?
replies the other. Nay—why you bind up Apocrypha with the Bible;
don't you?—Of a half:profane Joke this is one of the best I know.

I am panting all this while with Eager Expectation of Burkes
book; the News Papers tantalize one with extracts wch: increase
one's Appetite without gratifying it. There is such a Constellated
Radiance about all that Man writes, that Specimens are ridiculous;
'tis like peeping at the Galaxy thro' a Telescope when the grand
Idea is only to be gained in a clear Night by contemplating its
immense Sweep over the Horizon when 'tis widest.

What she read she liked to describe to her correspondents. The
Gothic romances of Mrs. Radcliffe and Monk Lewis—later,
such sensational works as *Frankenstein* and *Glenarvon*—the poems
of Southey, Crabbe, Scott, and Byron—all drew horrified or
rapturous comments, depending upon the mood of the moment
or her Johnsonian prejudices. Always personal, they represent
the candid opinions of a curious, eager reader.

Usually her anecdotes of people are short, admittedly suggested by something she had heard or seen. Thus a visit to an
exhibition of paintings in London brought the comment:

My Tears witness'd the Fondness I felt at Sight of poor Hogarth
& his Dog Trump—my Countryman Wilsons heavenly Landschapes
too! He used to *say* & my Father used to laugh at him for saying,
—'Ay Ay—They neglect poor Dick *now*: but Damn *me* if their
Grandchildren don't cover this Niobe with Guineas—and set them
edge-Ways too.'

When she does tell a longer story, it is almost always to illustrate
a point. As an old lady of seventy, she wrote to Queeney:

Lord Robert Manners, who I think you may possibly remember,
—when he felt Death approaching, called his old Valet:—and now
Matt (says he) I've led a Soldier's Life, and thought little about
t'other World; What dost thou think Matt that I should *do* now?—
just to Set Matters Straightish You see—before the Roll Call? Why
my Lord replies the Fellow There's fine Reading in my *Great Book*—
with an Intelligent Wink—for he durst not name the *Bible*; and if
your Lordship (seeing him so quiet) would hear me read The Twelve
minor Prophets—it might do some Good. how long is the whole
on't Matt? The Man fetch'd, and Shew'd him the Pages—Oh Devil!
—I shall never live to hear it half Thro'—and no more he did; but

expired, crying *Make haste* Matt, *Go on* Matt—with his last Breath. Risum teneas?

Well! Doctor Johnson said You know, that approaching Death would no more teach Piety to a Man devoid of previous Instruction, than it would teach Arithmetic to a Person who had never heard the Multiplication Table—but this Story illustrates his Axiom to a Nicety.

The question naturally arises: How dependable are her stories? Amusing anecdotes are all very well, but most of us wish old letters to be useful as historical evidence, as well as entertaining. Mrs. Piozzi's accuracy in her letters, as in her diaries, depends on the nature of each account: descriptions of contemporary events, written down when they happened, may in general be trusted; recollections of former days are apt to be vague. As a reporter on the spot she is excellent, but she had neither Boswell's ability nor his determination to remember the exact minutiae of past occurrences. The random remarks, the offhand references, the incidental quotations about famous acquaintances of her younger days which appear so often must consequently be accepted only for what they are. While the point of the anecdote will in all probability be correct, the trimmings may be suspected.

Her later letters were often interspersed with recollections of Streatham conversations—Johnson, of course, being the most often quoted. Almost anything might remind her of something he had said. Piozzi's illness provoked the comment to Queeney: 'For twenty hours he screamed like a woman in labour. I did not know (like Doctor Johnson and the Tart) that Gout could have been so bad.' In a letter to Dr. Thackeray a chance reference to the *Life of Savage* brought further remarks: 'but I have been credibly informed that after all you will read there he was *not* Lady Macclesfield's Son: Colonel Brett told Mr. Seward so himself. Dear Dr. Johnson was not difficult to be imposed on where the *Heart* came in Question.' And to her adopted son, Salusbury, a young boy at school, she wrote from North Wales: 'It is good to *see* as many Things, and *know* as many Things as we can; and my only reason for regretting our State of Retirement, is the Reflexion that whilst I am feeding my Chickens— (as poor Dr. Johnson used to say)—I am starving my Understanding.' These offhand remarks need not have the exactness of legal evidence; they were not intended as such. Their value is to add colour and interest to the writing.

Rarely in her letters is there even a touch of malice or spite. She might be scornful or contemptuous of what she thought silly or bad, but never mean or hateful. She enjoyed life too much to spend her time maligning others. Once she remarked to Mrs. Pennington that she 'never was good at *pouting* when a Miss; and after fifty years are gone, one should know the value of Life better than to *pout* any part of it away'. Delighted in watching the human comedy around her, she had few illusions that she could reform it either by exhortation or satire. Her function, as she interpreted it, was merely to describe for her correspondents the experiences and ideas that give piquancy and zest to an otherwise tragic world.

If, as many have contended, the art of letter-writing is the art of being oneself—of revealing personality more subtly than is possible in more formal authorship—then surely Mrs. Piozzi stands in the front rank of correspondents. Few can read her letters without gaining an intimate knowledge of the woman herself—her vigour, her courage, and her prodigious appetite for life. We understand her foibles, her eager curiosities—all the amusing qualities of her mind. Even for us who cannot sit in the same room and hear her effervescent talk, she comes to life as a real person.

THE POWER OF MEMORY IN BOSWELL AND SCOTT[1]

F. A. POTTLE

'THE Wizard of the North' is a title no serious critic would care to employ nowadays: it has a flavour of the sentimental or the comic or both together—something like the Wizard of Oz. Yet it is hard to see what epithet could fit Scott better. A wizard is a man who casts a spell: he enchants a country and it all seems changed. One walks dryshod where the map shows a river, and ascends mountains where uneasy memory records a fen. A wizard breaks the comfortable shackles of time, and the familiar scene, as in that disquieting narrative of the two ladies at Versailles, is frequented by forms that belong there, no doubt, but not now. Scott did precisely that to Scotland, and the spell has not lifted. For better or worse, Scotland as it is seen to-day is largely the creation of Walter Scott. And the best existing means of testing the extent of this transformation is the journal of James Boswell.

By an indiscriminate attention to significant and superficial resemblances, it would be possible to prove that James Boswell and Walter Scott were practically identical. Both were born in Edinburgh and spent the greater part of their lives there; both attended the University of Edinburgh; both were sons of lawyers, both became advocates and curators of the Advocates' Library; both were Tories, both were Masons, both belonged to The Club; both preferred the forms and doctrine of the Church of England to those of the Kirk; both had fine estates in the country; both wrote a great deal more than anybody knows, and are remembered to-day merely as literary men, and both, in their own time, would have been offended at being classed as authors by profession.

It would be possible to go on for a long time extending the

[1] The following short titles are employed throughout the notes:

Private Papers = *The Private Papers of James Boswell from Malahide Castle, in the Collection of Lt.-Colonel Ralph Heyward Isham*, ed. Geoffrey Scott and F. A. Pottle, privately printed, 1928–34, 18 vols.; *Life* = *Boswell's Life of Johnson*, ed. G. B. Hill and revised L. F. Powell, Oxford, 1934– , 4 vols. published; for vol. v (*Journal of a Tour to the Hebrides*) Hill's original text (1887) must be used; *Memoirs* = *Memoirs of the Life of Sir Walter Scott*, by J. G. Lockhart, 2nd ed., 1839, 10 vols. (the references by chapters apply to any unabridged edition after the first).

parallels, but such activity would be mere ingenuity, not criticism. There are, indeed, a surprising number of respects in which Boswell and Scott resemble each other to such a degree that by knowing the character of one it would be possible to predict the attitude of the other on a given issue. The similarity of their attitudes towards the law is very striking. Perhaps the best evidence of this is the inexhaustible usefulness of Scott's novels in annotating Boswell's journal. Neither Scott nor Boswell was so constituted as to become really prominent at the bar, but the reason was not any lack of aptitude. It was simply that both had other interests and were not willing to give them up. Men who wish to acquire fame and fortune as advocates must study in the vacations of the courts; they must not rush off the day the court rises on jaunts to London or raids into Liddesdale. Both Scott and Boswell (to use the words of one of them) defied the jealousy of the goddess Themis towards any flirtation with the Muses, but neither ever really meant to apostatize. Boswell groaned for manumission, not from the law but from the petty routine of the Court of Session and the General Assembly; always before his eyes hung the mirage of splendid success at the English bar. That mirage, at the age of 46, he characteristically pursued. Scott, a more hard-headed man who worked his romance off in best-sellers, accepted appointment as one of the principal clerks in the Court of Session. Both remained lawyers. Boswell, a year before his death, was outlining a legal education for his eldest son and chatting to him as one lawyer to another, while the sharpest letter Scott ever wrote to *his* eldest son was occasioned by some disparaging remarks which that young man had made about lawyers.[1] Scott continued his regular attendance in the Court of Session until 1830, and never did resign his sheriffship.

The politics of Boswell and Scott are also of a piece. Scott deflates his own self-importance with humour in a way that shows to great advantage beside the stiffness and pompousness of the political notes in the *Life of Johnson*, but like Boswell he

---

[1] 'The question which you put . . . is shrewd, and makes me believe you have a good law head' (Boswell to Alexander Boswell, 13 March 1794, *Private Papers*, xviii. 325); 'DEAR WALTER,—I have your letter of May 6th, to which it is unnecessary to reply very particularly. I would only insinuate to you that the *lawyers* and *gossips* of Edinburgh, whom your military politeness handsomely classes together in writing to a lawyer . . .' (Scott to Cornet Walter Scott, 15 May 1821, *Memoirs*, vi. 316, ch. LI, near end).

was a deadly serious intuitive Tory. Scott cherishing in his coat-tail the whisky-glass which the royal lips of George IV had touched, is hardly to be distinguished from Boswell melting in the seraphic smile of George III. And the touching scene of Scott on the Mound, bursting into tears and resting his head on the coping until he should have recovered his composure, when his Whig friends had tried to make a joking matter out of proposed reforms in the administration of justice in Scotland, is matched by Boswell in the vale of Glenmoriston weeping over Culloden.[1]

In their attitudes towards family and landed property they again see eye to eye. It is true that Boswell came of a long-established family, whereas Scott was establishing one himself; true also that Boswell could not bear to *live* on his property, whereas Scott was not completely happy anywhere else. But Boswell's tendency 'to think with sacred reverence and attachment of his Ancestors and to hope to aggrandize the Family' quite matches Scott's, and his appetite for land was little less reckless and insatiable. Every one knows that Scott overreached himself in his expenditure at Abbotsford and brought himself and his connexions to spectacular ruin, but it is not so well known that Boswell did what a lesser man could to involve his affairs. In order to purchase Knockroon ('I am willing to give more than any person whatever . . . I will *restrict* myself to any degree rather than fail') he had to borrow at a time when his affairs were 'sadly straitened'. In 1792, presumably to consolidate his debts, he granted a heritable bond for £4,000 on his lands of Dalblair to Quintin McAdam of Craigengillan. The bond, falling due on his death, could not be met, and Dalblair was lost for the mere sum of the debt. Sixty years later it sold for £17,300.[2]

To many this comparison will seem sophistical, if not in bad taste. It would be if we were concerned with the central practical issue. Scott from the earliest period at which we can discern him was a man of character: manly, courageous, confident to the point of rashness, self-controlled, and extraverted. So far as I can see, he had no vices at all, but my feeling for him has always been that of the sentimental pig, and perhaps is not to

---

[1] *Memoirs*, vii. 53–5, ch. LVI; *Private Papers*, xvi. 100–1; *Memoirs*, ii. 328, ch. xv, at end; *Journal of a Tour to the Hebrides*, ed. Pottle and Bennett, pp. 106–7 (1 Sept. 1773).

[2] *Private Papers*, xiv. 17, xviii. 287, 288 n.; James Paterson, *History of the Counties at Ayr and Wigton*, i. 201–2.

be trusted. Boswell in certain respects was a moral weakling: his vices are notorious, self-confessed, and unattractive. They all spring, unless I am mistaken, from a fundamental sense of insecurity, from a basic lack of confidence, caused by, or at least accompanied by, an extreme form of introversion. Here, certainly, the two men are diametrically opposed, and opposed in the most important respect. My concern in this essay, however, is not with conduct, but with a lesser matter, art; and I hope the reader will not be shocked if I say that in the sort of analysis which I propose to make of Boswell and Scott moral differences are largely irrelevant.

Scott, as I have said, cast a spell on the world; we know it by the world which Boswell has preserved for us. Between the two men there occurred a tremendous acceleration in the shift of sensibility which gradually transformed what we call the neo-classic mind into the romantic. A detailed and objective description of the essential differences between the sensibility of Boswell and the sensibility of Scott should be of some utility, for it would be material for a properly controlled generalization as to the nature of the neo-classic and the romantic expressions of the world. *Material*, of course, not a complete or trustworthy generalization. No one should expect to define romanticism except by extended historical statement, and one should not expect any particular author to be either completely 'neo-classic' or completely 'romantic'. These terms name imaginary or ideal embodiments of average characteristics.

A thorough study of the kind I propose would go far beyond the limits imposed upon this essay. I can give only a sketch. And the sketch will violate strict propriety of method. Though my purpose is in the main descriptive, I shall suggest rather more in the way of generalization than the material presented justifies.

It may be felt that the comparison is rendered futile at the start by the fact that Scott was a writer of fiction, Boswell a biographer and journalist. And indeed, unless one is willing to grant the fundamental assumption of the Crocean position—that all expression is art, and that the difference between a novel and a journal like Boswell's is a difference of degree and not of kind—there will seem to be no justification for the present study. It is precisely that assumption that will be made in what follows: that in analysing Boswell's journal we are concerned not merely with perception and memory, but also with imagination. To distinguish Scott from Boswell merely in the workings of the imagination is useful, but I should like to go farther back and see if even more interesting results could not be obtained if we began at the level of perception and continued on through the stage of memory. It may well be that memory will prove to be the most useful differential of all.

Did Boswell and Scott perceive the same sort of world to begin with? We have, as it happens, documents which should be capable of answering the question. They are Boswell's *Journal of a Tour to the Hebrides* and the journal of the tour to the Shetlands, Orkneys, and Hebrides which Scott made in 1814. The material is all similar in nature, and some of it—rather less than one would have expected—is quite parallel. Boswell's original manuscript has been recovered and printed; Scott's, so far as I know, is accessible only in the text given by Lockhart in the *Memoirs*, which seems to show some subsequent manipulation by Scott or his editor, but has probably not been sophisticated in any way injurious to our purpose.[1]

From Boswell's journal as a whole, it appears that his central interests were strongly humanistic. His perception was keen and full for all varieties of human nature (Johnson was merely his best subject), for social customs and practices, for human antiquities, for history and legends. For landscape and merely natural curiosities it was relatively languid. He remarks more than once that he has no skill in depicting natural objects, a clear indication that he did not see them with much detail. No author I know is more completely free from picturesque writing. Not that his perception of landscape is purely utilitarian, for he sometimes remarks aesthetic values in it. Landscape, however, is not by him perceived as involved in history and symbolic of it. It is probable that human antiquities such as Dunvegan or the ruins of Iona, though symbols of history, were perceived by him as *disconnected* from it, elements of a storied past gone beyond recall, a past which existed verbally but not in visual imagery tied to the scene.

Lockhart says that Scott's journal draws his character fully:

---

[1] 'Within the castle [of Dunvegan] we saw a remarkable drinking-cup . . . which I have described particularly elsewhere' (*Memoirs*, iv. 304, ch. XXXI). The 'elsewhere' is Note XII to *The Lord of the Isles*, of which the pertinent portion must have been written later than the journal. Lockhart, finding the description of the Dunvegan cup rather long and dull, probably modified the text at this point so that he could eliminate it from his printing of the journal.

'We have before us, according to the scene and occasion, the poet, the antiquary, the magistrate, the planter, and the agriculturist.'[1] It is easier to illustrate the antiquary, the magistrate, the planter, and the agriculturist than the poet. Scott shows the eager interest one would expect in brochs, tombs, drinking-cups, legends, trees, and crops—indeed, his interest in agriculture causes him to be much more detailed and intelligible on that topic than Boswell ever is—but the poetry of the journal is very low-pitched, so much so as to be almost a matter of inference. We see it because we come to the journal fortified with those passages from his autobiographical fragment which describe his early 'love of natural beauty, more especially when combined with ancient ruins, or remains of our fathers' piety or splendour', and his power to fill an old castle or a field of battle 'with its combatants in their proper costume'.[2]

In his journal, as one would expect, he gives a great deal of space to remarkable and terrific scenes: the Cave of Smoo, Loch Coruisk, 'Macallister's Cave' (Spar Cave), and Staffa—several extended and serious attempts at picturesque writing. And that, oddly enough, is just about what they remain. Loch Coruisk may have been overrun by tourists as a result of *The Lord of the Isles*, as Loch Katrine undoubtedly was because of *The Lady of the Lake*, but the passage in Scott's journal would not have effected such a result.

Similarly when Scott comes upon 'remains of our fathers' piety or splendour' (this particular tour was relatively barren in historical monuments) we sense the heightened interest we should have predicted. The best example is perhaps those ruins at Scalloway and Kirkwall connected with Patrick Stewart, Earl of Orkney.[3] But these, though extremely interesting, do not strike the reader as being intensely poetic.

The fact is that the two journals show much less difference in immediate perception of the world than one would have predicted. Boswell favours conversation (and would have even if Johnson had not been his companion), Scott favours scenery. But the central interests are so similar that not merely sentences but whole paragraphs could be interchanged without being detected by a casual reader. The two journals do not show respectively a typically 'neo-classic' and a typically 'romantic'

---

[1] *Memoirs*, iv. 371, ch. xxxiii, beginning.   [2] Ibid. i. 55, 72, ch. i.
[3] Ibid. iv. 213–15, 247–9, chs. xxviii, xxix.

perception of the world. Scott's throughout has the shrewd, humane, humorous tone of common sense that we associate with the eighteenth century.

Shall we conclude that the Wizard of the North was a charlatan, or at least an extraordinarily clever and deliberate showman—that he naturally and habitually *saw* Boswell's world, but by conscious literary devices tricked other people into seeing something else? That would be too simple a description of a very complex situation. Scott *did* perceive a normal, average world just about like Boswell's. But he constantly perceived another world behind and through it: the romantic world into which it could be transformed. He could hardly have written his description of Loch Coruisk without seeing it as sympathetic landscape for the meeting of Bruce and Cormac Doil—or at least for some melodramatic encounter; and it is safe to infer that when he saw Earl Patrick's ruined castle at Scalloway he was conscious of the lively presence of that rapacious prince in a way that Boswell would have considered enthusiastic. He does not *record* the romantic perception because he is recording fact, and he believes the romantic perception to be make-believe. It is very interesting to see at the basis of his artistic activity this clear, sharp, undistorted, 'realistic' perception of things, and his determination to keep it clear from the play of free imagination. It is the source of his strength and at the same time of his greatest weakness. One becomes impatient with an artist who is so genuinely convinced that fiction is merely make-believe that he can do himself justice only when the fiction sweeps him off his feet. But when it does, we get an imaginative presentation of such solidity and power as our language elsewhere hardly affords.

It is only when we turn to the *uses* that Scott made of his perceptions that we discern a sharp and striking difference between his mind and Boswell's. His memory works very differently. It will be easier to show this if we say something of Boswell first. The nature of Boswell's memory has been made the subject of a brilliant investigation by Geoffrey Scott, unfortunately in a work of limited circulation.[1] In what follows I shall draw freely on his conclusions, not pausing to indicate the places where I have modified and extended them.

Given the right kind of jog to his memory, Boswell had

[1] *The Making of the Life of Johnson*, vol. vi of the *Private Papers*.

something that looks like total recall. If he failed to make a written record soon after a series of events, he seems to have lost those events permanently, or at least to have had no greater power of recall than the next person. But given his written clue, and given time and patience, he could reconstruct accurately and in minute detail an account of practically everything that ever happened to him. The clues he relied on (when he did not write a full journal immediately) were rough and abbreviated notes jotted down on odd scraps of paper, often on the backs of envelopes. In these notes, which are in the highest degree fragmentary and cryptic, there appears to be no attempt to select what is important. Boswell simply jots down whatever rises first to his consciousness, knowing that one sort of hint will serve as well as another.[1] Once fixed in this fashion, the events may be recalled at will, the fullness of the recovery depending less upon the interval of time than upon his patience and ability to concentrate his attention.

The journal is generally written from these notes, after a lapse of time varying from days to years. When the notes and journal are compared (which is seldom possible, for Boswell's usual practice was to destroy his notes as soon as they had served their purpose), it will generally be found that something—sometimes a great deal—turns up for which there was no sort of hint in the notes, and not infrequently that some hints in the notes are ignored.[2] Suppressions of this kind in the journal I take to be due to several causes: inability to read the note; lack of time or patience to bring the scene back fully; deliberate rejection of remembered material as not worth recording. The material which turns up in the journal without warrant in the notes I can only conclude to have been *remembered*. It is of exactly the same sort as the material for which the notes furnish hints, and is just as circumstantial. When the circumstances are of a sort that will permit verification, they prove to be correct.

[1] 'A hint like this will serve to bring back to me all that past, though it would be useless to any one else' (Boswell's journal in the *Private Papers*—I have lost the reference).
[2] Good examples will be found in Geoffrey Scott's study. For the brilliant account of the evening at Lord Mansfield's, 11 April 1773 (pp. 107–11), the notes have only 'Lord Mans. Jenkins[on] there—Had him afterwards an hour alone. Etourdi again. Felt still that greatness and cold command can confuse me.' The journal gives a report of the hour's conversation, 750 words on six different topics, all highly detailed and circumstantial. For examples of hints recorded but not made use of, see the notes for 3 June 1784 (ibid. 53–6).

The process of recollection does not stop with the journal, but is still going on in the *Life of Johnson*. For one thing, the greater part of the extended Johnsonian conversations in which several speakers take part seems never to have been expanded in the journal at all. The only record Boswell had was frequently the rough note written many years before.[1] And even when he had before him a journal version which could have been transferred almost without change into the *Life*, one constantly finds additions which can only be explained, in my opinion, by assuming that even here he relived the scene as he copied it and recollected matter which had eluded him at the time he wrote the journal, or which he had then suppressed.[2]

The qualities which make the recall of Boswell remarkable are its wealth of detail and its circumstantial accuracy. Memory in people of education, particularly in artists, is usually a very inaccurate affair and deals cavalierly with circumstances. Very few people, moreover, can distinguish between what they have actually witnessed and what they have been told. Adults, no less than children, frequently convince themselves that they were spectators of events which for a time they were content to relate on the authority of others.

Yet the kind of memory here ascribed to Boswell, if it were merely a matter of detail and accuracy, would be no very rare thing. We have all met people who could remember everything, and we have shunned them. Who does not number among his acquaintance a narrator who bores his audience with interminable circumstantial detail, often of events of the

---

[1] 11 April 1773 exists in the journal in a form fuller, if anything, than the version in the *Life*. 13 April 1773 of the *Life* was written as late as 1787 from a rough note merely. In both cases (wages of female servants, 11 April; law reports, 13 April) Johnson is credited with remarks for which there is no warrant in the notes. A great deal, no doubt, depended on the fullness of the note. When, as in the latter portion of the *Journal of a Tour to the Hebrides* (ed. Pottle and Bennett, p. 346), Boswell complains of lack of freshness and fullness, he may have had only very brief notes to work from.

[2] In the nature of things, these additions are seldom of a sort to permit verification. One remarkable exception occurs in the account of 3 June 1784 as given in the *Life*. We are told there that Mrs. and Miss Beresford were Americans; that they were going to Worcestershire, where they resided; and that Mr. Beresford had been a member of Congress. None of this is recorded in the note (which happens to have survived) nor in the journal. But it is all correct. After a searching review, I have been unable to detect any difference in authenticity between expansions which Boswell made in the *Life* and those that he made in the journal; or, to state the problem more precisely, between additions made after an interval of years and additions made after an interval of days or months.

remote past? We do not doubt the accuracy of the detail or the power of the narrator, having got hold of his thread, to unravel it to the end of time. But accuracy of that sort is tedious. What we want, as we say, is for him to come to his *point*. We want selection; that is, we want him to pick out a few important things and sink the rest. To repeat, the memory which is tenacious of circumstantial detail is not uncommon, but it is usually associated with a low order of intelligence or a primitive culture.

The really remarkable feat of Boswell is that he has combined the full recall of the savage or the moron with the selectivity of the artist. His record, by its wealth of circumstantial detail, convinces us of its firm basis in reality, while by coming to the point he keeps us interested: that is, persuades us that what he is saying is significant.

What gives the peculiar quality of solidity and trustworthiness to Boswell's accounts is that he always presents his scenes in terms of average or normal experience. It begs the question to say that he presents things as they really were. There is a certain area in which all minds agree or in which agreement is ideally possible. The circumstantial detail which we have mentioned falls in this area. A particular conversation occurred on Thursday 3 June 1784 in the Oxford coach, or it did not; the ladies who accompanied Johnson were named Beresford, were Americans, were going to Worcestershire, or they were not; Mr. Beresford was a member of Congress or he was not. We may not always be able to verify things like this, but we shall agree that they are capable of verification and that only one answer is right. This is selection (for many more details could have been given) but it is not interpretation. When it comes to what Johnson *said* on any subject, if it was a matter of more than a sentence or two, it is obvious that Boswell gives us not merely selection but also interpretation, for you cannot condense or epitomize speech without deciding what, on the whole, it means. Boswell's interpretation moves on the plane of average or normal experience, with the result that in him we seem to see the past through no kind of medium at all, or at most through plate glass. The style that can achieve this result is one of the rarest things in literature. Much more common is the medium which colours or distorts—Carlyle's, let us say, or Scott's.

Boswell seems not in his own lifetime to have been regarded as a prodigy. Though he himself remarks with awe on the 'stretch of mind' which had enabled him to recover extended conversations, most readers of the *Life*, then as now, have thought of him as a stenographer. Scott's memory, on the contrary, was an object of general astonishment from the time he was six years old.[1] Like most memories which history chooses to distinguish as prodigious, his was essentially verbal and literary. He never pretended to be able to remember circumstantial details of his own experience or to report at length general conversations which he had once heard. But from childhood he could repeat from memory, without any conscious effort at memorization, a 'really marvellous quantity' of stanzas from the *Faerie Queene*, or ballads, or pages of history—in short, in any part of the field of his passionate antiquarian interest, to read or to have heard and to remember were the same thing.[2]

We have seen that Boswell, if he had a hint or clue, could recall past scenes of his life with remarkable fullness and accuracy. The clue he depended on was a *written* note; nothing else would serve. Scott seems never to have formed the habit of systematic notation. But we do have the tantalizing business of the notched twigs, and a great misfortune it is that we do not have from Scott himself a more satisfactory account of these extraordinary memoranda. Our authority is Robert Shortreed, Scott's companion in the Liddesdale raids. He was nine years older than Scott and predeceased him, but his son in 1824 had taken down his recollections in his own racy dialect. The passage about the notched sticks must be quoted in full:

J. E. S. 'Did Sir Walter keep a memorandum-book or take any notes, during your tours?'

FATHER. 'None that I ever saw. We had neither pens, nor ink, nor paper. But we had *knives* and they served the turn just as weel, for we took bits o' Cuttings wi' them, frae a broom Cowe, or an aller, or a hazel-bush, or whatever else might be at hand, and on thae bits o' stick (maybe tway or three inches lang they were) he made a variety o' notches, and these were the only memoranda I ever saw him take or have, of any of the memorable spots he wished to preserve the recollection of, or any tradition connected wi' them. And when he had notched them they were just slipt into our pockets, a' heads and thraws. When we cam hame frae some o' our trips, I hae seen us have a'maist haill wallets fu' o' them—wud aneuch to mend a mill as Burns says. I couldna think what he meant by this at first, and

---

[1] *Life*, i. 6 (Advertisement to the First Edition); *Memoirs*, i. 118–20, ch. II.
[2] *Memoirs*, i. 50, 53, ch. I.

when I asked him what a' thae marked sticks were for, he said "these are my log-book, Bob!"'

J. E. S. 'This is most amazing—And are you aware that he ever made any after use of them?'

FATHER. 'Yes I can satisfy ye on that point too. For I was frequently wi' him at his Father's house in Edinr. when he was preparing the Minstrelsy for publication, and I know, *for I saw it*, that as he went along he very often had recourse to *the notched sticks*. He had them a' hanging in their order above him, by a string alang the ceiling o' his room—(as you'll see Rhubarb in a gardener's house) —wi' mony mae o' the same kind about the Highlands, for ye ken he used often to gang on travels there too, about that time. I never saw a pen in his hand nor a piece o' paper a' the times we were in Liddesdale thegither, or in any other o' our Border rides, but twice, and that was when he took the two sketches that he made o' Hermitage Castle, and the one sheet o' paper he got frae Dr. Elliot, the other frae Willie o' Millburn.'[1]

It is very odd that Lockhart, who had Shortreed's manuscript before him and used it for other information, did not quote this highly interesting passage. He may have thought that it made mystery of a very simple matter. It has not, I think, been noted that there is a reference to the twigs by Scott himself in the autobiographical fragment which does seem on a careless reading to reduce them to the status of mere souvenirs. After relating his inability to learn to sketch the scenes that interested him, Scott says:

I endeavoured to make amends for my ignorance of drawing, by adopting a sort of technical memory respecting the scenes I visited. Wherever I went, I cut a piece of a branch from a tree—these constituted what I called my log-book; and I intended to have a set of chessmen out of them, each having reference to the place where it was cut—as the kings from Falkland and Holy-Rood; the queens from Queen Mary's yew-tree at Crookston; the bishops from abbeys or episcopal palaces; the knights from baronial residences; the rooks from royal fortresses; and the pawns generally from places worthy of historical note. But this whimsical design I never carried into execution.[2]

---

[1] W. E. Wilson, 'The Making of the Minstrelsy', in *Cornhill Magazine*, n.s. cxlvi. 281 (July–Dec. 1932). As Mr. Dobie has pointed out (*Transactions of the Edinburgh Bibliographical Society*, vol. ii, Part 1, p. 68 n.), there is at least one slight inaccuracy in Shortreed's account: the *Minstrelsy* was not planned until after Scott had left his father's house. But he had been recording ballads for a long time before he formed any plan of publication.

[2] *Memoirs*, i. 72–3, ch. 1.

Scott's 'technical memory' is, I think, equivalent to the 'artificial memory' which the *Oxford Dictionary* defines as 'a system of mnemonic devices', and illustrates from Hoyle (1747): *A Short Treatise on the Game of Whist . . . To which is added, An Artificial Memory: Or, An easy Method of assisting the memory of those that play at the Game.* The intention of making chessmen out of the twigs was probably second thought.

There is not much doubt, I think, that we have here a very interesting means of differentiating the modes of memory possessed by Boswell and Scott. Boswell had to consult verbal clues, and was unable or unwilling to reconstruct the past unless he was properly buttressed and limited by circumstance. Landscape he saw with little detail and made little or no effort to recall. For verbal material, Scott demanded no clues, but confidently constructed it out of his head as he wanted it. Picturesque landscape was a different matter. If he were to recall this, he must have some kind of clue. Written descriptions, such as those of the journal of 1814, would serve, but when he was in the field he was generally too busy enjoying himself to do any writing. He would have been willing to dash off a sketch, but drawing was something he could not master. The notched sticks were *landscape* memoranda, and served well enough for the broad effects he was partial to. But it is not likely that such memoranda could have furnished the circumstantial detail which ensures accuracy of memory.

And the fact is that Scott's memory, as contrasted with Boswell's, is wildly inaccurate. Imaginative construction is at work in it, and at work in the same way as in his fictions. Indeed, it is fair to say that the only difference between Scott's fictions and his anecdotal memories is that in the one case imagination is at work consciously and in the other it is not.

Consider first an instance where the professed object was merely to recall events and scenes of the tour of 1814. In the last of the *Letters on Demonology* (1830) he speaks of his experience in the haunted apartment at Dunvegan. The experience was in fact disappointing: the setting was impressive but nothing happened. What he has to say, therefore, concerns itself almost entirely with setting:

An autumnal blast, sometimes clear, sometimes driving mist before it, swept along the troubled billows of the lake, which it occasionally concealed, and by fits disclosed. The waves rushed in wild disorder on the shore, and covered with foam the steep pile of rocks, which, rising from the sea in forms something resembling the human figure, have obtained the name of Macleod's Maidens, and, in such a night, seemed no bad representatives of the Norwegian goddesses, called Choosers of the Slain or Riders of the Storm. [He goes on to mention the ancient battery of cannon on the platform beneath his window, the view of the two flat-topped mountains called Macleod's Dining Tables, and the noise of the cascade known as Rorie More's Nurse.][1]

This is impossible, even granting that one could discern features of the landscape so clearly at twelve o'clock of a misty night. Macleod's Maidens are not visible at Dunvegan; they stand eight miles away as the crow flies on the southern shore of Duirinish; that is, on the other side of the Dining Tables. Scott did not actually see them until the day *after* his experience of the haunted chamber. His memory has here done just what his imagination would have done if he had been constructing a fiction: that is, has blended a collection of impressive objects and given something more striking and romantic than actual fact. Scott himself once described his habit of modifying everything that went through his brain in a phrase that will serve as a sort of witty summary of the nature of his constructions, whether deliberate or unconscious: '[Clerk] is continually saying that I change his stories, whereas in fact I only put a cocked hat on their heads, and stick a cane into their hands—to make them fit for going into company.'[2]

Consider a group of recollections that are of particular importance for a comparative study of Scott and Boswell: the Boswellian anecdotes which Scott wrote for Croker's edition of the *Life of Johnson*. Here we have Scott in Boswell's own field. It is true that we cannot be entirely certain of the extent of his variations, for he gives an oral source for one of the stories and none at all for the others. An analysis of two of them, however, should convince any one that even if he had had his stories from Boswell himself, they would have come back riddled with 'circumstantial inaccuracy'.[3]

In the much-quoted note on the Douglas Cause Scott repre-

---

[1] Quoted by Lockhart in *Memoirs*, iv. 306, ch. XXXI.
[2] Ibid. i. 276, ch. VII.
[3] I omit consideration of the account (which he ascribes to Professor John Miller) of an altercation between Johnson and Adam Smith at Glasgow in Oct. 1773. Croker himself reprobated this anecdote, though not until after Scott's death. See *Life*, v. 369 n. 5.

sents Boswell ('I know not on what authority') as having 'headed
the mob which broke the windows of some of the judges, and of
Lord Auchinleck, his father, in particular'.[1] I think I can name
his authority: it was his friend John Ramsay of Ochtertyre, one
of the originals of Jonathan Oldbuck. Ramsay left voluminous
manuscript collections, of which a substantial portion has since
been published under the title *Scotland and Scotsmen in the Eighteenth Century*. Scott's Boswellian anecdotes may derive from
Ramsay's conversation, but I think it more likely that they go
back to the manuscript.[2] There, in a chapter of reminiscences
of Lord Auchinleck, Ramsay gives an account of the window-
breaking which is circumstantial and plausible. But of course
it does not say that Boswell broke his father's windows, for the
good reason that Lord Auchinleck, who had voted *for* Douglas,
was one of the heroes of that riotous evening. It was the windows of the Lord President and the other judges who had voted
against Douglas that suffered. What Ramsay had written was
that Boswell 'headed the mob which broke the judges' windows,
and insulted them in the most licentious manner'.[3] Scott, knowing that Lord Auchinleck was one of the Fifteen, and knowing
furthermore that he was not on the best terms with his son,
constructed a memory which was more dramatic than actual
fact. This is a clear case of the cocked hat.

The longest and most famous of the notes, besides giving a
good deal of miscellaneous information about Lord Auchinleck,
records two of his remarks. The first expresses Lord Auchinleck's
low opinion of Boswell's Corsican adventures and of Johnson:
'There 's nae hope for Jamie, mon. Jamie is gaen clean gyte.—
What do you think, mon? He 's done wi' Paoli—he 's off wi' the
land-louping scoundrel of a Corsican; and whose tail do you
think he has pinned himself to now, mon? A *dominie*, mon—an
auld dominie; he keeped a schule, and cau'd it an acaadamy.'
The second describes confidently the altercation at Auchinleck
between Johnson and Lord Auchinleck which Boswell had suppressed. It seems that Johnson asked Lord Auchinleck what
good Cromwell had ever done to his country, and the old judge

---

[1] *The Life of Johnson . . . by James Boswell*, ed. J. W. Croker, 1831, iii. 48 n.

[2] See the statement made by Dr. Gleig, an acquaintance, to Ramsay's editor:
'The MSS. which you are preparing for the press had been his recreation for years,
and he never failed to read a portion of them to every visitor whom he could prevail upon to listen' (*Scotland and Scotsmen*, i, p. xix).

[3] Ibid. 173.

replied, 'God, doctor! he gart kings ken that they had a *lith* in their neck.'[1]

When we read in Ramsay that Lord Auchinleck was offended with Boswell for going to Corsica, and that in 1774 he told Ramsay 'with more warmth than common, that the great Dr. Johnson ... was just a *dominie*, and the worst-bred dominie he had ever seen', we need have little doubt that we have found the source of all that is genuine in the first of these famous speeches. But Ramsay's manuscript furnishes nothing that could have served as the kernel of the second. 'Very different accounts', he says, 'were given of their famous altercation at Auchinleck. All that could be collected was that the disputants were equally hot and bigoted.'[2] Here, I think, Dr. G. B. Hill has given us the needed clue. 'Lord Auchinleck's famous saying had been anticipated by Quin, who ... had said that "on a thirtieth of January every king in Europe would rise with a crick in his neck." '[3] Anticipated indeed! My firm conviction is that Scott's account rests on nothing whatever except his memory of Boswell's own text and that anecdote about Quin. I do not mean that he consciously invented it. Knowing from Boswell that the altercation concerned Cromwell and Charles I, his mind played with the problem, searching for something appropriate. Sooner or later Quin's remark came into his consciousness, was reshaped slightly, and fitted in. The result was a brilliant historical fiction which, after telling it once or twice, he remembered as a fact.[4]

Yet I should not like to give the impression that Scott never remembered accurately. It has seemed to me that I could distinguish areas in which the unconscious creative impulse was very active, and others in which it was relatively inhibited. Scott always shows the greatest licence in dealing with chronology, and with the names and traits of historical personages, but he cleaves to what he believes to be literal fact in costume, architecture, and topography. Contrast, for example, the mass of literal detail of costume and architecture in *Marmion* with the melodrama of the plot; or the extraordinary manipulations

[1] *The Life of Johnson . . . by James Boswell*, ed. J. W. Croker, 1831, iii. 78–9 n.
[2] John Ramsay, op. cit. (see p. 182, n. 2), i. 172 n. 2, 175–6, 176 n.
[3] *Life*, v. 383 n.
[4] The practice of taking a telling speech or phrase from one context and fitting it into another is so characteristic of Scott's method in the novels that it hardly needs illustration. It was this trait of Scott's, no doubt, which caused Hazlitt, somewhat unjustly, to say that where Shakespeare *created*, Scott *compiled*.

of chronology and identity in *Kenilworth* with the insistence that the reader follow the story with an actual ground-plan of the castle in his hand. This cleavage is exactly what one would expect, but we can discuss it better after a somewhat general consideration of the relations of perceiving, remembering, and imagining.

Perceiving is not a simple mechanical process operating similarly in two minds faced with an identical situation.[1] It is shot through with imaging, with valuing, even with judging. 'It is directed by interest and by feeling, and may be dominated by certain crucial features of the objects and scenes dealt with.' That is, some features of the situation will stand out over the others, and will form a sort of nucleus about which the rest of the detail will shape itself. Temperament, interests, and attitudes often determine what will be perceived. And a great part of what is believed to be perceived is in fact inferred. Social conventions may affect powerfully not merely what one imagines but even what one perceives. A shift of sensibility such as that which separates Pope from Wordsworth does not mean merely a different taste in poetry; it means ultimately the perception of a different world.

At the basic level of perception Scott and Boswell show less difference than one would have expected. Scott still perceived the world with eighteenth-century eyes. But we infer that he must have had a double vision: side by side with the world which he would have agreed with Boswell in calling the 'real' world was another which he would probably have called the world of romance. The romantic vision did not completely cover the field of the 'real' world; there were some features (features corresponding to Scott's strong antiquarian and collecting interests) which appear in only one mode. Scott, like Byron, held the romantic mode to be 'a factitious state';[2] he published romances because they amused people and made him money, but he made no claim to be considered a seer or a teacher.

We commonly think of the brain as a storehouse, and memory as the setting forth of things actually stored. Every specific event, on this assumption, makes a literal, physical trace in the

---

[1] The psychological theory in what follows is from F. C. Bartlett, *Remembering, A Study in Experimental and Social Psychology*, Cambridge, 1932, especially pp. 31-3.

[2] *Don Juan*, IV. xix.

substance of the brain, which recollection somehow gets at and
re-excites. If recollection cannot get at the trace, we say a
person has 'forgotten'. If what is presented as recall is de-
monstrably at variance with historical fact, we say that the
person has 'imagined' it.

So long as it was believed that Boswell was a stenographer
who took down conversations verbatim on the spot, there was
no great difficulty in accepting his records for what they pur-
ported to be. But when the recovery of his materials made
clear in the most unequivocal manner that his first or basic
notations were generally hints or clues, his claim to have remembered so amply and with such detail naturally roused
incredulity. Some scholars have believed that a good part of
the *Life of Johnson* is not 'memory' but 'imagination'. The notes
or journal, it is said, furnished him with an outline which he
filled in much as a playwright expands a scenario. The problem
of defining Boswell's use of imagination is the most difficult and
delicate of this entire study. I have no doubt that the pages of
the *Life are* an imaginative reconstruction, but I wish to differ-
entiate his controlled use of imagination from that free imaginative play that results in fiction. I wish, in short, to maintain that
a man can use his imagination and yet remember 'accurately'.

What is not realized, I think, by those who have written
about Boswell's memory is that certain distinguished modern
students of psychology believe that imagination inevitably plays
a part in *all* remembering, just as it does in all perceiving. The
theory of literal traces in the brain is now sharply attacked.
Recollection, according to F. C. Bartlett, 'is an imaginative reconstruction, or construction, built out of the relation of our
attitude towards a whole active mass of organized past reactions
or experience, and to a little outstanding detail which commonly
appears in image or in language form'. The outstanding detail
gains its prominence through a valuation of items, depending
upon the person's interests. Memories do not come out of a
storehouse; they are *constructed* as we need them, and in most
cases they do not correspond at all closely to historical fact.[1]
But granted an overwhelming *interest* in a certain kind of details,
and granted the right kind of 'organized setting', the imaginative
construct would reproduce history. Boswell himself said that at
first he had some difficulty in recalling Johnson's conversation,

[1] Op. cit. (see p. 184, n. 1), pp. 213–14.

but that after he got himself 'strongly impregnated with the Johnsonian aether' he could retain and recollect it 'with more facility and exactness'.[1] This is only a witty and literary way of putting Bartlett's theory. Granted the purity of the 'Johnsonian aether', the imaginative reconstruction could be trusted to be not merely appropriate but as close to what Johnson really said as any condensed or selective report could be. Details in which Boswell was strongly interested would be sharply and fully perceived, and would furnish the nucleus for his recollection. Through his method of notation this detail, by being early verbalized, would become even more strongly anchored, so that the imaginative reconstruction would operate within an area which was at once rich in material and restricted in scope. The principal difference between recall and constructive imagination is that in recall one specially organized mass remains central, while in constructive imagination no particular scheme is central, and there is freer range from interest to interest. Boswell's detail kept him anchored to his central setting and kept his imagination to the limits within which 'accurate' reconstruction is possible. The vividness of his writing shows that imagination has been at work, while his circumstantial accuracy shows how scrupulously he has limited its operation.

For Boswell was one of those extremely rare persons who have a conscience about anecdotes and will discard the results of constructive imagination when reference to an earlier recording shows that the story has developed into something better than the truth. His awareness of the progressive improvement of stories is constant, and his honesty in trying always to get back to unimproved versions is remarkable.[2] Compare him with his rival Lockhart—I use the word deliberately, for I am not sure sometimes that I do not *like* Lockhart's book better than Boswell's. Pick out a succession of passages from Lockhart that you want to read aloud to people: the run keg of brandy and the young minister ruefully closing the Bible; the moving hand in the candlelight piling up the pages of *Waverley*; the sentimental pig; the furious letter about Blackwood's proposed alterations of *The Black Dwarf*; the deathbed[3]—they are all

---

[1] *Life*, i. 421, 1 July 1763.

[2] See the testimony of Dugald Stewart, quoted in G. B. Hill, *Johnsonian Miscellanies*, ii. 425. For a typical example from Boswell himself, see *Life*, v. 339 n. 5.

[3] *Memoirs*, i. 270–1, ch. VII; iv. 171–3, ch. XXVII; vi. 239–42, ch. XLIX; v. 157–9, ch. XXXVII; x. 217–18, ch. LXXXIII.

wonderful and you cannot trust any of them. You know that if you investigate them, they will evaporate. It will turn out that there is some truth in them, but that things didn't 'really' happen that way. Circumstantial detail has been altered for striking effect. But when you read one of the Johnsonian conversations which Boswell gives on his own authority, you know that so far as any human testimony can be trusted, that can.

Scott felt a clear distinction between the products of what I have called average or literal perception and those of constructive imagination, and derived the keenest pleasure from the juxtaposition of the two. No other English author, I should suppose, has ever taken such delight in exposing his *sources*: here are the real facts, here is what I made of them. Wordsworth furnishes a strong contrast. *The White Doe of Rylstone* is based upon matter precisely like that which Scott used in *The Lay of the Last Minstrel*, and, if it had been written by Scott, would have been accompanied by voluminous antiquarian notes, showing in detail just how the original history had been cooked. Wordsworth was rather angry when Scott offered to send him a batch of this material while he was at work on the *Doe*: he did not wish his conception of the poem to be affected by it, and he certainly did not intend to print it.[1] But Scott, having presented a romance, seems almost to feel under obligation to deflate it by parallel columns of history. It is a paradox something like Byron's alternations of romance and satire in *Don Juan*.

But we cannot say 'history' and leave it at that. Scott was more a child of the new sensibility than he himself realized. He was not aware of the fact that much of the matter in his parallel columns was coming out of his memory, and that his memory had already romanticized it strongly. No man wrote more pleasant or vivid notes than Scott, and for a good reason: they were often half fiction. In fact, to a mature reader the professed fictions often suffer by comparison with the unacknowledged ones. I have never been able to free myself from a feeling that the Introduction to *The Bride of Lammermoor* steals the show.

How far, one asks in conclusion, dare one go in generalizing from these observations? Have we anything more than a description of two highly unrepresentative individuals? Is Scott's imaginative memory any different from that of the anecdotist

[1] Wordsworth to Scott, 14 May 1808 (*The Letters of William and Dorothy Wordsworth: The Middle Years*, ed. E. de Selincourt, i. 458 e).

of any period? And was not Boswell so much *sui generis* that it would be futile to take him as typical of anything?

The objection as concerns Boswell seems the stronger. The mental organism with which he was endowed was certainly abnormal. And no other writer of whom we have record seems to have followed his peculiar method of journalizing or to have submitted his memory to so much deliberate self-discipline. As Mr. Bronson has pointed out, there are the youthful exercises in mimicry;[1] there are the reiterated memoranda to himself urging restraint and reasonableness; there are the regular nota-tions in his collection of anecdotes, 'I was present'; finally there is the lifelong discipline of the journal, in some respects the most ambitious ever undertaken. Of what other journalist can it be said that he sat up four entire nights in one week recollecting and writing in his journal what he thought worthy of preserva-tion?[2] If any one would train himself by the Boswellian system, would take notes persistently and consult them scrupulously, he would certainly astonish himself and his friends by the rich-ness and accuracy of his circumstantial recall.

Yet if we indulge for a moment in a game of speculation, I think we shall agree that it would be most remarkable to find a man pursuing such discipline in the nineteenth century but not at all surprising to find one doing it in the eighteenth. All the devices leading to circumstantial memory: the note-taking, the journalizing, the review and re-review, are as much symptoms as causes. People then were generally *interested* in personal detail. Boswell is the extreme example, but he fits into his time. There was tremendous social pressure on the individual mind to perceive in the average mode and to eschew free imagination in recall. Any scholar who has attacked biographical problems in both centuries knows how different in quality the basic materials for the two periods are. It is hardly too much to say that, given time enough, one can find the answer to any factual question concerning an eighteenth-century author. The records, both manuscript and printed, are abundant and trustworthy. Men and women then wrote informative letters and kept de-tailed journals. Newspapers and magazine accounts were fac-

[1] B. H. Bronson, *Johnson and Boswell*, University of California Publications in English, vol. iii, pp. 404–5.
[2] *Life*, i. 461, 30 July 1763. 'An exertion', he continues, 'which, during the first part of my acquaintance with Johnson, I frequently made.'

tual, and though they swarmed with faked news, the genuine and the spurious were not blended. People really feared the dangerous prevalence of the imagination. In the nineteenth century, biographical material is often scanty, sometimes voluminous to the point of embarrassment, and never trustworthy. If Byron had lived fifty years earlier, is it conceivable that we should be in doubt as to the nature of his deformity, even as to which of his feet was deformed? Could an author of the prominence of Shelley present so many unsolved biographical riddles if he had been a contemporary of Gray? The power to admire the average, the norm, the area of sanity in human experience; the power to hold this by a kind of memory in which the imagination was made to work within the limits of literal circumstance; finally, the power to express this in words —these things were given Boswell by his time. In many respects wildly romantic, he was in his re-creation of the past the fullest expression of the Age of Reason.

The characteristic mode of the Romantic period is strongly imaginative recall: Wordsworth's *Prelude*. There is no longer powerful social pressure in favour of average perception and 'accurate' memory. It becomes not merely permissible but praiseworthy to mingle a larger amount of inference in perception, as of imagination in recall. 'Facts' of life become less important than what is conceived to be their 'real' meaning.

In this Scott is a bridge figure, much less advanced in his sensibility than Wordsworth, but with enough of the new temper to understand and like the people on both sides of him. While his perception is rooted firmly in the eighteenth century, his imagination in the mode of fiction has freed itself completely from the restrictions which that century imposed. But he does not, like the more advanced Romantics, believe in the creative imagination as revelatory of truth. Fiction, for him, is make-believe and amusement. Hence, even in his most magnificent writing, he seldom escapes a tone of humorous self-exposure. It was in the mode of memory, where the workings of the imagination were unconscious, that his mind was most completely at one with itself.

ROBERT BURNS

R. DEWAR

IT was at the age of fourteen, during the harvest of 1773, that Burns—in his own phrase—'first committed the sin of RHYME'. The occasion is described, frankly and at some length, in his autobiographical letter to Dr. John Moore.

You know our country custom of coupling a man and woman together as Partners in the labors of Harvest.—In my fifteenth autumn, my Partner was a bewitching creature who just counted an autumn less.—My scarcity of English denies me the power of doing her justice in that language; but you know the Scotch idiom, She was a bonie, sweet, sonsie lass.—In short, she altogether unwittingly to herself, initiated me in a certain delicious Passion, which in spite of acid Disappointment, gin-horse Prudence and bookworm Philosophy, I hold to be the first of human joys, our dearest pleasure here below.—How she caught the contagion I can't say; you medical folks talk much of infection by breathing the same air, the touch, &c. but I never expressly told her that I loved her.—Indeed I did not well know myself, why I liked so much to loiter behind with her, when returning in the evening from our labors; why the tones of her voice made my heartstrings thrill like an Eolian harp; and particularly, why my pulse beat such a furious ratann when I looked and fingered over her hand, to pick out the nettle-stings and thistles.— Among her other love-inspiring qualifications, she sung sweetly; and 'twas her favorite reel to which I attempted giving an embodied vehicle in rhyme. . . . Thus with me began Love and Poesy.

Burns never printed the song, 'O once I lov'd a bonny lass', which, thus inspired, marks the beginning of his career as a poet.[1] But when, in 1783, on awakening to a clear consciousness of his gift and vocation, he began his first Commonplace Book, this piece was the first he transcribed. A 'very puerile and silly' performance Burns thought it in 1783: its transcription and the detailed criticism he appended to it in the Commonplace Book are all the more significant. Not its art but its origin earned it this recognition. In 1783, as at the later date of his letter to Moore, the opening word of the bard's story proper must con-

---

[1] It had to wait till Currie's edition of 1800: from which apparently Johnson copied it (some four years later, and with one or two misprints) into his *Scots Musical Museum*, vol. vi, no. 551; for the tune to which it is set in Johnson is not the 'reel' to which Burns wrote it—viz., 'I am a man unmarried'.

cern 'the feelings of green eighteen in the company of the mistress
of his heart' and announce his belief in 'some connection between
Love, and Music and Poetry'. The lasses of his parish world,
the tunes they danced to and the songs they sang—these, rather
than printed books, were the reading that inspired and committed Burns to poetry. And Burns himself seems to have
wished this fact to be emphasized in his story, to have attached
greater importance to it than most of his critics and expositors
have.

Evidence of this is not confined to the places cited. The motto
on the title-page and the opening words of the preface to his
Kilmarnock edition, his preference for the word 'Bard' rather
than 'Poet' to describe his character, his anxiety—even at the
height of his fame, in Edinburgh—to avoid being taken for a
learned well-read writer (not so much of a pose as some have
thought it to be); these whispered hints plainly bid us remember
the years 1773–83, as well as the *annus mirabilis* 1785, if we would
render a just account. We can point also to the reply he sent,
in March 1787, to Mrs. Scott of Wauchope. Her lively verses,
which occasioned it, expressed a doubt that Burns had been

> Wi' ploughmen schooled, wi' ploughmen fed.
> I doubt it sair, ye've drawn your knowledge
> Either frae grammar-school or college.

But no word of indebtedness to schoolmaster or to books occurs
in Burns's reply. All we get is another allusion to the harvest-
field episode of 1773.

But to return to the letter to Dr. Moore, most important of
all documents for the student of Burns's character, whether as
man or as poet. This is the best evidence of any, if only we can
avoid the common error of reading it piecemeal. Read as a
whole and in the light of previous letters that passed, this 'honest
narrative' (as Burns calls it) is seen to be reminiscent throughout, and all but born of the wish that men would not forget the
bard of 1773 in the poet of 1785.

Burns and Dr. Moore never met. Their correspondence was
due to their common friend, Mrs. Dunlop, and to the interest
she awakened in Moore by her gift of a copy of the Kilmarnock
Poems. This interest prompted him, as the more experienced
man of letters, to offer advice. And this advice, as Burns knew
only too well, chimed exactly with much he heard to the same

purpose among the literati of Edinburgh. In a letter which Moore dispatched while Burns was on his Border Tour, and which he probably did not receive till his return to Mauchline in early June 1787, it forms the chief feature. Alluding to the Edinburgh *Poems*, which apparently confirmed Moore in his opinion of Burns's genius, he writes: 'Some of the poems you have added in this last edition are very beautiful, particularly the *Winter Night*, the *Address to Edinburgh*, *Green grow the Rashes*, and the two songs immediately following,[1] the latter of which is exquisite.' Next come three sentences that must have warmed the cockles of Burns's heart, till he discovered how incidental they were in Moore's thought of him: 'By the way, I imagine you have a peculiar talent for such compositions, which you ought to indulge. No kind of poetry demands more delicacy or higher polishing. Horace is more admired on account of his *Odes* than all his other writings.' Then, blotting out any hopes he had raised, and proceeding to his main purpose:

But nothing now added is equal to your *Vision* and *Cotter's Saturday Night*. In these are united fine imagery, natural and pathetic description, with sublimity of language and thought. It is evident that you already possess a great variety of expression and command of the English language; you ought therefore to deal more sparingly, for the future, in the provincial dialect—why should you, by using *that*, limit the number of your admirers to those who understand the Scottish, when you can extend it to all persons of taste who understand the English language. In my opinion, you should plan some larger work than any you have as yet attempted. I mean reflect upon some proper subject, and arrange the plan in your mind, without beginning to execute any part of it till you have studied most of the best English poets, and read a little more of history.

And so on, to the more specific hints that Burns read the Greek and Roman stories in some abridgement, make himself master of the heathen mythology, and study with more attention the history of France and Great Britain from the beginning of Henry the Seventh's reign. 'I know very well', he concludes encouragingly, 'you have a mind capable of attaining knowledge by a shorter process than is commonly used, and I am certain you are capable of making a better use of it, when attained, than is generally done.' Now all this, kindly meant though it was, must have surprised, and perhaps disappointed, Burns not a little.

---

[1] i.e. 'Again rejoicing Nature sees', and 'The gloomy Night was gathering fast'.

The very first letter he had written Dr. Moore, only six months earlier, implied the futility of such advice in his case.

The hope to be admired for Ages [he had said] is, in by far the greater part of what are even Authors of repute, an unsubstantial dream.—For my part, my first ambition was, and still my strongest wish is, to please my Compeers, the rustic Inmates of the Hamlet, while everchanging language and manners will allow me to be relished and understood.—I am very willing to admit that I have some poetical abilities; and as few, if any Writers, either moral or poetical, are intimately acquainted with the classes of Mankind among whom I have chiefly mingled, I may have seen men and manners in a different phasis, which may assist originality of thought. —Still I know very well, the novelty of my character has by far the greatest share in the learned and polite notice I have lately got; and in a language where Pope and Churchill have raised the laugh, and Shenstone and Gray drawn the tear; where Thomson and Beattie have painted the landskip, and Littleton and Collins described the heart; I am not vain enough to hope for distinguished Poetic fame.

Unless we bear in mind these earlier letters, we miss the point of the 'honest narrative' that Burns composed in August 1787. It was addressed to a man whom he regarded as a 'Judge of the first character'. Nevertheless, its one aim and purpose was to correct, however obliquely, Moore's estimate of his talent; and to show him what the *Poems* and their previous correspondence had apparently failed to make clear—that the person he advised was not at all the sort of man or poet whose fame could be established, or whose nature was likely to take a better ply, if he accepted and tried to follow the advice given.

It is true that, here at last, Burns discovers to us the full extent of his reading, and frankly admits some indebtedness to books for what he calls 'critic-craft'. But too much can be, and is generally, made of these passages of his narrative. However useful and interesting in themselves, they are, when all is said, but eddies in the stream. The impression they leave, even taken altogether, is that Burns felt his acquaintance with such aids and sources of knowledge to be inconsiderable—certainly nothing to boast of in one who was himself an author of some mark. First and last, the thing Burns emphasizes is, not his reading habits, but his 'strong appetite for sociability', a 'social disposition', which (as he says), 'like our catechism definition of Infinitude, was "without bounds or limits" '. This, and its consequences during his youth and early manhood, are the ruling idea and central theme of his writing. As numerous and extended as any allusions to reading and study, and more significant, are the episodes that provoked such confessions as these:

The great misfortune of my life was, never to have An Aim.

Till my twenty-third year—Vive l'amour et vive la bagatelle, were my sole principles of action.

What else ought one to expect in an autobiography that begins by remarking the writer's resemblance to Solomon—'excepting the trifling affair of Wisdom', and that runs down on the warning: 'You can now, Sir, form a pretty near guess what sort of a Wight he is whom for some time you have honored with your correspondence.—That Fancy and Whim, keen Sensibility and riotous Passions may still make him zig-zag in his future path of life, is far from being improbable'?—Yet there never was a truer piece of self-portraiture: and for the moment, it seems to have shaken the confidence of Burns's mentor. There is no record of further advice from Dr. Moore till June of 1789. If, then, it is merely the old say—'abandon the Scottish stanza and dialect and adopt the measure and language of modern English poetry'—the blame must be shared by Burns. In reopening the correspondence, in the preceding January, he had written like a man half-converted, and enclosed his 'Epistle to Fintry, requesting a Favour'—an experiment in the manner of Pope; following it a few months later with a still more English, though poorer thing, the 'Ode to the Memory of Mrs. Oswald of Auchencruive'. These were clearly Moore's cue.

Now, coming upon this evidence, the question one asks is: Why did Dr. Moore, and not only he, but the whole world of taste of Burns's day, fail to acknowledge the Bard, and persist in lauding instead the book-taught, derivative Poet in Burns? The answer is that the advent of Burns—his sudden passage from obscurity to fame during 1786-7—unfortunately stamped him, for his own generation and for many a student since, as, before all else, the author of a single book: the *Poems*. And the *Poems*, whether in its Kilmarnock or in its several Edinburgh editions, is not remarkable either for the number or for the quality of its songs. Some dozen pieces in all—only half of them love-songs and perhaps not half of these worthy to rank with his best—this tiny sheaf is all of the harvest Burns carried to market in 1786–7 that revealed the man with whom Love and Poesy began together. All the rest, bulk for bulk eleven times as much, and in quite other kinds than song, excellent and characteristic though it often is, betrays a Burns more self-conscious and ambitious than the naïve singer of parish love-themes to parish tunes, a Burns at once disciple and rival of the old masters in the Scottish vernacular, the deliberate and in-spired artist rather than the simple Bard. Very naturally, of the two men thus announced to the world, it was not the author of the few unequal pages of songs who excited most remark, but his giant-like neighbour. Nor, when his book was 'enlarged' in 1793 (the only enlargement it received during his lifetime), did Burns do anything to correct this disproportion of its parts. The new pieces then added—all but one—could only confirm and deepen the impression already current, that wit and satire, rather than song, was this man's natural mode of speech and response to life. It was an erroneous impression none the less.

Suppose we take a look at the two men, the song-wright, and the wit, as they appear in the *Poems*. Here are some verses from the tinier portion of the book, the songs portion—from 'My Nanie, O':

1. Behind yon hills where Stinchar flows,
     'Mang moors an' mosses many, O,
   The wintry sun the day has clos'd,
     And I'll awa to Nanie, O!

2. The westlin wind blaws loud an' shill;
     The night's baith mirk and rainy, O;
   But I'll get my plaid an' out I'll steal,
     An' owre the hill to Nanie, O. . . .

5. A country lad is my degree,
     An' few there be that ken me, O;
   But what care I how few they be,
     I'm welcome ay to Nanie, O.

6. My riches a's my penny-fee,
     An' I maun guide it cannie, O;
   But warl's gear ne'er troubles me,
     My thoughts are a', my Nanie, O.

7. Our auld Guidman delights to view
     His sheep an' kye thrive bonie, O;
   But I'm as blythe that hauds his pleugh,
     An' has nae care but Nanie, O.

Or take these, from 'Green grow the Rashes', which Dr. Moore
so liked:

1.   There's nought but care on ev'ry han',
        In ev'ry hour that passes, O:
     What signifies the life o' man,
        An' 'twere na for the lasses, O.

2.   The warly race may riches chase,
        An' riches still may fly them, O;
     An' tho' at last they catch them fast,
        Their hearts can ne'er enjoy them, O.

3.   But gie me a cannie hour at e'en,
        My arms about my Dearie, O;
     An' warly cares, an' warly men,
        May a' gae tapsalteerie, O!

These pieces, like all one would care to quote from this part
(at most, perhaps as much again), were tune-born, in a world
obviously narrow, but satisfying and ample enough for the
man who made them. They may stand for the earlier Burns,
to show how he felt and wrote in the days before he dared even
to dream of printing. Over against these let us set some passages
from the other, the witty and more imposing, part of his book,
and let them refer to and recall (as distinctly as may be) the
little world of the songs. Here is a glimpse of a cottage interior
from 'The Twa Dogs', part of Luath's attempt to convince
Caesar that poor folk are 'no sae wretched 's ane wad think':

     That merry day the year begins,
     They bar the door on frosty wins;
     The nappy reeks wi' mantling ream,
     An' sheds a heart-inspiring steam;
     The luntin pipe, an' sneeshin mill,
     Are handed round wi' right guid will;
     The cantie, auld folks, crackin crouse,
     The young anes ranting thro' the house—
     My heart has been sae fain to see them,
     That I for joy hae barkit wi' them.

Next, a thumb-nail sketch of Burns himself at the end of a day's
toil, from 'The Vision':

2.   The Thresher's weary *flingin-tree*,
        The lee-lang day had tir'd me;
     And when the Day had clos'd his e'e,
                Far i' the West,
     Ben i' the *Spence*, right pensivelie,
                I gaed to rest.

3. There, lanely, by the ingle-cheek,
    I sat and ey'd the spewing reek,
    That fill'd, wi' hoast-provoking smeek,
            The auld, clay biggin;
    And heard the restless rattons squeak
            About the riggin.

4. All in this mottie, misty clime,
    I backward mus'd on wasted time,
    How I had spent my youthfu' prime,
            An' done nae-thing,
    But stringin blethers up in rhyme
            For fools to sing.

5. Had I to guid advice but harkit,
    I might, by this, hae led a market,
    Or strutted in a Bank and clarkit
            My cash-account:
    While here, half-mad, half-fed, half-sarkit,
            Is a' th' amount.

One more quotation, just for a glance at this world out of doors
—the going home of the crowd from Mauchline Holy Fair or
annual celebration of the Sacrament, a day of interminable
sermons, relieved (according to taste) by bouts of hard drinking,
or the planning of assignations, or maybe both:

26. Now *Clinkumbell*, wi' rattlin tow,
            Begins to jow an' croon;
    Some swagger hame, the best they dow,
            Some wait the afternoon.
    At slaps the billies halt a blink,
            Till lasses strip their shoon:
    Wi' faith an' hope, an' love an' drink,
            They're a' in famous tune
                    For crack that day.

27. How monie hearts this day converts
            O' Sinners and o' Lasses!
    Their hearts o' stane gin night are gane,
            As saft as ony flesh is.
    There's some are fou o' love divine;
            There's some are fou o' brandy;
    An' monie jobs that day begin,
            May end in Houghmagandie
                    Some ither day.

Here the wit begins to turn satirical, and to fetch up that

coarseness of allusion, which more men could digest in 1786
than in our time. The satirical in Burns leans a good deal that
way: but it must serve here to state the fact, to refer to things
like the speech of Death in 'Death and Dr. Hornbook', and to
remind ourselves that the well-worn tag

> O wad some Pow'r the giftie gie us
> *To see oursels as others see us!*

is the moral appended to a poem 'To a Louse, on seeing one on
a Lady's Bonnet at Church'.

These illustrations of and allusions to the wit and satire which
so predominated over song in Burns's book—that is to say, in
the writings by which he published himself to the world between
1786 and 1794—have been chosen (as I said) for the closeness
of their reference to the parish world of the songs. On trial they
will be found to be all the more justly representative of this
phase of his genius; to be drawn from the poems which are most
Scottish and at the same time most characteristically Burnsian.
What is the mighty difference, then, between the two voices we
have heard, that Burns's contemporaries should have favoured
one and ignored the other? Has the resort to Ramsay and
Fergusson—more especially Fergusson—for new measures and
a wider range of topics done more than make Burns aware
of his faculty? 'Crooning to a body's sel' ' (his own phrase)
describes exactly the ambition that made the songs. Tell that
ambition that a predecessor, Fergusson, when not a year older
than Burns and really no more gifted, had successfully published
a book; give it, in a word, an eye to an audience beyond itself:
are not the poems a probable result? Is not this sense of an
audience their chief distinction from the songs? A change of
direction and aim there may be, but nothing surely to imply a
break in our author's character as a writer. The wit of the
poems, though perhaps muffled and subdued, was yet not entirely absent from the songs. And when at last let go, it ought
not, therefore, to have been mistaken for the ordinary type—
born of a sense of superiority to and revulsion from life. Jovial,
rollicking, insolent rather than venomous, it loves life passionately; the follies and vices of men as much as, perhaps more
than, their virtues. It is a wit that might well be defined as song
gone wrong. But there was the book, so disproportionately
built, its halfpennyworth of song to so vast a deal of wit. How
did Burns come to lay this trap for the deception of men's

judgements? The brief answer is that, like so much else in his
career, Burns's book was largely a child of impulse.

We have seen, from the letter to Dr. Moore, that till his
twenty-third year Burns contrived to live without much thought
of his future. His motto had been *Vive l'amour et vive la bagatelle.*
He named that year because it was in the winter of 1781–2 that,
wishing at last 'to set about doing something in life',[1] he went
to Irvine to learn and practise the trade of flax-dressing. The
experiment, through no fault of Burns, was a bad failure; and
the spring saw him back on the farm, where, to add to his
misfortunes, he found a father past work and rapidly declining
in health. Indeed round about his twenty-third birthday proved
to be one of the most unlucky periods in Burns's life: everything seemed to go most wrong, just when it was most desirable
—considering the temperament of this recent convert to seriousness—that everything should have gone specially well. There
can be little doubt that the increasingly 'regardless' conduct of
the man after his return to Lochlea was largely due to the
misery and disappointments of this time, crowned as they were,
in February 1784, by his father's death in almost bankrupt
circumstances. And yet, in recounting the Irvine experiment
and its consequences, it is not upon these 'acts of God' that
Burns lays the stress. The stark honesty of the man refused to let
him excuse himself so easily and as another man might have done.
It had made him confess, at the risk of becoming a laughing-
stock, the calf-love that occasioned his first verses. At this
greater crisis, it drove him to face the graver risk of being
despised. 'The principal thing which gave his mind a turn'
during the Irvine period was, we are told,—not the failure of
the flax-dressing business, but—'a bosom-friendship with a young
fellow', the seaman, Richard Brown. A brief reference to this
man's adventures and misfortunes, and Burns sketches his
character and its influence upon himself as follows:

This gentleman's mind was fraught with courage, independance,
Magnanimity, and every noble, manly virtue.—I loved him, I admired him, to a degree of enthusiasm; and I strove to imitate him.—
In some measure I succeeded: I had the pride before, but he taught
it to flow in proper channels.—His knowledge of the world was vastly
superiour to mine, and I was all attention to learn.—He was the only

[1] His brother Gilbert, with a likely hit at the truth, says explicitly that Burns
wished to marry.

man I ever saw who was a greater fool than myself when WOMAN
was the presiding star; but he spoke of a certain fashionable failing
with levity, which hitherto I had regarded with horror.—Here his
friendship did me a mischief.

The consequence was (he goes on to say) that soon after he
resumed the plough, he wrote the poem we know as 'A Poet's
Welcome to his love-begotten Daughter'. The piece itself has
both beauty and charm enough to counter-balance its very outspoken sallies of wit: it is a real poem, and by no means a bad
testimonial to the fundamental soundness of character of the
man who wrote it. But Burns's citation of it in his autobiography
—like his earlier citation of his first song—was for the sake of
the occasion that gave rise to it, not for the sake of the poem
itself. And that occasion, the birth of his first illegitimate child
in November 1784, was unfortunately not the only error of this
kind that he was led to commit through his 'bosom-friendship'
with Richard Brown. Neither the unpleasant notoriety that he
achieved by this first slip—the fact that the parish 'teased his
name in kintra clatter'—nor the discipline of the cutty-stool
which the church administered as the police-authority of the
time, served to steady him; they seem rather to have stung him
to further rebellion. We need not stop to draw a chronological
table of these *affaires* in Burns's life, even though it might not
leave us, as it left Robert Louis Stevenson, 'comparatively
speechless'. But one more must be chronicled here, because,
by almost extinguishing his chances of success as a man of the
world, it led indirectly to the publication of the *Poems*. Within
eighteen months of the birth of Betty Paton's child, Burns found
himself faced with Jean Armour and a similar complication.
And this time, his pride as well as his conscience was wounded:
for after salving the latter by giving Jean a written declaration
of marriage—it was the best, if also the least, he could do in the
circumstances—he had to learn that Jean's father absolutely
refused to have him for a son-in-law, and compelled Jean to
mutilate her 'paper'. This was the 'shocking affair' of the letter
to Moore, which even then Burns confessed he could not 'bear
to recollect', and which so darkened his prospects at home that
he decided to emigrate at the first opportunity to Jamaica.

That, as Burns himself would have us read it, is the story of
the downward course of his fortunes from the day he departed
for Irvine, determined to 'set about doing something in life',

till the middle of 1786, when his fortunes touched their nadir. The fire that burnt down his shop in Irvine, the fight with bankruptcy and then his father's death at Lochlea, bad seed and bad harvests after the move to Mossgiel—these blows of fate are duly recorded by him. But, as he looked at himself and the issue in 1786, he saw truly that the root-cause of all was his weakness for 'rapture-giving Woman', and the 'mischief' which that weakness had allowed Richard Brown to do him.

And Richard Brown, therefore, in his degree—as well as the poet Fergusson—must stand sponsor to the Kilmarnock *Poems*. His 'mischief' maimed, for the time being at least, the innocent singer of love that Burns had been in his beginnings: a great part of the coarseness one finds in some of the poems derives more probably from this than from anything Burns found in Fergusson's writings. These last, which he seems to have come by for the first time after the return to Lochlea, did Burns nothing but good: they practically saved the poet from going down with the man. For rhyme had been given up by Burns in the serious fit that took him to Irvine. And after his return, as the fit passed and his days became more aimless and whim-ridden than ever, the poet in him seems also to have been allowed to rot in idleness—till (in his own words) 'meeting with Fergusson's Scotch Poems, I strung anew my wildly-sounding, rustic lyre with emulating vigour'. It was the one piece of good fortune that befell Burns during these bad years: and from sheer gratitude, he could never praise Fergusson enough. What he found in this poet—and for the first time in all his career—was an example of sustained and really distin-guished use of the Scots vernacular he loved—applied, more-over, to the portrayal of the life and manners of a chosen class and a defined locality, the burgess-life of the author's Edinburgh. It was nourishment precisely suited to his genius; and the pity of it is that Burns's meeting with Fergusson did not precede his 'bosom-friendship' with Brown. So the poet and the man might have proved better teamsters than they did. As it was, Fergus-son's potency to rouse the poet came in time, at least to break the fall of the man. Why, Burns asked himself, should he not do for his own Ayrshire parish what Fergusson had done for his Edinburgh? And so the years of his most riotous living, between 1783 and 1786, produced a harvest of legitimate poetry as well as of illegitimate children. And faced with Jamaica and exile because of the latter, Burns decided to solace himself, if not to rehabilitate his character, by publishing the former.

On this impulse and in these circumstances did Burns produce his book. That he had an eye, perhaps, to men's opinion of his character, as well as to his own solace, may be inferred from the selection he made from his manuscripts. In several of the pieces chosen, echoes of his wayward life may easily be detected: something of pride as well as of honesty, no doubt, made him print these; Richard Brown should peer at us over Fergusson's shoulder. But the remarkable thing is that the louder and more obvious echoes were silenced by him altogether. He might give the 'Epistle to John Rankine', with its cloaked allusion to his Betty; but the more direct and more poetical 'Welcome' was held back. 'Adam Armour's Prayer', 'The Court of Equity', even 'The Jolly Beggars' (which some to-day account his masterpiece) also remained in manuscript. It is very noticeable also that while plenty of fun is made of theology, and while numerous incidental passages show his disrespect for the discipline of the Church, 'Holy Willie's Prayer', the finest and most acid attack he ever made upon the spying interference of ministers and their kirk sessions, was another poem withheld. Rebel as he was and had been in his life, Burns apparently was just a tiny bit willing to avoid shocking the world quite as much in his new character of the poet, as he had shocked it in his own person. He spruced and tidied himself, a little—the little that the Lucifer in his nature would permit. Perhaps, after all, the mood that rejected so much of his stock of wit might have moved him to give us more songs than he did, if only his stock of these had been more ample. But most of the songs he had by him in 1786 belonged to the pre-'mischief' period of his life; and apart from his knowledge that their fount had been muddied, his interest in them had no doubt cooled from his contact with, and eager emulation of, the maturer style of Fergusson during more recent years. However it was—and even though, in 1787, the little parcel of songs was swelled to thrice its size in 1786—the book Burns rose by remained disproportionate in its parts, and a less clear index to his poetical character than we could wish.

For what was Burns's reaction to the world's reception of his book? He had made it principally for the sake of being thought 'a clever fellow', though an exile. And success, however much it gratified his vanity, did not at once change his purpose of emigrating. The profits of the Kilmarnock edition, he says, were 'near twenty pounds.—This . . . came very seasonable, as I was about to indent myself for want of money to pay my freight.—So soon as I was master of nine guineas, the price of wafting me to the torrid zone, I bespoke a passage in the very first ship that was to sail.' But, as everybody knows, that ship never sailed for Burns. The new friends his book made him in his own neighbourhood and county began to talk of a second edition; and, when his Kilmarnock publisher refused this venture on the only terms Burns could afford to offer, news that his fame had reached Edinburgh determined him to chance finding a publisher there. From a business point of view, the move to Edinburgh in November 1786 proved in the end a lucky gamble. Through the patronage of the Ayrshire gentry in the capital, and especially of Glencairn, Burns was soon helped both to a publisher and to subscribers; and the Edinburgh edition of the *Poems*, which appeared in April 1787, put money in his pocket. But the lure of Edinburgh for Burns was fame, not wealth. And long before the new edition was ready, he was sure he had brought his wares to the wrong market. Lionized and made welcome everywhere, even at the tables of the noblest and most learned in the land, the ploughman-poet from Ayrshire, who amazed and captivated Edinburgh by the strength and shrewdness of his mind in talk, and by his very presence, saw almost at once, and more and more clearly as time went on, that homage was paid, not to the poet and his writings, but to the prodigy he appeared to be in his new surroundings. In a city half-English in culture and the ape of London, if men of repute took any notice of the writer, it was to hint their regret that his preference for the vernacular and for old-world Scottish themes made some parts of his book 'exceptionable' in tone. What they praised most freely was not the pieces Burns knew to be most original, most clearly stamped as of his minting, but pieces almost English in vocabulary, grave and unctuous, like 'Man was made to mourn' and 'Winter, a Dirge' (the earliest of his writings here printed), or pieces like 'The Cotter's Saturday Night', 'To a Mouse', 'To a Mountain Daisy', where the vernacular suiting was pieced out with some Sunday rags from English poets like Gray and Blair and Young. The literati of Edinburgh, in short, regarded Burns in their hearts as a genius who had been unfortunate in his reading and education, as one whose talents had been largely wasted on out-of-date themes and a dying language. As the world wagged then for Scotsmen, who shall blame them? Edinburgh, as it happened, knew far more how things were driving than did Kilmarnock, or Ayr, or for that matter any other town or district in Scotland. It was nothing but kindness and a desire to secure the future of their discovered genius, that moved these men to counsel Burns as they did. Their mistake was that they failed to take the measure of their man, to see that—young as he was in years—he was already old in opinion, proud, too set to take a new ply, that there was nothing for it but to let him run his own course. He refused to expunge the offending words and passages they criticized, but their prestige seems to have affected his choice of additional poems for the 1787 edition; and it seems to have scared him also into diminishing the Scotchness of his book in print by getting rid of the phonetic spelling devices of the 1786 *Poems*. If Burns could have settled accounts with his publisher Creech—notoriously dilatory in such matters—it is pretty certain that he would have left Edinburgh for good as soon as his new edition appeared. Even before that date he sought, and preferred to that of his official patrons, the company of convivial wits, such as the Crochallan Fencibles, whose meeting-place was at Daniel Douglas's tavern in Anchor Close, and who provided a more sympathetic audience for his venturesome wit and recital of old indecent songs. And after the Tours[1] which enabled him to kill May to September 1787 of the waiting-time away from Edinburgh altogether, on his return to town, the Fencibles and their like seem to have been his principal social resort till the end of March 1788, when Creech's procrastination at last let him wind up his Edinburgh affairs, and depart to marry Jean Armour and turn farmer and exciseman at Ellisland and Dumfries.

To Burns himself, then, the Edinburgh bid for fame must have seemed, on the whole, only less of a failure than his Irvine bid for wealth and worldly goods. All the gain to the poet— the gain of being trumpeted through the land as the protégé of such distinguished patrons—was his more completely after six months' stay in the capital than after sixteen. During those ten

---

[1] The Borders, 5 May–8 June; The West Highlands, June; The Central Highlands, 25 Aug.–16 Sept. 1787. Later, there were also (Oct. 1787) Harvieston, and (March 1788) Dalswinton.

months more that he lingered there, off and on, his growing
conviction that this patronage was his to keep and profit by
only on conditions impossible to one of his gift and temperament,
gave rise to conduct that must have estranged many and debited
his account. And yet, though the Crochallan Fencibles, by
cooling the enthusiasm of his patrons, did Burns immediate
harm, dashing what remained of his former hopes, the luckiest
of all his Edinburgh days was to be one spent in their company.
The hopes they dashed, after all, were false hopes: the harm
they did affected only the poet that Edinburgh imagined Burns
to be. The best thing that Edinburgh did for Burns was to make
him acquainted with James Johnson, the illiterate but enthusiastic engraver of *The Scots Musical Museum*; and that happened,
as was foreordained, in Daniel Douglas's tavern. The disillusioned
author of the *Poems*, who left Edinburgh in 1788, confirmed in
his year-old fear that the 'many intimacies and friendships' he
had formed there with the great, were 'all of too tender a con-
stitution to carry a hundred and fifty miles', if only he could
have wakened completely from the bad dream of it all, might
have discovered, and been comforted to know, that Edinburgh
had been kinder than appeared; that, through his humble friendship with James Johnson, it had unwittingly assigned his pen its
appointed task, brought him again—after five years of erring
trespass—into the road he was travelling when Poesy first met
him. For *The Scots Musical Museum* was Johnson's device for
preserving, before it was too late, the folk-music and the folk-
songs of his native land. It was not a work designed to catch the
eye of the learned and fashionable society that patronized Burns:
both to satisfy his enthusiasm for the things he wished to publish,
and to recoup himself, Johnson aimed to capture a larger public
than that; and the chief problem that confronted him was
how to produce his volumes at a price low enough to suit the
pockets of the less *élite*. His solution was to invent a cheap
process of engraving both the words and the music of his proposed corpus of Scottish song; and already before he met Burns,
the greater part of the first volume of a hundred airs was through
the press. Only two pieces by Burns were included. The remaining volumes, however, are sown thick with Burns's work.
And it is clear from his correspondence, from holograph lists of
songs and airs, and from annotations on his own song-manu-
scripts, that from the autumn of 1787 till his last illness in 1796

it was a labour of love with Burns to promote Johnson's scheme by every means in his power. For the second, third, and fourth volumes—all that appeared before his death—Burns practically acted as literary editor. A letter he wrote Johnson near the end asking for 'proofs (if they are ready)' of the fifth volume, has one sentence which may be quoted here as showing the value Burns set upon this part of his writing, and suggesting how much more likely we are to catch the real Burns in Johnson's pages than in the several editions of the *Poems*. 'Your Work', he writes, 'is a great one; and though, now that it is near finished, I see if we were to begin again, two or three things that might be mended, yet I will venture to prophesy, that to future ages your Publication will be the text-book and standard of Scottish Song and Music.'

And there is yet another book of Burns's post-Edinburgh years that can rival the *Poems*, for those who know when they have met their man. The effect of his attachment to Johnson was not only to enlarge *The Museum* far beyond the original intention of its projector, but also apparently to make the singing of Scottish songs a praiseworthy accomplishment with some at least of the polite world that first welcomed Burns to Edinburgh. It was for these converts in particular that George Thomson, Clerk to the Board of Trustees for the Encouragement of Art and Manufactures in Scotland, and well known in Edinburgh drawing-rooms for his singing and violin-solos, planned, in 1792, his elaborate *Select Collection of Original Scotish Airs*. He engaged Pleyel—he was later to engage even Beethoven—to compose the accompaniments, which he meant to be the outstanding feature of his book. So that one ought not, perhaps, to be surprised at the tone of the letter in which he invited Burns to help with the words.

To render the work perfect [he wrote] we are desirous to have the poetry improved wherever it seems unworthy of the music; and that it is so in many instances is allowed by every one conversant with our musical collections. The editors of these [there can be little doubt that he had Johnson's *Museum* principally in his mind] seem in general to have depended on the music proving an excuse for the verses; and hence, some charming melodies are united to mere nonsense and doggrel, while others are accommodated with rhymes so loose and indelicate as cannot be sung in decent company. To remove this reproach would be an easy task to the author of *The*

Cotter's Saturday Night. . . . Tell me frankly then, whether you will devote your leisure to writing twenty or twenty-five songs, suitable to the particular melodies which I am prepared to send you. A few songs, exceptionable only in some of their verses, I will likewise submit to your consideration; leaving it to you, either to mend these, or make new songs in their stead.

Whether or not it weighed with Burns that here at last was his opportunity to please his former patrons in the character of an 'unexceptionable', but still Scottish, poet—of proving that his rejection of their advice and desertion to the Crochallan Fencibles was not mere ingratitude but had some ground in reason—none can tell. But, considering that apart from heavy duties in the Excise, upon which he now depended entirely for his livelihood, he was, at the moment, setting out upon Johnson's fifth volume, and busy also with the additions for Creech's 'enlarged' (1793) edition of the *Poems*, it is difficult not to suspect some such motive behind the combined enthusiasm and discretion of his instant acceptance of Thomson's proposal.

It is almost impossible to over-emphasize the importance for the student of Burns of these two collections of Scottish songs. From the autumn of 1787 in the one case, from the autumn of 1792 in the other, and in both cases till the end of his working days, Burns wrought at Johnson's *Museum* and at Thomson's *Airs* with a zeal and energy even greater and more unflagging than the zeal with which Fergusson had inspired him throughout 1785. During the years at Ellisland and Dumfries, the *Poems*, for Burns, were practically a thing of the past, a sort of half-relevant episode in his career more and more dimly recalled. When Creech first wrote proposing a new and enlarged edition, in 1791, Burns took 'no notice', but let him ask again before he troubled to reply on 16 April 1792. And even then it was to offer only fifty pages of new material, and to suggest that the copy for the whole book should be submitted to Alexander Fraser Tytler for his 'strictures' and the supervision of the press-work. In consequence, the *Poems* of 1793 appeared more Anglified than ever in spelling, and it was perhaps no great loss that, of the twenty new pieces, only three or four were at all characteristic—though these included, it is true, 'On the late Captain Grose's Peregrinations thro' Scotland' and 'Tam o' Shanter'. But this bored, lackadaisical poet of Creech's was not the man who did business all these years with Johnson and with Thomson.

These publishers set him a congenial task, and one in which he knew himself qualified to lead, not follow. The old folk-tunes of Scotland that both admired and were so keen—each after his fashion—to preserve and bring again into general use, had been Burns's use since childhood and a principal part (as we saw) of the schooling that had made him a poet. By Johnson, the less educated enthusiast of the two, Burns's assumption of command was apparently taken for granted and unquestioned from the first. The chief interest of the *Museum*, therefore, is that it shows how completely tune-ridden Burns was as a song-maker; so tune-ridden, indeed, that—lacking in this case a critic to nudge him for some of his verses—he wrote sometimes as if the words mattered hardly at all. It is his own confession to Thomson that the principle which guided him in his *Museum* pieces was that 'it is better to have mediocre verses to a favorite air than none at all'. His excuse must be that Johnson was the first to employ him on such work, and at a time when poetic employment of a kind suited to his gifts seemed a forlorn hope; whereas the reassured and happier Burns whom Thomson engaged was also, by then, five years old at song-craft. If the *Museum* songs of Burns are much more unequal than those in Thomson's *Airs*, this is largely because the eager tune-ridden beginner was content —perhaps found it easier—at first to tinker and adapt old words than to create new ones for his purpose. There is a picture of him song-making in a letter to Thomson of 1793.

Untill I am compleat master of a tune, in my own singing, (such as it is) I never can compose for it.—My way is: I consider the poetic Sentiment, correspondent to my idea of the musical expression; then chuse my theme; begin one Stanza; when that is composed, which is generally the most difficult part of the business, I walk out, sit down now and then, look out for objects in Nature around me that are in unison or harmony with the cogitations of my fancy and workings of my bosom; humming every now and then the air with the verses I have framed: when I feel my Muse beginning to jade, I return to the solitary fireside of my study, and there commit my effusions to paper; swinging, at intervals, on the hind-legs of my elbow chair, by way of calling forth my own critical strictures, as my pen goes on.—Seriously, this, at home, is almost invariably my way.

The tune is still the starting-point for Burns. But that 'way' of his can have come only by degrees and in practice: he had to learn first how to make himself 'compleat master' of the tune in hand.

And many a *Museum* number of his suggests that the tune was his master, rather than that Burns was 'compleat master' of it. So the *Museum* is the chief storehouse of Burns's vamps of existing words—songs like 'We're a' noddin' and 'My love, she's but a lassie yet', or the first sets of 'Whistle, an' I'll come to ye, my lad', 'Ca' the yowes to the knowes', and 'Duncan Gray', which he was to work over and improve still further for Thomson's *Airs*—for Thomson saw to it that he had the pickings that suited his need out of the collection of his despised rival. But we must have a care, lest we underrate *The Museum*, by comparison with Thomson's *Airs*, because it exhibits so frequently the 'prentice' hand of Burns. Vamps are not all of it. And even the vamps show genius on occasion, ranging so near in quality to Burns's best as to deserve a better classification, if one could be devised. In some of them, as he works on the old words, he seems to lift nearer to that 'mastery' of the tune which his 'way' demanded, and achieves a thing almost his own, that calls to be sung as a strathspey calls to be danced. And I am not sure (after allowance made for the fact that Thomson, as I say, poached some of the best things in Johnson) that the *Museum* does not exhibit this trade-mark of Burns as a song-writer more often and more richly than the *Airs*.

For Thomson, though more educated than Johnson, was not really more wise than he about Scottish song: he was only more opinionated. The man who had no qualms about telling Beethoven where his score was wrong naturally did not hesitate to instruct Burns how to improve his idea of a tune or the poetry of his verses. On the verses, Burns, by a sort of tacit consent, let him have his way more often than he ought. But there were occasions when he stuck out for his own wording; and their correspondence reveals, again and again, how opposite the two were in their notion of the style most proper to a Scottish song or ballad. 'Give me leave', Burns counters in one dispute, 'to criticise your taste in the only thing in which it is in my opinion reprehensible: (you know I ought to know something of my trade) of Pathos, Sentiment, and Point, you are a compleat judge; but there is a quality more necessary than either in a Song, and which is the very essence of a Ballad, I mean Simplicity—now, if I mistake not, this last feature you are a little apt to sacrifice to the foregoing.' Once he 'declared off from Thomson's taste' still more bluntly—'What pleases me, as simple and naive, disgusts you as ludicrous and low.' But it was on the tunes that Burns found Thomson most stupid and unteachable. A very early letter of his begins:

If you mean, my dear Sir, that all the Songs in your Collection shall be Poetry of the first merit, I am afraid you will find difficulty in the undertaking more than you are aware of.—There is a peculiar rhythmus in many of our airs, and a necessity of adapting syllables to the emphasis, or what I would call, the feature-notes, of the tune, that cramps the Poet, and lays him under almost insuperable difficulties.

And he goes on to illustrate how what he calls a 'random clink' is the most that can be hoped for some very fine and characteristic airs. Where there was so much of pull-devil, pull-baker in the collaboration, it says a deal for Burns's patience and tact that Thomson's *Airs* represents him no worse than it does. But the fact remains, you cannot depend on Thomson, as you can on Johnson, for a verbatim text of what Burns wrote. And independent of this, it is clear that a sense of the audience he addressed through Thomson, and Thomson himself—whose respectability shivered at every piece of 'native humour' Burns sent him—have kept Burns too consistently serious in this collection of his songs. This was a pity; for Burns serious was ever apt to be Burns English. And it is unfortunately true, that what troubles the sensitive reader most in the songs that Burns made definitely for Thomson—a very few excepted—is their needless, extra-gilt finish of Englishry. It can intrude, at times, so far upon the Scotch as to make that seem the stranger note—

> Ye banks and braes and streams around
>   The castle o' Montgomery,
> Green be your woods, and fair your flowers,
>   Your waters never drumlie!
> There Summer first unfald her robes,
>   And there the langest tarry!
> For there I took the last fareweel
>   O' my sweet Highland Mary!

Four or five words and a hint of syntax is the Scottish sum-total of that stanza—just enough to make it felt as an excrescence. It is a disease, this Englishry of style, that has threatened Scottish writers ever since the country sold its soul to John Knox and his imported English Bible: Scots have been condemned ever since to do the bulk of their serious thinking in a foreign idiom. And Burns was smitten with his worst attack of it by George Thomson. The interest of the *Museum*, I said, was its revelation of the need to sing Burns rather than say him. The interest of Thomson's *Airs* is the more negative one of suggesting the limitations of our author's genius even in song—a genius for the ring not of English but of Scottish words, and that worked best from the life, echoing things heard and seen and done more truly than things it had only read of in books. Burns is nothing if not the poet of the folk among whom he was born, the folk of the harvest-field of 1773, the simple folk of his native Kyle and their likes elsewhere in the workaday Scotland of his time. And for all who would know him rightly and appreciate his peculiar virtue, the true path of approach must be—Johnson, Thomson, the *Poems*.

The poems -
his 1st
simple work
perhaps
Burn's truest
work to show his
literary genius.

FANNY BURNEY'S NOVELS

LORD DAVID CECIL

FEW first novels have been more successful than *Evelina*. Not only was it a best-seller, but it won enthusiastic praise from the most distinguished minds of the age. 'Worthy of Richardson at his best,' said Burke: Dr. Johnson majestically expressed a desire to meet its author. Nor was *Evelina*'s success a flash in the pan. *Cecilia*, appearing a few years later, met with, if possible, greater acclamation. And though her third and fourth novels—*Camilla* and *The Wanderer*—were less admired, Fanny Burney's reputation remained very high. In fact, no less a person than Jane Austen thought *Camilla* a masterpiece. To-day, it must be admitted, all this enthusiasm seems exaggerated. Compared with the greatest novels, Fanny Burney's look a trifle thin. All the same they are still enjoyable. And, moreover, it is possible to see why they made such a sensation among contemporaries. For they were something new. In Fanny Burney's hands the novel took a step forward which was to have enormous consequences. Her stories represent the entry of the woman, or perhaps one should say the lady, into English fiction.

The English novel was created—as every history of literature tells us—by Richardson and Fielding. They conceived it on different lines. Richardson was the first dramatic novelist. His subject is the clash of character; and he exhibits it by an elaborate analysis of the processes of heart and conscience in a given situation. Fielding is the first panoramic novelist. His aim is to give a broad humorous picture of the varieties of the human scene. His plots are merely the framework on which he stretches this picture. Fanny Burney derives from both, but more from Fielding. Here she was like most of her countrymen. Richardson's influence was strongest on the Continent; but the English, the lazy, unintrospective English, with their delight in humour and their suspicion of any entertainment that demanded a strenuous intellectual effort, tended to follow Fielding. Fanny Burney had a typically English talent; she was a bright, light, humorous observer of the outward scene, not a psychological analyst; and, like Fielding,

what attracted her about the novel form was the opportunity
it provided for giving an entertaining picture of the world about
her. In their main lines her novels are of the Fielding type,
satirical panoramas of society centring upon an agreeable hero
and heroine, and held together rather loosely by a symmetrical
plot, culminating in their happy marriage. Perhaps the shortest
way to sum up her place in the history of English Letters is to
say that she was the first writer to translate the Fielding type
of novel into the feminine key.

This meant altering it considerably. Fielding was an
intensely masculine character: Fanny Burney was equally intensely feminine, using the word, it must be owned, not wholly
in its best sense. She was an English lady of a recognizable
type, lively, civilized, and, within certain limits, extremely
observant, but petty, fussy, a slave to convention and far too
easily shocked. Evelina, we recall, is so horrified at the coarseness of *Love for Love* that she is quite unable to get any pleasure
out of its brilliance. This is not at all like Fielding: and such a
difference of outlook imposed a very different perspective on
her creator's panorama of English society. Inevitably it is much
narrower. Fielding is free to move his heroes all over the place:
now they are talking to squires, now to gamekeepers, now they
are flirting with ladies of title in London boudoirs, now drinking
at the tavern with the postboy, now at a ball, now at a gaming-
house, now following the hunt, now in Newgate jail. Their
sisters—Miss Burney's heroines—were shut off from all these
phases of life except those to be observed at the squire's house,
the boudoir, and the ball. Even there the scope of her observation
was limited by convention. She heard only such parts of the
conversation as were thought suitable for a young lady's ears.
In compensation, however, she had time to examine in great
detail what she was permitted to see—Fielding's young men
never observed the texture of social intercourse so minutely—
and, under the microscope of her undeviating attention, one
aspect of the social scene stood out as it had never stood out
to him. This was its social distinctions. Social distinctions,
no doubt, are a feature of the picture of life presented by Miss
Burney's predecessors: for England in the eighteenth century
was—even more than it is now—a hierarchical society. Differences of rank were one of its outstanding characteristics.
But Fielding and Smollett and the rest of them surveyed the

world with too broad a sweep to note more than their salient features. It was different for a woman. She could only satisfy her adventurousness and curiosity within the confines of the different social worlds into which respectable girls were allowed to go. She could not visit Newgate, or the tavern, or the gaming-house; she could only move from country society to town society, from the fashionable to the dowdy, from the elegant to the vulgar, from the aristocratic to the professional classes. The diversity of her panorama was limited by the diversity she could find included in this area. It was not a fatal limitation. By nature, women are observers of those minutiae of manners in which the subtler social distinctions reveal themselves. Fanny Burney seized her opportunity with avidity. In her hands, for the first time in the English novel, social distinctions are the dominant subject of the story. She is the first novelist—though very far from being the last—to make a thorough study of snobbery.

Further, although her plots are constructed within the same convention as Fielding's, their emphasis is different. The Fielding type of plot turns on love and marriage; but Fielding was not particularly interested in the feelings of his hero and heroine for each other. Tom loves Sophia; Sophia loves Tom. From time to time Sophia learns of some lapse of Tom's which temporarily puts her off him. But when it is explained, or apologized for, back her sentiment flows into its original channel without comment on the part of her creator. Fielding, like most very masculine men, has no objective interest in observing the process of courtship. Fanny Burney had; and she gives up a great deal of her space to tracing it.

It is in her treatment of this aspect of her theme that she reveals the influence of Richardson. Though she did not see life as a whole dramatically, one drama did interest her: the central drama of any young lady's life—the drama of getting married. Confronted with this spectacle she becomes for the time being a psychologist. How does a young lady feel on first meeting a marriageable young man? How does she discover her growing sentiments towards him? What steps does she take to check or to cherish them? How far by observing his behaviour, governed as it is outwardly by the rules of formal good manners, is she able to interpret the fluctuation of his feelings towards her? In Fanny Burney's novels, for the first time, the process of an ordinary, legitimate, everyday courtship becomes the central theme of an English novel.

Richardson was bound to be her master here. He was the master of any English novelist who sought to analyse feeling. In *Sir Charles Grandison* he had used his skill to illuminate the complicated hopes and fears, the scruples of honour and modesty and refinement, which agitated the breast of Miss Harriet Byron at the sight of the awful perfections of Sir Charles. However, Miss Burney is no mere imitator of Richardson. A woman herself, she could enter into a girl's feelings much more realistically than he could. And anyway Richardson's mind tended always to pierce beneath a particular drama to explore the fundamental moral situation that it illustrates. Besides, with him, analysis of character occupies most of the book. With Fanny Burney the courtship which is the subject of analysis is merely the central theme of the action; and the action is, as we have seen, secondary to her picture of society as a whole.

Fanny Burney's range, then, the area of experience in which her creative talent shows itself, is that concerned with respectable society and respectable courtship. Her three chief books all follow the same plan. An inexperienced young girl—Evelina or Cecilia or Camilla—is cast into the social world. We see it through her clear innocent eyes in all its variety.[1] Soon—for Fanny Burney's heroines are usually both lovely and financially eligible—a cloud of suitors surrounds her. By the end of the book she has chosen a husband. In the meantime she has visited London, the country—usually a spa—has moved in good society and bad. By the end, in addition to getting married, she has managed to acquire a knowledge of the world.

It is an excellent subject for a novelist, and in many ways Fanny Burney was well equipped to do it justice. She had a vigorous, varied, vivacious talent that could control and vitalize a great deal of diverse material. Further, she was a natural story-teller: she gets the plot going at once, and sustains it by an unflagging talent for inventing incidents. Even though these are sometimes unconvincing, they do not bore the reader. Always they are related with spirit. And anyway no

[1] The original conception of this theme seems also to have been suggested by *Sir Charles Grandison*, which opens with Harriet Byron's introduction, as an inexperienced young girl, to London society. But Richardson is not interested in the social scene, and does not explore the possibilities for describing it suggested by his scheme.

single one goes on too long. After the long-windedness of many eighteenth-century novels Fanny Burney's come as a welcome relief. Moreover—it was her outstanding talent—she was extremely observant of the surface of existence. Fanny Burney can bring to life not only her central figures but the whole world they live in. To open *Cecilia* or *Evelina* is to be transported straight into eighteenth-century London, crowded, shrill, diverse, bustling, with its curious blend of elegance and crudeness, of ceremoniousness and brutality. Now we are with the middle classes, gossiping with a merchant in the room behind his shop, or out for an evening's pleasure with a flashy city beau at the shilling ball at Hampstead; now we are moving in the *beau monde* at a masquerade, or at Ranelagh rubbing shoulders with languid fops, rattle-pated ladies; now crowding up the stairs to the Italian Opera, now at a fashionable concert overhearing the conversation of two frivolous débutantes:

. . . though there was an excellent concert in which several capital performers played and sung, she found it impossible to hear a note, as she chanced to be sitting just by Miss Leeson, and two other young ladies who were paying one another compliments upon their dress and their looks, settling to dance in the same cotillon, guessing who would begin the minuets, and wondering there were not more gentlemen. Yet in the midst of this unmeaning conversation, . . . not one of them failed, from time to time to exclaim with great rapture 'What sweet music!'—'Oh how charming!'—'Did you ever hear anything so delightful?—'

In each place Fanny Burney picks out infallibly the particular detail of scene or speech that brings it alive and stirring before our mental eye. And she relates what she sees with just that touch of slight caricature, that stroke of Hogarthian style, which gives it aesthetic life and quality.

Nor is her observation confined to the general scene. She had a lively gift for drawing individual character. It shows itself in two ways. Her most typical successes are in that tradition of realistic humorous portraiture which she learnt from Fielding and Smollett, and which they in their turn had inherited from the comic drama—'character parts', to use a stage phrase, made up of one or two strongly marked idiosyncrasies, drawn in a convention of slight caricature, and revealing themselves directly in dialogue: Evelina's vulgar cousins, the Branghtons, and their friend Mr. Smith; the fashionables who aroused the contempt of Cecilia, Miss Larolles, Miss Leeson, the absurd Mr. Meadows who thought it dowdy to appear to enjoy anything, Captain Aresby with his conversation all scattered over with French phrases, the miserly Mr. Briggs. Fanny Burney does not present them with subtlety. The Branghtons are always vulgar, Meadows is always bored, Miss Larolles is always chattering like a magpie. All the same, they are not mere conventional types. Their creator had an extremely sharp ear for dialogue, for the particular accent of silliness or pomposity which distinguishes one fool from another. She may represent these figures only in one aspect, but that aspect is drawn straight from life; and life still throbs in it.

Listen to the Branghtons persuaded by their genteel cousin to attend an opera for the first time.

At the end of the first act, as the green curtain dropped to prepare for the dance, they imagined that the opera was done; and Mr. Branghton expressed great indignation that he had been *tricked* out of his money with so little trouble. 'Now if any Englishman was to do such an impudent thing as this,' said he, 'why, he'd be pelted;— but here, one of these outlandish gentry may do just what he pleases, and come on, and squeak out a song or two, and then pocket your money without further ceremony.'

However, so determined he was to be dissatisfied, that, before the conclusion of the third act, he found still more fault with the opera for being too long; and wondered whether they thought their singing good enough to serve us for supper.

During the symphony of a song of Signor Millico's, in the second act, young Mr. Branghton said, 'It's my belief that that fellow's going to sing another song!—why, there's nothing but singing!— I wonder when they'll speak.'

This song, which was slow and pathetic, caught all my attention, and I lean'd my head forward to avoid hearing their observations, that I might listen without interruption: but, upon turning round, when the song was over, I found that I was the object of general diversion to the whole party; for the Miss Branghtons were tittering, and the two gentlemen making signs and faces at me, implying their contempt of my affectation.

This discovery determined me to appear as inattentive as themselves; but I was very much provoked at being thus prevented enjoying the only pleasure, which, in such a party, was within my power.

'So Miss,' said Mr. Branghton, 'you're quite in the fashion, I see; —so you like operas? well, I'm not so polite; I can't like nonsense, let it be never so much the taste.'

'But pray, Miss,' said the son, 'what makes that fellow look so doleful while he is singing?'

'Probably because the character he performs is in distress.'

'Why, then, I think he might as well let alone singing till he's in better cue: it's out of all nature for a man to be piping when he's in distress. For my part, I never sing but when I'm merry; yet I love a song as well as most people.'

When the curtain dropt they all rejoiced.

'How do *you* like it?'—and 'How do *you* like it?' passed from one to another with looks of the utmost contempt. 'As for me,' said Mr. Branghton, 'they've caught me once; but if ever they do again, I'll give 'em leave to sing me to Bedlam for my pains: for such a heap of stuff never did I hear; there isn't one ounce of sense in the whole Opera, nothing but one continued squeaking and squalling from beginning to end.'

'If I had been in the pit,' said Madame Duval, 'I should have liked it vastly, for music is my passion; but sitting in such a place as this, is quite unbearable.'

Miss Branghton, looking at me, declared, that she was not *genteel* enough to admire it.

Miss Polly confessed, that, if they would but sing *English* she would like it *very well*.

The brother wished he could raise a riot in the house, because then he might get his money again.

And, finally, they all agreed, that it was *monstrous dear*.

This is dreadfully convincing; no wonder poor Evelina felt awkward at being seen with such companions. Indeed, Fanny Burney is never better than when conveying social embarrassments of this kind. Evelina, confronted at this very Opera by the dashing Sir Clement Willoughby; or, on another occasion, forced by the Branghtons to ask the awe-inspiring Lord Orville to give her the use of his carriage—in these scenes embarrassment is portrayed with such vividness as to render them painful to read about. Perhaps too painful: Evelina could hardly have suffered more had she been caught committing a crime; and, after all, it is not a crime to be found by genteel people in vulgar company. Hard though Fanny Burney was on other snobs, I am afraid she herself cannot be altogether acquitted of snobbishness. A social lapse was to her a tragedy. Still, the emotion she puts into them makes her accounts of such lapses more convincingly realistic. To a shy young girl, taking her first tentative steps on to the stage of the great world, a social lapse has its tragic side.

Fanny Burney's mastery over character is not exclusively confined to these satiric types. At times she shows also an insight that enables her to penetrate beneath the surface of personality.

And if Mr. Delvile was shunned through hatred, his lady no less was avoided through fear; high spirited and fastidious, she was easily wearied and disgusted, she bore neither frailty nor folly—those two principal ingredients in human nature! She required, to obtain her favour, the union of virtue and abilities with elegance, which meeting but rarely, she was rarely disposed to be pleased; and disdaining to conceal either contempt or aversion, she inspired in return nothing but dread or resentment: making thus, by a want of that lenity which is the milk of human kindness, and the bond of society, enemies the most numerous and illiberal by those very talents which, more meekly borne, would have rendered her not merely admired, but adored!

In proportion, however, as she was thus at war with the world in general, the chosen few who were honoured with her favour she loved with a zeal all her own; her heart, liberal, open, and but too daringly sincere, was fervent in affection, and enthusiastic in admiration; the friends who were dear to her, she was devoted to serve, she magnified their virtues till she thought them of a higher race of beings, she inflamed her generosity with ideas of what she owed to them, till her life seemed too small a sacrifice to be refused for their service.

This analysis is confined within the limitations imposed by the period in which Fanny Burney lived. It is concerned wholly with the moral elements in Mrs. Delvile's nature: no account is taken in it of those imponderables of temperament and taste which in reality make so important a contribution to the composition of personality. But, as far as it goes, it is very shrewd, and reveals an unusual power to isolate and sum up the basic elements of character. The lack of balance in Mrs. Delvile, which made her, in spite of her virtues, an unpopular figure with the world at large, is stated with a clear, firm certainty, perceived with an easy mature worldly wisdom. Here Fanny Burney shows the advantages that went along with the limitations of the eighteenth-century outlook. The fact that it failed to take in large parts of human experience gave it all the more time and energy to concentrate on those aspects it did observe. Fanny Burney was a woman of the world, though this world was a little narrow. The average second-class female novelist in the nineteenth century, nervously aware of more elements in life than she can get into focus, retains a youthful uncertainty, a jejune vagueness of vision.

Fanny Burney had one more weapon in her armoury, extremely useful for the presentation of the 'courtship' element in her stories; an instinctive delicate perception of the processes of feeling in a young girl's heart. Sensitively she can perceive the significance of the small gesture, the almost imperceptible movement indicating the hidden trend of emotion. How justly she describes Cecilia's gradual discovery that her heart is lost to young Delvile! With what a succession of convincing touches she portrays the scene in which the innocent Evelina, already attached to Lord Orville, is found by him stealing home from an apparently compromising interview with Mr. Macartney!

. . . I have reason to believe Lord Orville, from the parlour-window, saw me tottering along; for, before I had taken five steps, he came out, and hastening to meet me, said, 'I fear you are not well; pray allow me (offering his arm) to assist you.'

'No, my Lord,' said I, with all the resolution I could assume; yet I was affected by an attention, at that time so little expected, and forced to turn away my head to conceal my emotion.

'You *must*,' said he, with earnestness, 'indeed you must,—I am sure you are not well;—refuse me not the honour of assisting you'; and, almost forcibly, he took my hand, and drawing it under his arm, obliged me to lean upon him. That I submitted was partly the effect of surprise at an earnestness so uncommon in Lord Orville, and partly, that I did not, just then, dare trust my voice to make any objection.

When we came to the house, he led me into the parlour, and to a chair, and begged to know if I would not have a glass of water.

'No, my Lord, I thank you,' said I, 'I am perfectly recovered'; and, rising, I walked to the window, where, for some time, I pretended to be occupied in looking at the garden.

Determined as I was to act honourably by Mr. Macartney, I yet most anxiously wished to be restored to the good opinion of Lord Orville; but his silence, and the thoughtfulness of his air, discouraged me from speaking.

My situation soon grew disagreeable and embarrassing, and I resolved to return to my chamber till breakfast was ready. To remain longer, I feared, might seem *asking* for his enquiries; and I was sure it would ill become me to be more eager to speak, than he was to hear.

Just as I reached the door, turning to me hastily, he said, 'Are you going, Miss Anville?'

'I am, my Lord,' answered I; yet I stopped.

'Perhaps to return to—but I beg your pardon!' He spoke with a degree of agitation that made me readily comprehend he meant to *the garden*; and I instantly said, 'To my own room, my Lord.' And again, I would have gone; but, convinced by my answer that I understood him, I believe he was sorry for the insinuation: he approached me with a very serious air. . . .

Power of story-telling, of character-drawing, ability to trace the process of feeling—with these gifts why should Fanny Burney not have done better than she did? No doubt it is primarily due to a weakness in the essential quality of her talent. The lack of subtlety in her character-drawing, the impression of thinness she makes as compared with the greatest authors, are symptoms of a fundamental lack of mental distinction. Vivacious though her scene may be, it lacks that peculiar individuality of vision which stamps the work of the great creative novelists. So, we feel, might any clever eighteenth-century lady have described the world, had she possessed a turn for writing. Fanny Burney must inevitably have been a minor novelist, for she had not been endowed with a major talent. This, however, is no reason why she should not have been consistently good at her own level; but she is not even that. Even at her best—even in *Cecilia* and *Evelina*—her work is marred by serious faults. For one thing, she could not make her different talents pull together, fuse them in a harmonious whole. This weakness appears conspicuously in her treatment of character. She had, as we have seen, a talent for analysis and a talent for comic presentation: but she never applies both to the same figures. Her comedy characters—the Branghtons and the Larolles—though vividly dramatized, are shallowly conceived. They talk vivaciously and convincingly, but we are never allowed to penetrate beneath that talk to discover the combination of qualities which went to produce their comic exterior. What they are like we see vividly, but not why they were like that. Mrs. Delvile, on the other hand, is diagnosed but not dramatized. A serious type, unsuitable for presentation in a comic convention, she required a far more subtle talent to make her personality vivid on the stage than was needed for the Branghtons. Fanny Burney did not possess such a talent. Her observation was not intelligent enough to enable her to vitalize a deep complex nature whose demeanour was uncoloured by any obvious idiosyncrasies. The

consequence is that, though we understand Mrs. Delvile, we
never 'see' her.

Fanny Burney's books also suffer from the fact that she does
not stay within the limitations of her talent. She could have
been pretty certain of success if she had only sought to show her
reader what a young lady could see: her view of the social scene,
her vision of her own heart and its emotions. But she refused
to be bound down in this way; in the Madame Duval and
Captain Mirvan episodes in *Evelina* she attempts the brutal
masculine farce of Smollett: in the Macartney episodes she has
a try at tragic drama involving suicide and despair. Fanny
Burney, in fact, frequently commits the novelist's greatest sin;
she goes outside her true creative range. It was not altogether
her fault. The Fielding formula for novel-writing was not a
fully matured instrument; it had not solved the problem of reconciling form with fact. In order to give unity and pattern to his
realistic panorama of contemporary life Fielding had imposed
on it an artificial symmetrical plot copied from that stage
comedy in which he had served his apprenticeship as a writer,
centring upon a hero and heroine and consisting of a formal
intrigue which solves itself neatly in a happy ending.

Where Fielding failed Fanny Burney was not likely to succeed.
Her plots are clumsy as well as improbable. To what extraordinary lengths and improbabilities is she forced to go to
prevent Cecilia marrying Delvile before the end of the last
volume ! Moreover, the fact that she imposed a stagy plot on
a realistic picture of life involved her in all sorts of material
outside her range; and unluckily she was not so powerful and
creative an artist as to be able to sweep the reader away so
irresistibly that he overlooks her lapses. Indeed she is hardly an
artist at all in the fullest sense of the word. The novel to her was
not the expression of an imaginative conception, but merely a
means of recording her observations of the world, which she
organized into an artificial unity by using any convention of
story-writing she found to her hand. Only if she had lived in
an age that had presented her ready-made with a thoroughly
sound model for a plot could she have achieved consistently
good work. As it was, she was a victim of any influence that
crossed her path. *Evelina*, her first book, reveals her at her best
and her worst. There is a peculiar charm exhaling from this first
fresh sparkling gush of her talent. The Branghton scenes show

her comedy at its brightest; Evelina's relation to Orville reveals
Fanny Burney's perception at its most sensitive. Both these
strains in her story are conceived well within her range.

Alas, this cannot be said of its other elements. The story of
the courtship and the picture of the social scene are incongru-
ously combined first of all with an unsuccessful essay in Smollettian farce—the Captain Mirvan–Madame Duval scenes—and
secondly with a melodramatic romance in the manner of the
novelist of sensibility, featuring a brother saved at the last
moment from suicide by the intervention of a hitherto unknown
sister and a father plunged into repentant tears at the sight of
his long-lost and also tearful daughter. By the time she wrote
Cecilia, Fanny Burney had learnt to prune her books of the
wildest of these extravagances. There is no more Smollettian
farce, and not so much sentimental melodrama. The plot is
conceived in a quieter tone. But in its quiet way it is extremely
improbable, turning as it does on the idea that two devoted
lovers are prevented from marrying because the young man
would have to change his surname to something less aristocratic
if he did marry. Moreover, plot and character are not so
integrated that one seems directly the result of the other. Here
Fanny Burney shows conspicuously her inferiority to Jane Austen:
she imposes her plot on a picture of life; the action does not
arise inevitably from the situation. The Monckton intrigue, for
instance, is nothing but a piece of machinery invented to keep
the story going.

Furthermore, her prejudiced, enthusiastic, feminine spirit had
only escaped from one influence to fall under another. Since
she wrote *Evelina* no less a person than Dr. Johnson himself had
taken notice of her. She had read his wonderful books with
absorbed awe; and now she had begun to shape her own unpretentious talent on his august model. Alas, Dr. Johnson was
no better example to her than Smollett. Dr. Johnson was a
professional moralist: Fanny Burney thought that she ought to
be one too; with the result that she proclaims insistently the
moral of her story instead of letting it emerge tacitly from the
action. Worse still, the easy colloquial speech of *Evelina* is translated into stately 'Johnsonese'—all abstractions and polysyllables
and antitheses—a magnificent instrument in Johnson's own
hands but comically inappropriate as an expression of Fanny
Burney's homely and sociable little personality. All the same,

Cecilia is the most sustainedly successful of her books; though it lacks the dewy freshness of *Evelina*, it maintains a steadier level and reveals a deeper insight into character. *Camilla* and *The Wanderer* written some years after show a decline in every respect. The moralism is more aggressive than ever, and the language more stilted; even the comedy is by comparison fatigued and laboured. Whatever Jane Austen may say in its defence, *Camilla* has sunk from the noble stature of a novel to the mean stature of a tract.

No—Fanny Burney was not an artist, she was not even an efficient craftsman; she approached her work without understanding the capacities either of her own talent or of the form which she had chosen. Responsive and undiscriminating, she lay open to any literary influence that came her way; with the consequence that the harmony of her work, even at its best, is jarred by the introduction of incongruous elements.

Yet she deserves an honourable place in the history of English literature. In her first two books, at any rate, the flame of her creative talent still burns bright enough to keep the whole alive and delightful: and her influence on the course of the novel is yet more important than her achievement. She was the first writer to detect how it might be possible to combine the methods of Richardson and Fielding. *Cecilia*, in particular, is both a novel of analysis and a comic picture of social life. Fanny Burney had not a strong enough talent herself to fuse the two with complete success. For that the English novel had to wait for Jane Austen. Still, it is a credit to anyone to have suggested an idea to Jane Austen. Nor did Fanny Burney's influence stop there. The feminization of the Fielding type of novel was to prove a momentous step in the history of English literature. From the next century onwards novels were written largely by women and, still more largely, for women. Women have remained passionately interested both in the drama of respectable courtship and the varieties of the social scene. In consequence, a huge proportion of the novels published in the nineteenth century took as their subject a picture of a society seen through the clear, unsophisticated eyes of a young girl freshly launched into it and grouped round the story of her courtship. Such stories indeed are written still. They are all Fanny Burney's children.

ELEGANT EXTRACTS

EDMUND BLUNDEN

VICESIMUS KNOX, who died in the same year as Keats, was a very young man when he experienced the kindness of Dr. Johnson. At that time he was beginning to make something of a name as an original writer, with a collection of essays; and Johnson expressed himself upon these to their publisher 'in terms of high panegyric, and predicted the future reputation of the author'. Popular as these papers were for many years— there were some twenty editions—the chief interest belonging to them now is that they brought the author into Boswell's list of imitators of Johnson's style. There are no signs that any other compositions by Knox, collected as his *Works* in seven volumes in 1824, are more attentively regarded, humane and enlightened and busy as he was. But a certain glimmering of fame or illustrious obscurity has persisted about the set of volumes wherein, as headmaster of Tonbridge School, he made so great an attempt to ensure that English schoolboys should form a lasting acquaintance with English literature—the trio of anthologies which bear the general title *Elegant Extracts*.

The mere physical mass of these productions is testimony to the overflowing zeal of their editor. They generally occur in three tall octavos, and portly as tall; and even so the contents are disposed in double columns. Their daily cartage must have helped the bodily as well as mental and spiritual development of their young recipients. The polished tree-calf in which copies are so often seen bound reflects the value which parents and guardians, schoolmasters and no doubt schoolboys themselves, set on these collections. They defy the tendency which exists to suppose that before Palgrave came to the rescue with the *Golden Treasury* there was no anthology to be had by the child with a longing for good reading. Their wide circulation is evidenced in one or two striking passages by noted authors. William Wordsworth pays respect to that at least when he complains in the 'Essay upon Epitaphs' (1810):

In a bulky volume of Poetry entitled *Elegant Extracts in Verse*, which must be known to most of my Readers, as it is circulated everywhere and in fact constitutes at this day the poetical library of our Schools, I find a number of epitaphs in verse, of the last century; and there is scarcely one which is not thoroughly tainted by the artifices which have over-run our writings in metre since the days of Dryden and Pope.

The avowed aim of William Hazlitt's *Select Poets of Great Britain* (1825) was

to improve upon the plan of the Elegant Extracts in Verse by the late Dr. Knox. From the length of time which had elapsed since the first appearance of that work, a similar undertaking admitted of considerable improvement, although the size of the volume has been compressed by means of a more severe selection of matter. At least a third of the former popular and in many respects valuable work was devoted to articles either entirely worthless, or recommended only by considerations foreign to the reader of poetry.

Hazlitt's book was not very fortunate.

Such being the established place of Knox's *Elegant Extracts* in England for a period which extended over the entire lifetime of Keats and Shelley, the effects on general reading taste are self-evident, and only a slight review of what Knox set before his public is necessary. The succeeding editions varied from each other, yet the prevailing character of *Elegant Extracts* remained; and it does not greatly matter which edition is inspected since the essentials are in all. That of 1809 stood already on the reputation of a quarter of a century—I speak of the anthology of verse, *Elegant Extracts : or, useful and entertaining Pieces of Poetry, Selected for the Improvement of Young Persons*. The Trade clearly approved of it, for the names of forty-nine publishing firms are set out on the title-page, beneath a pretty oval vignette from a drawing by E. F. Burney. In a scene of roses and evergreens with a Gothic hall behind, and a game of cricket going on not far off, an elegant boy reads a book and at the same time superintends a fishing rod; another with quill in hand looks aloft for inspiration; a third is preoccupied with three immense volumes, presumably the anthologies of Dr. Knox.

Utility and innocent entertainment are the sole designs of the Editor. . . . He is ready to confess, that almost any man willing to incur a considerable expense, and undergo a little trouble, might have furnished as good a collection.

Knox at any rate incurred the expense and underwent the trouble before anyone else thought of it. His aims were to assist schools 'in recitation, transcription, the exercise of the memory, or in imitation', but he did not lack a certain vision on the nature of poetry and its place in civilized life. With a floridity of speech which he perhaps thought was his legacy from Dr. Johnson, he dilated on this subject.

Through the pleasant paths of Poetry [he argued] many young persons have been gradually led to the heights of science: they have been allured, on first setting out, by the beauty of the scene presented to them, into a delightful land, flowing with milk and honey; where, after having been nourished like the infant at the mother's breast, they have gradually acquired strength enough to relish and digest the solidest food of philosophy.

He admitted that 'many sensible persons in the world' objected to the young reading poetry, because 'it interfered with an attention to what they called the MAIN CHANCE'; but he was not intimidated.

There is no good reason to be given why the mercantile classes, at least of the higher order, should not amuse their leisure with any pleasures of polite literature. Nothing perhaps contributes more to liberalize their minds and prevent that narrowness which is too often the consequence of a life attached, from the earliest age, to the pursuits of lucre.

Wordsworth was soon to express something like this conviction, but not quite in this style.

Another point made clear, or detachable from the flowers of speech, in Knox's Preface is that he intended to stick to pieces 'publicly known and universally celebrated', even if it meant inserting things now and then 'entirely in submissive deference to public opinion'; which (he adds, and we hear a mightier voice insisting through his words) 'when general and long continued, is the best criterion of merit in the fine arts, and particularly in Poetry'. He said that his selections, familiar as they were to older readers, would naturally be new to young ones, and he evidently meant to fit the latter as well as he could for the society and the conversation of the time. On that score, it is historically interesting to see how he classified his extracts and what in his thousand pages, double-columned, he chose.

The First Book is headed 'Sacred and Moral'. Milton is admitted here with the 'Morning Hymn of Adam and Eve', but that is all we see of him; perhaps the poor old soul had been pushed from his throne as according to report he has again been lately. There are several paraphrases from Psalms, not by him, but by competent persons like James Merrick and Christopher Pitt, and even Miss Williams, that great supporter of the French Revolution. Her inclusion is a sign of the fame that she, and even her verses (one hardly knows why), had acquired. The extent to which prize poems were read during the eighteenth century appears especially in the republication among others of Christopher Smart's five Seatonian compositions (already many years old) on the attributes of the Supreme Being. In these the boys had a certain amount of the material of the 'Song to David' without the inspiration, and were safely schooled in the judgement of the day. If, even so, some casual touch of glory and mystery alarmed them in Smart, they had the 'Visions' of Dr. Cotton to turn to, the physician who was good to William Cowper:

> A rural landscape I descried,
> Drest in the robes of summer pride;
> The herds adorn'd the sloping hills,
> That glitter'd with their tinkling rills;
> Below, the fleecy mothers stray'd,
> And round their sportive lambkins play'd.

Or they could, with more hope, pass to the 'Fables, by the late Mr. Gay', or 'Fables for the Female Sex' by Mr. Moore, or sundry other specimens of this kind of rhyming. A mass of mostly celebrated passages from Young's *Night Thoughts* was there at their service, though they had probably received *that* work from solicitous aunts as a Christmas gift.

In this 'Sacred and Moral' section are seen Gray's *Elegy* next to Porteus on Death, which the young must have found less bearable: it begins less pastorally,

> Friend to the wretch whom every friend forsakes,
> I woo thee, Death!

In case Porteus on Death did not strike home, Blair's *Grave* was at hand. *The Vanity of Human Wishes* was duly given, and another noble poem which needed no graveyard spectres to be moral was not forgotten, the 'Know Thyself' of John Arbuthnot. This last perhaps, as a piece then demanded by general taste, in spite of its remote date, is a little unexpected, but not so much so as two poems by Robert Burns: 'Despondency, an Ode,' and 'A Prayer in the Prospect of Death'. These illustrate the reason of Burns's great early reputation in a light which perhaps is not observed enough at the present time.

Knox's Second Book is allotted to the 'Didactic, Descriptive, Narrative, and Pathetic', and it is extensive. It is not subject to very rigid rules of selection; into it he bundles all the Odes of Gray, and *The Splendid Shilling* of J. Philips. There are indeed large supplies of odes in this book, Tom Warton's, Smollett's, Ogilvie's, but curiously enough not those of Collins. We shall come to those. Here is plenty of Dryden and Pope, and clearly the taste for some seventeenth-century couplet-writers had not declined: Waller, Denham, Buckingham appear. The boys have Somerville's *Chace* and Armstrong's *Art of Preserving Health* to train them in blank verse, besides parts of *The Seasons*, and selections from Cowper. A great deal of liberal opinion comes out in Knox's choice, and he will include, for the sake of its humanitarian doctrine, an occasional piece which even at the time was not well known. Such is 'Morning; or, The Complaint. An American Eclogue', ascribed simply to 'Gregory'. In form and manner it is modelled on Collins's *Persian Eclogues*, in substance it is a grim attack on slave-owners. The pieces following it are from Crabbe's *Village*, and these too may be supposed to have 'put ideas into the boys' heads'. We are not surprised to find Chatterton represented, and it is a triumph of general feeling for poetry that one of the selections was—that is, had to be—

> O! synge untoe my roundelaie.

Towards the end of the book it is found, with less congratulation, that Samuel Rogers has made himself a very comfortable name in the closing years of the eighteenth century; not only his *Pleasures of Memory* but two or three of his little idyllic pieces are gathered in, and the school of simplicity is commended to notice not by Wordsworth's Lucy but by his:

> Around my ivied porch shall spring
> Each fragrant flower that drinks the dew;
> And Lucy at her wheel shall sing,
> In russet gown and apron blue.

The Third Book, ushered in with a vignette of a boy enthralling some of his schoolfellows in the classroom with a little acting, is 'Dramatic, chiefly from Shakespeare'. This is the section probably which especially disappointed Charles Lamb, who wrote to Coleridge at the end of June 1796:

I wish you would try and do something to bring our elder bards into more general fame. I writhe with indignation when in books of Criticism, where common place quotation is heaped upon quotation, I find no mention of such men as Massinger, or B[eaumont] and F[letcher], men with whom succeeding Dramatic Writers (Otway alone excepted) can bear no manner of comparison. Stupid Knox hath noticed none of 'em among his extracts.

But Lamb was neglecting Knox's preface and the limited purpose which is stated there. Knox supplied, besides extracts, the whole of Addison's *Cato* and, what is more surprising, the whole of Edmund Smith's *Phaedra and Hippolitus*—surprising, if it signifies that the public still called for it, and also because Dr. Johnson thought that they did not and agreed with them. 'It is a scholar's play.' That may be the point on which Knox dwelt in considering Johnson's remarks.

At length Knox brings on his rag-bag, the Fourth Book, 'consisting of Odes, Sonnets, Classical Songs, Ancient and Modern Ballads, Comic Tales, Epigrams and Epitaphs, various amusing little Poems, Prologues and Epilogues'. It is at once observable how the 'minor poems' of Milton continued to bewitch the reader as they had for long done. Johnson being by this time out of reach, Knox could even represent the Sonnets. The descriptions in Spenser are next presented, and then a specimen or two of Fairfax's Tasso—a prelude to the revival of that almost great work. No such revival was awaiting Glover's *Leonidas*, an epic which it may be suspected was honoured mainly out of timidity, deference, and indolence. As for sonnets, which had had so curious a history since Milton's appeared, the spirit of the age had elected to create them, and Knox as best he could was following that spirit. So the boys had a fair share of Charlotte Smith's pensive utterances, and here too Helen Maria Williams had her place; her 'Sonnet to Hope' is among the examples, 'To Twilight' also. In 1833 Wordsworth advised Dyce that 'Miss Williams's Sonnet upon Twilight is pleasing; that upon Hope of great merit'. And it would have been odd if Tom Warton's sonnets were not brought out again in such a setting. Suddenly in this section Knox plays a trick on his audience by thrusting in the 'Odes' of Collins, and it is all the more odd since he had previously made use of Joseph Warton's 'Ode to Evening', and might have passed then to Warton's friend and competitor. Once again we find what Burns's greatness was in the eyes of his English contemporaries. 'To a Mouse' and 'To a Mountain Daisy' are included, and the humanitarian movement will have been greatly strengthened by this means.

If the place of Swift among the poets has been by now unjustly lessened, it is no fault of Knox and his book. Forty tall columns are allotted to Swift's verse. The kindly anthologist, in truth, employs it partly in reference to the last word in the title of his Fourth Book: 'Sentimental, Lyrical, and Ludicrous'; games were in his mind, and the riddles of Swift are very good games.

> We are little airy creatures,
> All of diff'rent voice and features:
> One of us in glass is set,
> One of us you'll find in jet;
> T'other you may see in tin,
> And the fourth a box within;
> If the fifth you should pursue,
> It can never fly from you.

But the greater Swift has the larger province. *On the Death of Dr. Swift* is there. The inimitable parodies, the 'Description of the Morning' and 'Description of a City Shower', may lead to a slight reflection on the flourishing taste throughout Knox's lifetime for parody and imitation. It 'was not counted stain' that a man, or the child the father of the man, should enjoy within a few pages the original 'L'Allegro', and 'L'Allegro; or Fun, a Parody'.

> Off, blubbering Melancholy,
>   Of the blue devils and book-learning born,
>   In dusty schools forlorn,
> Among black gowns, square caps, and books unjolly.
>   Hunt out some college cell
> Where muzzing quizzes mutter monkish schemes,
>   And the old proctor dreams;
> There in thy smutty walls, o'ergrown with dock,
>   As ragged as thy smock,
> With rusty, fusty Fellows ever dwell.

This connexion of university life with parody is seen also in Knox's choice from the many imitations of Gray's *Elegy*; that, namely, by Duncombe, 'An Evening Contemplation in a College'. A curiosity is the imitation of imitation, and having given *The Splendid Shilling* a dignity among the Didactic (or Pathetic) class Knox supplies two pieces which it suggested, Bramston's 'Crooked Sixpence' and Mrs. Pennington's 'Copper

Farthing'. Not to stay too long among these varied pieces, we just notice the effect of Percy's *Reliques* on a representative anthology and the obvious success with all kinds of people of the songs of Dibdin.

Altogether, Knox with all his muddles and (it must be added of the later editions) all his misprints succeeded in making a useful book of English verse, a small library of it in a single volume. It is in the main a book of eighteenth-century verse, and has still a value apart from its being a register of taste; for one can find almost everything in it that is likely to be wanted in the ordinary way, besides a number of things that have become difficult of access in other forms of publication. It may deserve more attention from authorities on the history of our education than it has had, and that would of course be what the anthologist, an enthusiast for the useful and agreeable in teaching, would have liked. It was part of a campaign. As for any claim that might have been made for it in point of fine discernment and proportioned choice, it will scarcely be made in a period which possesses the *Oxford Book of Eighteenth Century Verse*.

The edition of Knox's corresponding *Elegant Extracts: or useful and entertaining Passages in Prose* which is available to the present writer is the seventh (1797), and it has a special 'Advertisement' which emphasizes Knox's chief designs. 'This whole Set of Extracts, more copious, more convenient in its form, and valuable in its materials, than any which have preceded it, certainly conduces, in a very high degree, to that great national object, the PUBLIC INSTRUCTION, to promote which has been the primary object of the compiler.' Another purpose included within that was to correct a disproportion: in the past, Knox asserts, 'the ENGLISH PART of education (to many the most important part) was defective even in places most celebrated for classic discipline; and boys were often enabled to read Latin perfectly, and write it tolerably, who, from the disuse, or the want of models for practice, were wretchedly qualified to do either in their native language'. An enormous quantity of materials was now set before their sons.

The Moral and Religious passages begin with Addison's 'Vision of Mirza' and end with the Lord's Prayer. Within these boundaries Knox sets a multitude of writings most of which to-day are little known and seldom seen. He draws freely indeed

upon the great periodicals which continue to be valued and
enjoyed, the *Spectator* and *Tatler* and *Guardian*, the *Idler* and
Rambler and *Adventurer*, and some of his other moralists are at
least respected by literary historians; but I do not know where
else I should easily find Queen Anne's Prayer, Prince Eugene's
Prayer, the Physico-Theological Reflections of Ferguson, and
excerpts from Dean Bolton's *Works*. James Ferguson, mechani-
cian and astronomer, eventually had Sir David Brewster for his
editor; a glance at his delightfully lavish accounts of God's works
brings to mind such physico-theological schoolboys as Shelley
and Tennyson. Robert Bolton, Dean of Carlisle, is able to make
exhortations against intemperance in eating and on the employment of time quite attractive in his plain prose and with his
knowledge and humour. The extraordinary passion of the
eighteenth century for disguises and imitations is declared by
the inclusion entire of that very ambitious scriptural production,
the *Economy of Human Life*:

The piety of a child is sweeter than the incense of Persia offered
to the sun; yea more delicious than odours wafted from a field of
Arabian spices by the western gales.

The Second Book of these Prose Extracts is 'Classical and
Historical'. It is largely intended to form a general critical
taste, and to assist the young in making judgements on particular
authors and works. Within its wide bounds there is space for
such masterpieces as Johnson's Preface to Shakespeare and
Pope's Preface to his Homer. With these Knox places 'An Essay
on Virgil's Georgics, prefixed to Mr. Dryden's Translation', by
Mr. Addison, and its virtues do not disappear by reason of the
juxtaposition. Yet this book's instruction is often of a more
philosophical kind, and the names of the treatise-spinners,
Blair, Harris, Usher, abound in the list. Spence's estimates of
ancient authors are freely used. A name less familiar even to the
scholarly now is Henry Felton, once Principal of St. Edmund
Hall, among whose commendations there is one on Shakespeare
beginning, 'Shakespeare is a wonderful genius'. Packed away
among such contributions is a history of the heathen deities,
which probably was more often consulted than the abstract
principles of criticism.

Then comes a Book of celebrated Orations, translated from
the Greek or Latin, or selected from British eloquence (and

Knox does not forget his Shakespeare in that selecting). With these are assembled out of the ancient and modern historians many characters of eminent men and women; there are no fewer than four of the elder Pitt. An anonymous author shall remind us of the manner of those times in defining a remarkable man:

Upon the whole, there was in this man something that could create, subvert, or reform; an understanding, a spirit, and an eloquence, to summon mankind to society, or to break the bonds of slavery asunder, and to rule the wilderness of free minds with unbounded authority; something that could establish or overwhelm empire, and strike a blow in the world that should resound through the universe.

From these stately altitudes the boys could soon turn to the Fourth Book containing 'Narratives, Dialogues, &c. with other Humorous, Facetious and Entertaining Pieces'. Here they had (Sterne's) Yorick and Falstaff; they were not allowed the humours and situations of Fielding and Smollett, but they could voyage to Lilliput and to Brobdingnag, and study the biography of Martinus Scriblerus. Such items as an 'Essay on Suicide' might not be very easily accepted as entertaining pieces, and even if Burke wrote it, 'Terror, a Source of the Sublime' could scarcely be a holiday task; the way of Vicesimus Knox is often mysterious. But he was liberal with his favourite papers from the periodical essayists, and among others from Bonnell Thornton, who did his work so skilfully and pleasantly. His 'Family Going to the Seaside' is not so good, we know, as similar studies by Charles Lamb or Charles Dickens, but at an age when they were not it must have had a similar effect.

Now the *Elegant Extracts in Prose* might have been considered complete but for the fact that it was the age of Linnaeus—and an Englishman may add, of White of Selborne. There was therefore an Appendix, 'to accustom young People to the innocent and agreeable Employment of observing Nature', and it contained Benjamin Stillingfleet's 'Calendar of Flora', and a series of descriptions from Pennant's *Natural History*, particularly a 'Synopsis of British Dogs'. With these, and with a chronological table of events, discoveries, inventions, besides a catalogue of men of learning and genius, the volume concludes.

One more of its kind remains at its side. This is *Elegant Epistles: or, a Copious Collection of Familiar and Amusing Letters.* It had its vogue; the present comments are chiefly made on the first edition dated 1790. Later editions were very much altered and enlarged, notably with Knox's finds among the letter-writers of France. Perhaps an extended account of the *Elegant Epistles* is not called for. Some of the writers would hardly be given as much of a benefit to-day as Knox expected for them in 1790. Dr. Rundle, Archbishop Herring, Bishop Gibson, Lady Russell, the Countess of Hertford might not now be inspected at all closely by an anthologist of letter-writing. They knew something about the art, and on this occasion an observation by Archbishop Herring may well be gleaned: of Pope he says, 'His acrimony was the sting of the bee, for such he was, rather than a wasp.' But Howell, Pope, Gray, Sterne, and their correspondents are also in Knox's bag, and a whole section was set apart for the letters between Dr. Johnson and Mrs. Thrale and some others of Johnson's—at a date before Boswell's *Life* was achieved. This was almost business efficiency! Later on Knox would be bringing in some of the letters to Boswell, and adding 'copious' examples of other excellent hands like Steele and Shenstone—and always, of course, his book provided an array of the letters, done into English, of the ancients who have left any.

Before the publications of Knox had altogether ceased to be in favour, his title was borrowed by other compilers. Those who are acquainted with his own repository may also have observed a row of pocket volumes printed at Chiswick by C. Whittingham between 1823 and 1827, partly called *Elegant Extracts* and partly *New Elegant Extracts*. The editor was R. A. Davenport, that obscure figure who seems to have spent his life in sifting out literary odds and ends, and among other things conducted that sleepy annual *The Poetical Register*. I believe that he was one of the opium-eaters of that period, and died forlorn in a house overflowing with books and spiders' webs. As for *his* 'Elegant Extracts', he refers at the outset to the 'many Selections, with the name, or on the plan' of Knox's work, but his own aim was different. Davenport asserts that his predecessors had been giving, one after another, 'almost the identical mixture which has often been poured out before'. Besides, his collection of pieces not contained in them was not meant for schoolboys but for grown-up readers. It ranges over poetry (our own and our translations), prose, and epistles. It is like all the queer miscellaneous literary gatherings of the Romantic period, chaotic and perhaps all the more interesting on that account. Things may be found in it by the literary inquirer with a special object which would be otherwise even less likely to be traced, or thought of at all, than anything in Knox's volumes.

To the Rev. Vicesimus Knox, however, the conclusion of this slight account of one of his numerous enterprises is due. Boswell dined with Johnson, Knox, the poet Beattie, and others at Mr. Dilly's on 24 June 1784, but leaves no record of Knox's personal characteristics or share in the conversation. When he includes Knox in the list of perpetual imitators of Johnson's style, he treats him to a longish footnote, and begins in none too friendly a manner. He is displeased with some attacks made by Knox, even if they were restricted to 'certain particulars', on his *alma mater*, the University of Oxford. Boswell, however, goes on to say:

While I animadvert on what appears to me exceptionable in some of the works of Dr. Knox, I cannot refuse due praise to others of his productions; particularly his sermons, and to the spirit with which he maintains, against presumptuous hereticks, the consolatory doctrines peculiar to the Christian Revelation. This he has done in a manner equally strenuous and conciliating. Neither ought I to omit mentioning a remarkable instance of his candour: Notwithstanding the wide difference of our opinions, upon the important subject of University education, in a letter to me concerning this Work, he thus expresses himself: 'I thank you for the very great entertainment your *Life of Johnson* gives me. It is a most valuable work. Yours is a new species of biography. Happy for Johnson, that he had so able a recorder of his wit and wisdom.'

In all this, no word of *Elegant Extracts*; and yet those three volumes probably exhibit the spirit of Knox at its best, in its vernal mood. They are faintly touched with absurdity, but they announce an ideal, and perhaps set up a sort of mirror in which the modern educator may look and see not so much the absurdity of Knox as the uncertainties of our own practice. Knox had in mind not the boy who can deal adroitly with examiners but the future citizen; he wanted him to read for the good of his character and his command of life, within himself and without. Imagination can hardly paint the boy, even among Dr. Knox's own pupils at Tonbridge, who could have engulfed the whole, or half, or a quarter of the tremendous dispensation of moral advice freely flowing in *Elegant Extracts*. But, as has been seen, there were other refreshments in the house, and the spirit of the whole was 'equally strenuous and conciliating'. As Charles Lamb said in his own way, from the literary point of view Knox might have been something else; and the boys who had enjoyed and taken pains with the reading of his three volumes were still, so far as that experience went, unaware of a great deal of our finest prose and verse. (They might never have heard of Ben Jonson.) They would nevertheless be versed in about a century of very clear and various and wise writing, and presumably the man who had made that possible by his labour and ingenuity —anticipating the 'five-foot bookshelf'—may be forgiven for being 'stupid', as he is in points of arrangement apart from chosen boundaries. One further point occurs to me. It is in modern America that extensive school anthologies something after the model of Knox's have been appearing in our own day. Listening lately to an American broadcast programme for the troops, I heard allusions to Shakespeare, Chaucer, and Milton, joking of course included; but I could not help feeling that it was no insignificant thing for these allusions to be made at all on such an occasion, with the implication that they would mean something to the majority of the audience. 'Comparisons', as Knox would have unhesitatingly said, 'are odious.' But somehow I was thinking that the teaching of English literature here in respect of the widest audience had missed the boat, and that the humaner, the more social and more life-fulfilling idea tried in *Elegant Extracts* had gone overseas.

'THE OLD CUMBERLAND BEGGAR' AND THE WORDSWORTHIAN UNITIES

H. V. D. DYSON

IT would be a pity if a collection of studies in eighteenth-century literature did not include at least one on Wordsworth. In Wordsworth so many characteristics which we associate with the literature of this century meet, combine, and are fulfilled. That strong awareness of the artistic, social, and spiritual significance of everyday commonplace people and affairs, the intricate elaboration of emotional sensibility, the preoccupation with moral issues, the deep sense of discipline and order and respect for traditional ways of life are all found in him, freshly presented and with a new impetus, and moving in new directions. Wordsworth is so often strong where the century is strong and weak where it is weak. Like Addison he is often trite and like Swift perverse; the emotional eccentricity which in Sterne is so often a wonder and delight disfigures some of the weaker poems in *Lyrical Ballads*.

His view of society was at once dynamic as was fitting in the age of the French Revolution and imbued with a deep reverence for customs and institutions appropriate in a contemporary of Burke. If we care to contrast his outlook with that of Pope, society's most admired and eloquent entertainer and spokesman in the early part of the eighteenth century, we shall, I believe, find that civilization meant less to him than to Pope, and culture, both of the individual and of the community, more. He saw man moving in a larger, more complicated context and saw him in a simpler if a profounder way. One of the three genuinely prophetic writers which the century produced, he spoke of wider issues than Burke and to a wider audience than Blake. His prophesying found its characteristic note well before the century's close. It is fully heard in 'The Old Cumberland Beggar', a poem which although not printed until the first month of the nineteenth century when it appeared in the second volume of *Lyrical Ballads*—dated 1800—was probably composed in 1797–8, during the earlier gestatory processes of the poem we now know as *The Prelude*. Indeed it may well have been conceived at first as an episode of the longer poem which Wordsworth still thought of as *The Recluse*. The old beggar might have figured amongst the notable solitaries of the great epic and would not have seemed incongruous.

'The Old Cumberland Beggar' has affinities with some of the poetry of the previous twenty years. It has not less acute observation and accurate detail than *The Village*; like the much more massive *Task* it is discursive and speculative, moving easily in regions well known to and long observed by the poet. Of all the poems in *Lyrical Ballads* it is the least lyrical in impulse and the least ballad-like in movement; it is no doubt one of those referred to on the title-page as 'other Poems'. We feel that it is rather shaped by the experience it records than imposes shape upon it. For all his knowledge of English poetry and deep interest in theories about his art Wordsworth is of our great poets the one least controlled by formal tradition. His great technical triumphs in ode and lyric and sonnet are late and, on the whole, we do not bear in mind the outward patterns of most of his work. The term 'lyrical ballad' as applied to his work is really meaningless, and the mighty *Prelude* itself is almost casually set down. It is by the brilliant balancing of elements inside the poem, one theme against another, that Wordsworth achieves his poetic intensity. 'The Old Cumberland Beggar' is one of those many poems in which the versification is incomparably the least interesting and least important part. Nor is the diction of particular note. What interests us is in the main his power of describing in a matter-of-fact way carefully seen objects and interpenetrating this description with arresting spiritual commentary. It is a piece of intense poetic observation enriched by profound moral insight and has so far escaped being overmuch 'clapper-clawed with the palms' of devout Wordsworthians. He is not yet the master of memorable images, there is here nothing like that figure—old man, sea-beast, huge stone on mountain—which is one of the special glories of 'Resolution and Independence', a poem which develops certain possibilities here hinted at. 'The Old Cumberland Beggar' opens with matter-of-fact directness. We are shown the old man seated on a low structure of rude masonry at the foot of a huge hill. Size, remoteness, and the immobility of old age are closely associated and introduce us to the atmosphere of the entire poem. But though they reinforce, they do not illustrate one another as in the image in the later poem; Wordsworth is not yet ready for that way of writing. A slowly moving old man in a sparsely inhabited country of great hills—that is the outer fabric of the poet's vision. His slowness is emphasized here as always. Scarcely can the tremor of his hand, the first movement to catch the eye, keep at a distance the small mountain birds which share his meal. We have him more or less in sight during most of the poem from his first emergence, scarcely distinguishable from his environment, to the benison of his final dismissal. He is nearly as intimately related to the landscape through which he moves as the figures in a Blake engraving are to the settings from which and into which they seem to flow. There he has lived, there he will die. It is not quite clear what to die 'in the eye of nature' means. Probably no more than that he shall not die in a workhouse—

> May never House, misnamed of industry,
> Make him a captive.

The priest in 'The Brothers' may well have voiced Wordsworth's own view when he declared that

> The thought of death sits easy on the man
> Who has been born and dies among the mountains.

Perhaps the vast gorgeous display of winds and vapour which triumphed in the heavens shortly before the passing of another poor mountain-dweller will at the end honour the dissolution of this 'old mendicant':

> Glory beyond all glory ever seen
> By waking sense or by the dreaming soul!
> The appearance, instantaneously disclosed,
> Was of a mighty city—boldly say
> A wilderness of building, sinking far
> And self-withdrawn into a boundless depth,
> Far sinking into splendour—without end!
> Fabric it seemed of diamond and of gold,
> With alabaster domes, and silver spires,
> And blazing terrace upon terrace, high
> Uplifted; here, serene pavilions bright,
> In avenues disposed; there, towers begirt
> With battlements that on their restless fronts
> Bore stars—illumination of all gems!
> By earthly nature had the effect been wrought
> Upon the dark materials of the storm
> Now pacified; on them, and on the coves
> And mountain-steeps and summits, whereunto

The vapours had receded, taking there
Their station under a cerulean sky.
  Oh, 'twas an unimaginable sight!
Clouds, mists, streams, watery rocks and emerald turf,
Clouds of all tincture, rocks and sapphire sky,
Confused, commingled, mutually inflamed,
Molten together, and composing thus,
Each lost in each, that marvellous array
Of temple, palace, citadel, and huge
Fantastic pomp of structure without name,
In fleecy folds voluminous, enwrapped.
Right in the midst, where interspace appeared
Of open court, an object like a throne
Under a shining canopy of state
Stood fixed; and fixed resemblances were seen
To implements of ordinary use,
But vast in size, in substance glorified;
Such as by Hebrew prophets were beheld
In vision—forms uncouth of mightiest power
For admiration and mysterious awe.[1]

But Wordsworth is not yet the pageant-master to supervise such ceremonies, and more probably one day the poet, or another, will find the old man

> seated by the highway side
> On a low structure of rude masonry

and the small birds, their 'destined meal' long eaten, no more afraid to venture 'within the length of half his staff'. He will have become a portion of the surrounding country-side as unobtrusively as he once emerged from it.

But quite certainly Wordsworth was in grim earnest about the workhouse. No one was more acutely aware than he of the threats to traditional human relationships involved in the haphazard regrouping of men and women in a rapidly changing social and economic order, and no one protested more emphatically against the inhumanity of the new Poor Law. He knew well enough the danger and evil that lay in treating men as things. In his well-known letter of 14 January 1801 to Charles James Fox which accompanied a set of the volumes in which this poem first appeared, his comments have particular reference to 'The Brothers' and 'Michael'. But 'The Old Cumberland Beggar' illustrates equally well a somewhat different aspect of

[1] *The Excursion*, ii. 832–69.

the problem, describing as it does a long-settled community life which is threatened by the new order of things. This is the relevant paragraph of the letter.

It appears to me that the most calamitous effect, which has followed the measures which have lately been pursued in this country, is a rapid decay of the domestic affections among the lower orders of society. This effect the present Rulers of this Country are not conscious of, or they disregard it. For many years past, the tendency of society amongst almost all the nations of Europe has been to produce it. But recently by the spreading of manufactures through every part of the country, by the heavy taxes upon postage, by workhouses, Houses of Industry, and the invention of Soup-shops &c. &c. superadded to the encreasing disproportion between the price of labour and that of the necessaries of life, the bonds of domestic feeling among the poor, as far as the influence of these things has extended, have been weakened, and in innumerable instances entirely destroyed. The evil would be the less to be regretted, if these institutions were regarded only as palliatives to a disease; but the vanity and pride of their promoters are so subtly interwoven with them, that they are deemed great discoveries and blessings to humanity. In the mean time parents are separated from their children, and children from their parents; the wife no longer prepares with her own hands a meal for her husband, the produce of his labour; there is little doing in his house in which his affections can be interested, and but little left in it which he can love. I have two neighbours, a man and his wife, both upwards of eighty years of age; they live alone; the husband has been confined to his bed many months and has never had, nor till within these few weeks has ever needed, any body to attend to him but his wife. She has recently been seized with a lameness which has often prevented her from being able to carry him his food to his bed; the neighbours fetch water for her from the well, and do other kind offices for them both, but her infirmities encrease. She told my Servant two days ago that she was afraid they must both be boarded out among some other Poor of the parish (they have long been supported by the parish) but she said, it was hard, having kept house together so long, to come to this, and she was sure that 'it would burst her heart'. I mention this fact to show how deeply the spirit of independence is, even yet, rooted in some parts of the country. These people could not express themselves in this way without an almost sublime conviction of the blessings of independent domestic life. If it is true, as I believe, that this spirit is rapidly disappearing, no greater curse can befal a land.[1]

---

[1] *Early Letters of William and Dorothy Wordsworth*, ed. E. de Selincourt (Oxford, 1935), pp. 260-1.

The poem here in question cries a warning against some of the tendencies of the time; the beggar and other remembered solitaries are loved vestiges of a way of life that is passing. Events here are not events as in tragedy, epic, or ballad, which are presented as exciting, or interesting for their own sakes or for the consequences that flow from them: there is here no change, no turn of fortune, no drama. Except in the opening paragraph there is scarcely a hint of an aorist; the dominant tenses are those of habit, present and imperfect, underpinned by an occasional pluperfect. We are examining life rather than lives, the life of a community as it affects the beggar and as it is affected by him. Almost all the happenings described are customary and habitual. Wordsworth's power of observation and accurate recording give them at once immediacy and definition.

I suppose we should not take the old man too seriously. He sometimes appears to be simply a function of age, indigence, and solitude. His personal sufferings are no part of the poem: as we see them they are translated into things rich and strange. He hardly shows the human consciousness or the human form:

> Bowbent, his eyes for ever on the ground,
> He plies his weary journey.

Unlike the similarly shaped leech-gatherer whose

> body was bent double, feet and head
> Coming together in life's pilgrimage

but who was reflective and articulate, he has nothing to say. At least we never hear him speak. His 'thank you' is in his continued existence and his teaching is indirect. He moves so slowly that he is almost motionless, the cottage curs grow weary of barking before he has passed, his feet hardly raise the summer dust as they shuffle along.

> Boys and girls,
> The vacant and the busy, maids and youths,
> And urchins newly breech'd all pass him by:
> Him even the slow-paced waggon leaves behind.

Almost imperceptibly he crosses our vision, a piece of detached and drifting landscape unpurposeful save in his continued living. Yet this solitary is a link between lonely households, the charities done to him movements in a social ritual; slow as he is, he is a quickener of people's hearts. No less than Oedipus in Sophocles' last play he is at once outcast and benefactor, bearing a secret blessing beneath his rags.

In his understanding of the nature and needs of poverty Wordsworth is almost Shakespearian. The sting of poverty is twofold. First the infinite lack which sheer beggary knows—the bitter want of necessaries. Lear's vision of the poor naked wretches and their houseless heads and unfed sides, their looped and windowed raggedness, aches at us like physical pain. Poverty's other hurt is also proclaimed by Lear, somewhat earlier in his progress to the state where he excites and no longer bestows charity. It is the lack of that *superfluity* which distinguishes man from beast: man is not to be defined in terms of the elementary needs of living. The king has been stripped of his authority and its symbols; the roll of his knights has been progressively diminished until Regan cries 'What need one?' Lear slowly moving in his rage and despair towards madness and wisdom knows the answer.

> O! reason not the need; our basest beggars
> Are in the poorest thing superfluous:
> Allow not nature more than nature needs,
> Man's life is cheap as beast's. Thou art a lady;
> If only to go warm were gorgeous,
> Why, nature needs not what thou gorgeous wear'st
> Which scarcely keeps thee warm!

'Allow not nature more than nature needs', that is the point. Even the poorest craves as token of his human status some slight unnecessary things to wear, to squander, or to bestow in pathetic charity. As Wordsworth puts it in this poem in which these two kinds of poverty meet and relieve each other,

> the poorest poor
> Long for some moments in a weary life
> When they can know and feel that they have been
> Themselves the fathers and the dealers out
> Of some small blessings, have been kind to such
> As needed kindness, for this single cause,
> That we have all of us one human heart.

This beggar is so poor that he can make the poorest rich: compared with his their poverty is wealth. Any passer-by that he may meet is better off than he, and can afford him alms and in so doing achieve a kind of promotion. In that free, remote society of the hills he has his place as a full human being at once receiving and bestowing bounty.

> Such pleasure is to one kind Being known
> My Neighbour, when with punctual care, each week
> Duly as Friday comes, though press'd herself
> By her own wants, she from her chest of meal
> Takes one unsparing handful for the scrip
> Of this old Mendicant, and, from her door
> Returning with exhilarated heart,
> Sits by her fire, and builds her hope in heaven.

Just as his poverty breeds a kind of wealth, so his completely solitary life is contrasted with and yet also appears as a valuable element in the social life of the district. The themes of solitude and unity are tightly interwoven.

In different forms unity is a leading subject of Wordsworth's poetry: it cannot be fully understood or appreciated unless this is realized. He never fully and finally stated his views on the unities of which he is so conscious; but there is scarcely a poem which does not suggest something of them. His vision of unity was, like Blake's system of imaginative interpretation, fourfold. But it was less symbolic than Blake's way of seeing things and at once more actual and more immediate. The finding, losing, and recovering of these major unities is the main business of *The Prelude*, and it is handled again more quietly, more coolly, and in the light of more orthodox references in *The Excursion*.

The most familiar is perhaps the unity of man with his physical environment, with the natural order. 'Tintern Abbey', *The Prelude*, and 'Intimations of Immortality' have familiarized us with different stages of Wordsworth's own experience of this. There is no need here to attempt a new survey in detail of Wordsworth's attitude to nature; it is enough to recall how varied and complex this relationship was. From the beginning it was of extraordinary intensity, and was perhaps his most powerful stimulus to contemplation not only of nature itself but of man. Hence it was that nature was so vital a function in his normal life. This external unity with things was at once a symbol and a pre-condition of his unity with himself and with his fellow men. Besides all that, it afforded splendid new material for poetry, the making of which is itself a unification of experience selected and shaped under high pressure.

Personal unity, the unity of man with himself, has for Words-worth two forms: an inner unity of the spirit, of intellect and imagination, will and knowledge, and a unity in time, 'the child is father of the man'.

The first kind can most easily be illustrated negatively. Its collapse is told most vividly in those lines which describe the divorce between the poet's intelligence and his imagination during the time of acute unhappiness which followed his return from revolutionary France,

> Dragging all passions, notions, shapes of faith,
> Like culprits to the bar, suspiciously
> Calling the mind to establish in plain day
> Her titles and her honours, now believing,
> Now disbelieving, endlessly perplex'd
> With impulse, motive, right and wrong, the ground
> Of moral obligation, what the rule
> And what the sanction, till, demanding *proof*,
> And seeking it in everything, I lost
> All feeling of conviction, and, in fine,
> Sick, wearied out with contrarieties,
> Yielded up moral questions in despair.[1]

The other kind of self-unity is unity in time. The two extre-mities of life's pilgrimage, like the head and feet of his leech-gatherer, are constantly together in Wordsworth's mind. Old age and early childhood fascinated him and we often find them associated in his poems. To Wordsworth, to be one with his own past, neither to deny it nor to forget it, was of great importance. In the light of the past, present happiness is enhanced, present misery endurable. There have been early splendours and they need never pass away entirely. It is no less fatal for a man to be separated from his past than for his intellect to give the lie to his imagination. We constantly find Wordsworth anxious that the years shall not annul his first experiences; he is incessantly exploring the past for lost happiness, and becomes continually dependent on those

> spots of time,
> Which with distinct pre-eminence retain
> A vivifying Virtue, whence . . . our minds
> Are nourished and invisibly repair'd.[2]

---

[1] *The Prelude*, 1805–6, ed. E. de Selincourt (Oxford, 1926), x. 890–901.
[2] Ibid xi. 258–65.

This placing together of crabbed age and early youth is not simply a reminder of how well they can get on together provided that the former has retained or recovered the other's unself-conscious and innocent faithfulness of vision; it is also an assertion of the continuity of our experience. To forget or deny or betray the past is to abandon hope for the future.

The last of these major unities is social, the community of man with his fellows. In all except the very earliest stages of Wordsworth's life this is really more important to him than unity with his physical environment. The quality of his dealings with nature was highly exceptional, perhaps unique; in his relationships with himself and his fellow men he was deeply sensible of needs shared, though not always understood, by everyone.

His readers are constantly made aware of the supreme importance of this social unity. In the time of his great trouble he was not only at war within himself, with the faith and glory of his own past, he was also sundered from other men. In the same book of *The Prelude* in which he speaks of his self-division he tells us of this other desolation which has overwhelmed him. The nations, England and France, which had conferred upon him their several freedoms were at war, and he found himself a stranger. The older, deeper allegiance tore at him most painfully.

> I, who with the breeze
> Had play'd, a green leaf on the blessed tree
> Of my beloved country; nor had wish'd
> For happier fortune than to wither there,
> Now from my pleasant station was cut off,
> And toss'd about in whirlwinds. . . .
>
> . . . It was a grief,
> Grief call it not, 'twas anything but that,
> A conflict of sensations without name,
> Of which he only who may love the sight
> Of a Village Steeple as I do can judge
> When in the Congregation, bending all
> To their great Father, prayers were offer'd up,
> Or praises for our Country's Victories,
> And 'mid the simple worshippers, perchance,
> I only, like an uninvited Guest
> Whom no one own'd sate silent, shall I add,
> Fed on the day of vengeance yet to come?[1]

[1] Ibid. x. 254–75.

From this personal disaster Wordsworth had fully recovered when he was writing 'The Old Cumberland Beggar': it was already a two- or three-year-old memory and he was in process of finding his main subject. He had become a great poet in fact as well as in desire, and this poem is one of the earlier fruits of his *vita nuova*. Different kinds of unity are here contrasted with and balanced by the solitude of the beggar, whose solitude at once illuminates them and preserves them.

This theme, of solitude interacting with these different unities, is developed throughout the poem. It is a solitude untouched with that 'visionary dreariness' which Wordsworth evoked when he turned his most intense personal experiences into poetry. For this is not one of his markedly personal poems. The significance of the events of 'The Old Cumberland Beggar' is not that Wordsworth saw them or that they marked some critical phase of his imaginative development but simply that they *were* as he described them. They matter in their own right, in the fact of their stark objective reality. We have nothing like the 'affecting incident' which ever afterwards associated in his mind

> The single sheep, and the one blasted tree,
> And the bleak music of that old stone wall,
> The noise of wood and water, and the mist
> Which on the line of each of those two Roads
> Advanced in such indisputable shapes

with his father's death, nor are we in the region of

> the naked Pool,
> The Beacon on the lonely Eminence,
> The Woman, and her garments vex'd and toss'd
> By the strong wind.

The apocalyptic solitude of the high Alps seems far away from the hills over which the beggar wanders: his fate troubles the poet's intelligence rather than his dreams, his solitude is compounded of common, Wordsworth might have called them vulgar, distresses. He travels

> Among the farms and solitary huts,
> Hamlets, and thinly-scattered villages,

of an extensive, lightly populated country-side. All of those whom he encounters, post-boy, toll-keeper, cottager, would themselves seem solitary to a townsman and their way of life remote from ordinary human traffic. But he is remote even amidst these remote people.

As noted above, his poverty is unique and so extreme that everyone else seems in comparison well-to-do. No other mortal is as poor as he, or is poor in the same way. He is a passive figure, hardly human save in his needs. We see him sit and walk and eat, but the light of his mind burns low, his consciousness is in eclipse,

> seeing still,
> And never knowing that he sees, some straw,
> Some scatter'd leaf, or marks which, in one track,
> The nails of cart or chariot wheel have left
> Impressed on the white road, in the same line,
> At distance still the same.

The slowness of his journey is unmatched by man or beast.

But above all he is solitary in his antiquity. Like some ancient document whose value is only in its date he records nothing. It is others who remember him. He is eventless history. Wordsworth wisely did not pursue the plan that he seems once to have entertained and make him a character in a story. It may be supposed that the fragment printed in *Lyrical Ballads* of 1798 called 'Old Man Travelling' is a memorial of this rejected plan. It was not a happy idea. What should our beggar do with a son dying of injuries received in a sea-fight? What should he know of hospitals? He knows, and is content to know, nothing; his mild imbecility is his passport and his security. Just as his poverty conferred a form of wealth on those by whom it was relieved, so his solitude strengthens the bonds of neighbourhood and community amongst the inhabitants of the country-side. Charity towards him is a common burden gladly borne and accepted as a matter of course; the thoughtless and the loveless show kindness and consideration to him. There is no one who has not at some time relieved his wants. Not only is his maintenance a common obligation, he is also a common memory. All know him and remember him as helpless and old; he has, it seems, scarcely been known as anything else. This service, love, and memory are ever in the minds and hearts of that hard-working, far-scattered community. He, a solitary, tempers the solitude of others. Having no personal history he is a perpetual reminder of past deeds of charity and forbearance. He has had

> no trivial influence
> On that best portion of a good man's life;
> His little, nameless, unremembered acts
> Of kindness and of love.

The continuity which he provides with the past is particularly emphasized.

> While thus he creeps
> From door to door, the Villagers in him
> Behold a record which together binds
> Past deeds and offices of charity
> Else unremember'd, and so keeps alive
> The kindly mood in hearts which lapse of years,
> And that half-wisdom half-experience gives
> Make slow to feel, and by sure steps resign
> To selfishness and cold oblivious cares.

In him the past is ever present, his age takes from others the sense of the movement of time: his years, slow as his footsteps, seem locust-proof.

> Him from my childhood have I known; and then
> He was so old, he seems not older now.

'Nor', might the poet have added, 'do I seem older when I behold him': time seems to have provided an antidote against oblivion. The old man too is a kind of guarantee against that selfishness which threatens a frugal, hard-working, rural community, the self-sufficient kindness of the not unprosperous peasant proprietor. Wordsworth has made him a poetic symbol of the kinship which men have with one another, of the ever-living, ever-present past which in individual lives is so important an element of spiritual integrity, of the intimacy of man with his physical environment, and lastly of that self-unity which is a basis of human virtue. He excites response but never question.

It is an early poem. Wordsworth will do much greater things soon, but we can already find in it many of his characteristic moral and poetic qualities, qualities never far apart in him. His power of balancing opposites and showing their reconciliation in action was never more successfully shown. I think few earlier eighteenth-century writers would not have accepted it gladly; Pope, lover of freedom and hater of corruption, would have discreetly applauded the sentiments; Johnson, recoiling a little from the setting, would have endorsed the morality. It might have seemed a little strange to many, but I doubt if any of them would have repudiated it altogether; they would surely have understood what Wordsworth was trying to do. And if at times we feel cynical about this beggar and the good works that hang about him and think that it is all too perfect and too far from the facts of 'real life', we can always find dismal amusement in the miniature monstrosity of 'Andrew Jones'. Wordsworth knew as well as we do that age and disability are often subject to mockery and pillage.

MATTHEW ARNOLD AND
EIGHTEENTH-CENTURY POETRY

GEOFFREY TILLOTSON

I

WHEN we read the writings of Matthew Arnold we should remember that the better part of his working day went in attending to his profession of school inspector, and that the fifteen volumes of his collected works are the product of what time was left over from that. All adverse criticism of their contents should be prefaced by the acknowledgement that those volumes do exist, and that they exist to the number of fifteen. Such acknowledgement is, as I say, prefatory: we praise Arnold's achievement as an unusual one, as an instance of authorship against odds. Yet we cannot choose but proceed to examine his writings as unaccommodatingly as if he had poured out his whole working day into them. Our knowing that they are by-products, or, if not that, co-products, merely provides their shortcomings with a convenient explanation. Those shortcomings are particularly noticeable when Arnold is dealing with the past, when he is employed in glancing back at older civilizations, at the world's poetry and theology. On those occasions we cannot help wishing that Arnold had studied closely enough to strike the proper balance between interpretation and facts, between intelligence and its material.[1] That balance is well struck whenever he speaks of his own age, since in that field an adequate number of facts came his way

---

[1] The distinction between these two elements underlies Arnold's remarks about Stubbs's *Constitutional History of England* in a letter to M. Fontanès of 15 Dec. 1878: 'Stubbs's book is a sound and substantial one, but rather overpraised by a certain school here, the school of Mr. Freeman, of whom Stubbs is a disciple. This school has done much to explore our early history and to throw light on the beginnings of our system of government and of our liberty; but they have not had a single man of genius, with the *étincelle* and the instinctive good sense and moderation which make a guide really attaching and useful. Freeman is an ardent, learned, and honest man, but he is a ferocious pedant, and Stubbs, though not ferocious, is not without his dash of pedantry.' (*Letters*, 1895, ii. 149; cf. ii. 123.)
Who but Arnold would ask that an historian, especially a constitutional historian, should provide sparkle? He himself always provided it, but not always enough soundness and substance.

inevitably. But he tells us little that we cannot dispense with about earlier ages, about the mysteries (for instance) of the Elizabethan age or of the eighteenth century. Arnold is a first-rate commentator on Victorian times (and an interesting one on our own, since he saw not only 'how the world is going', but also how the world 'must go');[1] but when his theme is times anterior to the Victorian, the hungry sheep look up, and are given merely the 'fragrant steams' of cooking.

II

Arnold's being a charming writer does not preclude his also being a writer given to pontificating: the charm is often priestly. He seems to have been the first critic to use the formula 'the most [beautiful] in the world',[2] a formula which both delights us with its all-out enthusiasm and disturbs us with its assumption of a supernatural omniscience and infallibility. Arnold's pontifical manner persists even when he is confessing that he is out of his depth. Usually he makes no such confession, and we therefore cannot usually tell when he is giving out what he has tested, and when he is giving out what he has seized on trust for the sake of a brilliant paragraph, a paragraph to 'startle', to shock, or to enchant, and so to contribute to the propaganda to which he devoted his life. In 'The Literary Influence of Academies' (1864) there is a passage (it is almost a melodramatic incident) which, when linked with remarks from the preface to his selections from Burke (1881), suggests that Arnold does not always hold his views about the eighteenth century as responsibly as his manner suggests. In this essay the eighteenth century in England is called provincial and second-rate, and the best that it can show is given as the 'Attic prose' of Addison. The Augustan age, and the whole English eighteenth century with it, drops into the category of provincial and second-rate because the peg of Addison's prose, though pretty, proves too light in substance, and collapses. Why, one asks, does not Arnold take Swift for his peg, a peg of oak from which the intellectual greatness of any age could hang in any wind? There seem to have been two main reasons why not, and both discredit Arnold's worth as an authority. The first is that Sainte-Beuve makes no use of Swift in the essay 'Qu'est-ce qu'un Classique?' to which Arnold at this

[1] *Letters,* i. 309 f.
[2] See, e.g., p. 272 below, n. 2.

point was indebted. That essay enthrones Addison among the 'Attics of every tongue and every nation', but alludes to the author of *Gulliver's Travels* only as the recipient of a certain letter from Bolingbroke. Perhaps, then, Arnold omitted Swift through reliance on his hero Sainte-Beuve. But there is another possible reason. Arnold sometimes seems to be accepting the lazy assumptions of those of his contemporaries who were under no obligation to think critically.[1] It was different, of course, where foreign literature was concerned: for instance, in 1887 Arnold predicted a future for Russian novelists which promptly came true, and there is plenty of up-to-date knowledge of contemporary French literature (though Arnold seems unaware of Baudelaire). Arnold comes near to confessing that he overlooked Swift because of his acceptance of man-in-the-street opinion when, in the preface to Burke, he puts himself in the position of having known no better than his grandfather on a subject about which his grandfather was mistaken:

Shakespeare and Milton we are all supposed to know something of; but of none of our prose classics, I think, if we leave stories out of the account, such as are the *Pilgrim's Progress* and the *Vicar of Wakefield*, are we expected to have a like knowledge. . . . Our grandfathers were bound to know their Addison, but for us the obligation has ceased; nor is that loss, indeed, a very serious matter. But to lose Swift and Burke out of our mind's circle of acquaintance is a loss indeed, and a loss for which no conversance with contemporary prose literature can make up, any more than conversance with contemporary poetry could make up to us for unacquaintance with Shakespeare and Milton.[2]

There seems to be no more responsible reason for Arnold's final estimate of Swift than that time has brought about a general improvement in his popularity, an improvement from which Arnold has benefited as well as everybody else.[3]

---

[1] Evidence supporting this interpretation comes in the essay on Wordsworth, which is as late as 1879. In that essay Arnold exalts Wordsworth above all English poets since Chaucer, with the two exceptions of Shakespeare and Milton, but does so by reference not to those rivals who alone count, but to a list of 'our chief poetical names' (i.e. the poets who in 1879 are thought to be poets by the man in the street) which includes Scott, Campbell, and Moore.

[2] *Letters Speeches and Tracts on Irish Affairs by Edmund Burke*, 1881, p. v f.

[3] Arnold told Thomas Hardy that 'the best man to read for style—narrative style—was Swift' (Florence Emily Hardy, *The Early Life of Thomas Hardy* (1928), p. 175). If Arnold intended the remark as a home-truth, it was lost on Hardy, who had made his own style for his own purposes, and very properly regarded both as sacred.

III

It is perhaps because so much of Arnold's day went in school-inspecting, and so much of his leisure in keeping abreast of his own age, that he achieved only a vague notion of the past. Vagueness is a disabling disease of the historian because the one thing certain about the past (we infer this from our own experience of the present) is that it was lived through particular by particular. It is the business of the historian to discover these particulars for himself and for us. He will not always, of course, present them as particulars; he will sometimes generalize. But generalizations are concrete things when derived from an adequate number of particulars. They are the pattern made by the particulars; they are the expression, to adapt a phrase of Wordsworth's, on the countenance of knowledge. Arnold's generalizations are not pattern, expression: they are the speculations of a mind interested in ideas independently of the material that alone should generate and govern them. When Arnold writes the phrase, 'blank with all the ennui of the Middle Ages',[1] we ask him for his evidence that there was more ennui at that time than at any other; we ask him to search for it in, say, Chaucer, i.e. in a piece of 'the Middle Ages' which is sufficiently big and detailed to count as an adequate representation of the life of the time. We ask Arnold if what he read as blank ennui was not rather the blank left by records which have disappeared, and the blankness of his own unfamiliarity with what medieval records have survived: these records are not so plentiful as those of later ages, and accordingly Arnold came across few of them in the general reading which was all he had time for. In so far as adequate records exist, ennui seems to have been no more endemic in the Middle Ages than in any other age, and what did exist should not have been called by that name, a name which had developed new connotations during the nineteenth century.

And then there are all Arnold's abstract terms. It is no business of the historian to deal in abstractions so near to no-meaning as many that Arnold deals in: 'the great open stream of the world's history', 'the mental history of mankind', 'universal history', the 'Middle Ages', the 'eighteenth century', 'things as they are', 'the way the world is going', 'tendencies', 'influences',

[1] *Essays in Criticism*, ed. 1869, p. 282.

'the Zeitgeist'. And take the term 'century'. In England it may well have been Arnold's doing that it became the specious term of generalization which it often still is: before Arnold's day, people had preferred to manage smaller quantities, to speak of the age of Elizabeth, of the reign of Queen Anne, and so on. But the enormous holds no terrors for Arnold. Burke, we remember, recoiled from pitting himself against odds that were too great: when faced with the French Revolution, he did not know how to draw up an indictment against a whole nation. No such arresting sense of personal insignificance, of being dangerously in a minority, struck Arnold, who saw no difference between attacking a line of a poem of Gray, or F. W. Newman's translation of the *Iliad*, or the *Daily Telegraph*, or the eighteenth century, or the Middle Ages. Occasionally he did find it necessary to distinguish the later from the earlier part of the eighteenth century, to insist on the contrasts between the ages of Swift and of Burke. But his usual practice was to bulk all the multitudinous detail surviving from those hundred years under the term 'the eighteenth century'.

One good result of his later theological studies was that they jolted him into seeing that the abstract, the enormous, and the vague were deceptive quantities. In *God and the Bible*, for example, he makes this discovery:

> To such a degree do words make man, who invents them, their sport! The moment we have an abstract word, a word where we do not apprehend both the concrete sense and the manner of the sense's application, there is danger. . . . And [a certain term] is . . . a dangerous term, because without clearly conceiving what it means, we nevertheless use it freely . . . we talk of our idea of a myriagon or ten-thousand-sided figure . . . but it is not a clear idea, it is an idea of something very big, but confused.[1]

This, of course, is excellent sense, a sense so excellent that it is beyond the power of any critic to live up to it altogether. It is useless, however, to argue that if Arnold had made the discovery earlier it might have effected his salvation as a secular historian. There is no evidence that, as a secular historian, Arnold had reached the point of wanting to be saved: he delighted in his vague quantities, and did not see that intellectually they were so much erring and straying.

[1] *God and the Bible*, ed. 1885, pp. 44, 51.

IV

Arnold, therefore, is not a victim: it was not a lack of leisure which imposed vagueness on him, but a preference for seeing vague things. The verse shows it equally with the prose, though vagueness, of course, is not so badly out of place in the verse as in the prose. (The distinction between Arnold's verse and prose is sometimes merely one of rhythm, and sometimes even that distinction is very nearly a distinction without a difference: see, for instance, such a poem as 'Heine's Grave' and such a prose-poem as that which concludes the essay on Falkland.) A gift for clarity of manner is often expended on presenting vague thoughts and a vague conception of the concrete. As a secular historian he remains vague to the end. The result is that much of his history exists in a sort of poetical sanctuary. Its impressionistic vagueness makes it inaccessible to argument. So that there is no need to examine his grandiose generalizations about the eighteenth century either when he praises it or, more often, when he attacks it as 'second-rate', 'provincial', 'arid of air', 'touched with frost', 'an age of prose', an age whose greatest poet conceived his poems in the 'wits' rather than in the 'soul'. We must interpret such vague charges as poetry, as the outcome of fits of dislike, or as 'language *thrown out* at an object of consciousness . . . which inspired emotion'.[1] They are expressions of individual distaste like the direct expression of it in one of his letters:

I am glad you like [my essay on] Gray; that century is very interesting, though I should not like to have lived in it. . . .[2]

They shed light on the subject feeling the distaste rather than upon its object. They express the distaste of Arnold and those of his contemporaries who were 'modern' enough to resemble him, of people who have only just managed to effect an escape; they are a part of Arnold's attempt to clear himself of that element in his intellectual ancestry which he found 'retarding', to push himself and his fellows farther into what remained of the nineteenth century. For instance, if he calls the air of the eighteenth century arid, that is because his own sense of freshness has been finely developed. We can observe that sense of freshness developing over the hundred years which separate Arnold from Gray,

---

[1] *Literature & Dogma*, ed. 1900, pp. 30 ff.
[2] *Letters*, 1895, ii. 187.

who sought out mountains in the Lakes and Scotland.[1] The Romantics followed Gray on foot and in imagination, and Wordsworth and Scott reap the benefit of being born and bred in the midst of country then at last properly appreciated. The sense of freshness seems to have been specially cultivated by the Rugby circle. Thomas Arnold and his favourite pupils spent all their available holidays in the Lakes or in Scotland, and developed a need for the air of fell and mountain which made the normal air of eighteenth-century haunts seem stuffy in comparison—the air of town, village, highroad, park, and garden. But the air of the eighteenth century was only arid by the northern standards of those whose nostrils had become abnormally sharp as a pen. And, again, when Arnold speaks of the English eighteenth century as provincial and second-rate, he tells us little about an age which led Europe, or which greatly influenced it, in theology, philosophy, industrial invention, geographical discovery, imperial expansion, trade, landscape gardening, domestic architecture, an age which produced Alexander Pope who, in 1739, seemed to an Italian writer to be the greatest poet living, an age which produced European household words like *Robinson Crusoe, Gulliver's Travels,* the *Essay on Man, Pamela,* the *Night Thoughts, Ossian,*[2] *The Vicar of Wakefield.* Instead of telling us anything about the eighteenth century, Arnold tells us of his own dislike for parochialism, and of his own wish that his fellows would take to bathing more freely in that much advertised Ganges of his, the current of European ideas.

V

Arnold, however, does not always write about the eighteenth century as a vague quantity. He writes about it also at particular points. For example, when he praises what its writers did for English prose, he provides instances which enable us to appreciate his praise closely. When he blames the lapses of

---

[1] It seems to have been Thomson and Gray who reintroduced the use of the term 'fresh', which became so popular in the nineteenth century, and which led to the use of such phrases as Arnold's 'torrent of freshness' (applied to his father's contribution to English thought: see *Letters*, i. 311). It is Gray's 'Ode on the Pleasure arising from Vicissitude' that Hurrell Froude quotes (or rather misquotes) when, away in the Barbados, he longs for a sight of the English spring: 'I wish I could be in England now, and see a little of "Nature's tenderest, freshest green"', &c.' (*Remains*, Part I, 1838, i. 367.)

[2] Arnold was well aware that 'All Europe felt the power of [the] melancholy [of Ossian]'. (*On the Study of Celtic Literature*, 1867, p. 154.)

Burke, whom he regarded as the greatest of English prose-writers, he quotes the lapses for all to see. We can also follow him closely when, commenting on eighteenth-century poetry, he centres his comment in a quotation. On that subject, however, it is usually a matter of following not praise but patronage.

There is enough evidence to show that Arnold knew eighteenth-century poetry fairly well,[1] and that to begin with he paid it at least that amount of respect which the ordinary Victorian reader felt to be its due. At his most handsome the young Professor of Poetry can even write of it like this:

Every one will at once remember a thousand passages in which
... the ten-syllable couplet [proves itself] to have nobleness. Undoubtedly the movement and manner of this;
> Still raise for good the supplicating voice,
> But leave to Heaven the measure and the choice—
are noble.[2]

But as he grew older he grew less ready to allow due value to the kind of poetry Pope wrote, and in the end could only speak of it as the kind of poetry that a 'true' poet like Gray needed to be rescued from, rescued by means of a critic's fantasy of what might have been. To begin with, Arnold perceived that Pope had 'a quick and darting spirit' and 'real nobleness',[3] but later could see him only as stiff, pompous, and inhuman, as a splendid high priest, as the splendid high priest, indeed, of an age of prose.[4] The results of Arnold's patronage are still with us, of course: in his later days his prestige as a critic was so high that his brilliant epigrams established themselves in the minds of younger critics as sentences, and in the minds of the incurious mass of readers as assumptions. The critics and readers who relied on his critical scheme—glorious Shakespeare, glorious Milton, an age of prose, fairly glorious Wordsworth—did not understand how precariously he climbed to the point at which he found mockery of eighteenth-century poetry possible. For, like most nineteenth-century poets and readers, Arnold never

---

[1] He knew it better than Professor Lowry recognized, who, when editing Arnold's letters to Clough, added an '[e]' to the name of Green under the impression that Arnold meant the author of *Friar Bacon and Friar Bungay* and not the author of *The Spleen*. (*Letters of Matthew Arnold to Arthur Hugh Clough*, 1932, p. 99.)
[2] *On Translating Homer*, 1861, p. 69. The instance is from Johnson's *Vanity of Human Wishes*, 351 f.
[3] *On Translating Homer*, 1861, p. 67.
[4] *Essays in Criticism Second Series*, 1888, p. 40.

got clear of eighteenth-century poetry. Most nineteenth-century poets and readers were in two minds about it, hating it one moment because it strangled what was new in their own poetry, and admiring it the next because it was so admirable. Tennyson saw Pope as a rival in the minute interpretative observation of what he considered as beautiful in external nature; and, to take a smaller instance, the poet David Gray, whom Arnold set beside Keats whom he set beside Shakespeare, freely exclaimed that when he opened his Thomson he despaired.

VI

In so far as Arnold's remarks on eighteenth-century poetry are concrete ones, comment is possible, and here are comments on three of them.

1. In the essay on Gray, Arnold, seeking something of Goldsmith 'in retaliation' for Goldsmith's disparagement of Gray, hits on the line,

> No chearful murmurs fluctuate in the gale,

and comments expansively:

there is exactly the poetic diction of our prose century! rhetorical, ornate,—and, poetically, quite false.

And he proceeds to 'apply', as a deadly touchstone,

> In cradle of the rude, imperious surge.

But if we turn to *The Deserted Village*, we find that the line belongs inseparably to a context remarkable for its fidelity to a complicated recollection, the recollection of an experience which for the senses was blurred, but which for the apperceptive intellect (sorting out and naming the 'mingling notes') was clear; a recollection of an experience of the senses and intellect which is prompted by a general emotion of pity for the decay of a society:

> Sweet was the sound when oft at evening's close,
> Up yonder hill the village murmur rose;
> There as I past with careless steps and slow,
> The mingling notes came softened from below;
> The swain responsive as the milk-maid sung,
> The sober herd that lowed to meet their young;
> The noisy geese that gabbled o'er the pool,
> The playful children just let loose from school;

The watch-dog's voice that bayed the whispering wind,
And the loud laugh that spoke the vacant mind,
These all in soft confusion sought the shade,
And filled each pause the nightingale had made.
But now the sounds of population fail,
No chearful murmurs fluctuate in the gale,
No busy steps the grass-grown foot-way tread,
But all the bloomy flush of life is fled.
All but yon widowed, solitary thing
That feebly bends beside the plashy spring;
She, wretched matron, forced, in age, for bread,
To strip the brook with mantling cresses spread,
To pick her wintry faggot from the thorn,
To seek her nightly shed, and weep till morn;
She only left of all the harmless train,
The sad historian of the pensive plain.[1]

Arnold expressly concerns himself with the 'poetic diction' of
the line which he tears from its place. I cannot believe he includes in his dislike the word 'fluctuate' (a word which he had
used more than once in his own poems): the accuracy of Goldsmith's use of it was as obvious in 1880 as it had been in 1770
and as it remains to-day. It was against 'cheerful' and 'gale',
then, that Arnold levelled his charges. The word 'cheerful'
was as necessary to the poets of the eighteenth century as the
words 'clear', 'light' (adjective), 'bloom' (noun), and 'lone'
were necessary to Arnold. It was an inevitable word for poets
who were conscious of the social group, and who fully prized
the consolations to be got from being accepted by the normal
run of their fellows. Much of their poetry is built on the assumption that the happiness of men glows most steadily in the family
and in a group of friends. Like so many other things, it is all
there in Gray's *Elegy*, where the warm precincts of the cheerful
day are set against dull forgetfulness and the solitude and
melancholy of

> And leaves the world to darkness and to me.

Goldsmith's poems are related to society as if by a fascination.
They concern the emotions of the stranger, the guest, the exiled,
the turned-away, the forsaken, the wanderer, the native returning. And so the 'cheerful' is what he longs for most.

If the eighteenth-century poets use the word too much, that

---

[1] *The Deserted Village ... The Second Edition*, 1770, p. 7 f.

is because they are preoccupied with the thing it signifies. To deny them this word cuts them off from the source of their best poetry. It would be as if we denied to modern poets the word 'history'.

Then the word 'gale'. By Arnold's time this word had developed a new and narrower meaning, that of a wind which was strong. For the seventeenth and eighteenth centuries, however, its connotation was more neutral: it meant 'a movement of air': and the preciser meaning of the context it appears in derives from the epithet which almost invariably accompanies it. We find a nautical writer in 1621 listing the following degrees: 'A calme, a brese, a fresh gaile, a pleasant gayle, a stiffe gayle'.[1] And Milton has the lines:

> ... and winds
> Of gentlest gale *Arabian* odors fann'd
> From their soft wings, and *Flora*'s earliest smells.[2]

Elsewhere Goldsmith himself wrote:

> ... sea-born gales their gelid wings expand
> To winnow fragrance round the smiling land,

where 'gales' can no more mean high winds than 'gelid' can mean icy.

Goldsmith's line, therefore, does not exhibit poetic diction at all. It exhibits eighteenth-century usage, whether in prose or verse. Arnold's quarrel is with the history of the English language, which is as unavailing as a quarrel with your family tree.

Moreover Arnold had no right to speak of the line as typical of eighteenth-century poetry. At the most it is typical of certain poems, and kinds and parts of poems.

2. The essay proceeds to attack Dryden's ode 'To the Pious Memory of ... Mrs. Anne Killigrew', citing Johnson's praise of it

---

[1] See *O.E.D.* s.v. 'gale'. The *O.E.D.*'s treatment of this word proceeds on the assumption that 'gale' has always meant what it means to-day, i.e. a stiff wind. But in most of its many instances the word is qualified by an epithet, and where not, means a movement of air rather than a brisk movement of air. When the word is qualified by an epithet connoting gentleness, the editors consider it to be used 'poetically'; but where the poetry comes in is in the epithet, in the gentleness, poets requiring to speak of gentle gales more often than of stiff ones.

[2] *Paradise Regained*, ii. 362 ff. It is worth remarking that when the twentieth-century reader encounters 'gales' and cries 'Poetic diction!' he should equally, when he encounters 'smell', cry 'How unpoetic!'; and then go on to discover the historical conditions which explain a great poet's use of both words.

as 'the noblest ode that our language ever has produced'. Arnold quotes a few lines, and comments:

The intellectual, ingenious, superficial evolution of poetry of this school could not be better illustrated,

and out comes a strip of litmus from Pindar.

Arnold does not properly evaluate the remark of Johnson. Johnson did not care for the ode as a kind of lyric poem, and praise from him on this subject amounts to little more than saying that Dryden's ode is the best of a poor lot. Unlike Johnson, Arnold admits too few categories, and so does not appreciate the restriction implied in Johnson's words 'noblest' and 'ode'. He therefore offers as the normal poetry of 'this school' what is most abnormal. Dryden's ode exhibits his breaking out into a baroque floridity which he manages as beautifully as Rubens managed that of his royal portraits. But the poetry which Dryden wrote habitually was very different. Instead of being florid, it was a sort of Adam and Eve poetry, masculine and feminine together, both on the grand scale and both on that grand scale which is also simple. Arnold saw this habitual poetry as so much admirable prose. Fortunately he supports his charge with an instance, the instance of

> A milk-white *Hind* immortal and unchang'd
> Fed on the lawns and in the forest rang'd.

To reinstate the couplet where it belongs, we need only remember that prose is not concerned with music. The music of Dryden's couplet, subtle without being fussy, substantial without being heavy, securely divides it off from prose.

3. In his lecture on Milton we get this paragraph:

Thomson, Cowper, Wordsworth, all of them good poets who have studied Milton, followed Milton, adopted his form, fail in their diction and rhythm if we try them by that high standard of excellence maintained by Milton constantly. From style really high and pure Milton never departs; their departures from it are frequent.[1]

I have ranged this among Arnold's particular criticisms of eighteenth-century poetry, but, apart from his using names, its place is among his vague ones. Of course Thomson and Cowper studied Milton: so have almost all English poets since Milton's day. But they did not adopt his 'form' (by 'form' I take it

---

[1] *Essays in Criticism Second Series*, 1888, p. 62. Arnold had already stated this view in *Mixed Essays*, 1879, pp. 267 ff.

Arnold means the blank verse of *Paradise Lost* with its characteristic use of pauses, and perhaps also the diction and syntax which are sometimes latinate). Dr. Johnson saw clearly that

[Thomson's] blank verse is no more the blank verse of Milton or of any other poet than the rhymes of Prior are the rhymes of Cowley.[1]

The same is true of Cowper, also. And if Thomson and Cowper do not adopt Milton's form, they cannot be said to depart from it, and the only sense in which they can be said to fail is the absolute sense: they may be said to be inferior to Milton as poets only in the way that, as a dramatist, Jonson may be said to be inferior to Shakespeare. Discipleship of Milton is precluded for Thomson and Cowper by their subject and by the literary kind which it required. Thomson is following Virgil, the poet of the *Georgics*, and Cowper the mock-heroic and Georgic poets. And in writing more humbly than epic poets, they succeed thoroughly. Both Thomson and Cowper write latinately, and do so as deliberately as Milton did; but for other ends. Arnold had raised an easy laugh against Cowper when he warned off the would-be translator of Homer from Cowper's latinate diction:

It must not be Cowper's blank verse, who has studied Milton's pregnant manner with such effect, that, having to say of Mr. Throckmorton that he spares his avenue, although it is the fashion with other people to cut down theirs, he says that Benevolus 'reprieves The obsolete prolixity of shade'.[2]

But that line is not taken from Cowper's own translation of Homer: it is taken from *The Task*. Of course no translator of Homer should imitate the verse and diction of *The Task*: Cowper himself had said as much by not doing so himself. Arnold's instance, therefore, serves no purpose except that of raising a laugh against Cowper, the sort of laugh we associate with the lecture-room. But Cowper had laughed before Arnold, and so laughs after him. The point of Cowper's line and of the many appropriately like it in a poem beginning 'I sing the Sofa', is that Cowper's words are selected fastidiously, and were recognized at the time as being so selected. Arnold speaks as if Cowper did not know that he was writing with exquisite cleverness, and so misses the chance of recognizing the quality of the

---

[1] *Lives of the Poets*, ed. G. Birkbeck Hill, 1905, iii. 298.
[2] *On Translating Homer*, 1861, p. 74.

product. *The Task* (especially when we remember that while writing it Cowper was *'very often most supremely unhappy'*[1]) demonstrates the quality of the particular civilization of the eighteenth century. At times Arnold fully appreciated this quality, but he did not see that Cowper's writings were an instance of it equally with the 'culture, lofty spirit, and greatness' of Lord Granville,[2] and the heavenly beauty of Esher.[3]

Arnold confounds the distinctions of times in his concern with absolute standards. But though Cowper is inferior to Milton when those doomsday standards are evoked, his deficiency is not one of style, of diction and rhythm, but of subject. Cowper accepted the absolute deficiency of his subject as inevitable. He knew he could not pile up the sublimities, and so, unlike Blackmore, did not try to. Instead, he did what he knew to be within his varied capabilities as Milton did what Milton knew to be within his own. The discrepancy, therefore, lies in the capabilities, not in the degree of their fulfilment. Cowper, who has several subtle discussions on style, claimed that he never wrote any line negligently, but made each line as good as possible before proceeding.[4] And it is because he always did thoroughly what he clearly discerned as good that his diction has a uniform integrity which, on this count, puts him beside such poets as Herbert, Herrick, Milton, Pope, Swift, and Tennyson. If Cowper fails in his diction, then they fail too, and there are no such things as principles and standards of expression.

In discussing these instances I have done no more than indicate that Arnold gave sentence in ignorance of the nature of the fact.

VII

I have already quoted Arnold's discovery that Pope, the translator of Homer, had 'a quick and darting spirit' and contrasted that discovery with the image of him later as a splendid high priest. About the same time as Arnold hit on this ecclesiastical image, he also made the statement that while 'genuine'

---

[1] Letter to Lady Hesketh, 16 Jan. 1786.

[2] See *On Translating Homer*, 1861, pp. 16 ff. Cf. *Mixed Essays*, 1879, pp. 20 ff.

[3] 'And Esher is a heaven upon earth for beauty' (*Letters . . . to Arthur Hugh Clough*, p. 89). Arnold echoes the praise which Pope and Walpole accorded this famous eighteenth-century garden (see Pope, Twickenham ed., iv. 367).

[4] Letter to John Newton, 18 Sept. 1781.

poetry is conceived and composed in the soul, Pope's poetry 'is conceived and composed in [the] wits'.[1] 'Spirit', 'soul', 'wits': Arnold is still being vague. But vagueness about an individual is at least preferable to vagueness about a century, and I think we can make something of his terms. If it is true that Pope conceived and composed his poems in his 'wits', he could still be said to have 'a quick and darting spirit' if the word 'spirit' were used in the sense of the spirit which issues in a witticism or a bagatelle. But this is not the sense of the word as Arnold applies it to Pope, because his 'quick and darting spirit' is seen as an appropriate endowment for one who is tracking down 'the swift-moving spirit of Homer'. If Pope had 'spirit' in this superior sense, then one would have thought that he had the beginnings, at least, of the 'soul' which Arnold denied him. Arnold, one concludes, has not worked out his meaning fully enough (I am assuming that his view of Pope had not changed during the twenty years that separate the former judgement from the latter two).

No one would trouble to deny that Pope's poems were conceived and composed in the wits if they were all made up of couplets like that instanced, confessedly at random, in Arnold's 'Study of Poetry':

Do you ask me whether Pope's verse, take it almost where you will, is not good?
    'To Hounslow Heath I point, and Banstead Down;
    Thence comes your mutton, and these chicks my own.'
I answer: Admirable for the purposes of the high priest of an age of prose and reason. But do you ask me whether such verse proceeds from men with an adequate poetic criticism of life, from men whose criticism of life has a high seriousness, or even, without that high seriousness, has poetic largeness, freedom, insight, benignity? Do you ask me whether the application of ideas to life in the verse of these men, often a powerful application, no doubt, is a powerful *poetic* application? Do you ask me whether the poetry of these men has either the matter or the inseparable manner of such an adequate poetic criticism; whether it has the accent of
    'Absent thee from felicity awhile . . .'
or of
    'And what is else not to be overcome . . .'

[1] *Essays in Criticism Second Series*, 1888, p. 95. Arnold may owe to Schiller the introduction of the term 'soul' into his critical vocabulary: 'Goethe's *Iphigeneia* . . . that noble poem which Schiller so exactly characterised when he said that it was "full of soul".' (*Merope*, 1858, p. xl.)

or of
> 'O martyr souded in virginitee!'

I answer: It has not and cannot have them; it is the poetry of the
builders of an age of prose and reason. Though they may write in
verse, though they may in a certain sense be masters of the art of
versification, Dryden and Pope . . . are classics of our prose.[1]

We need not take Arnold's list of indispensable qualifications
too seriously since most people agree that they discredited themselves in discrediting Chaucer. But, as it happens, Pope's poetry
does satisfy three of Arnold's arbitrary desiderata: it has high
seriousness (if by high seriousness is meant the intense application of the mind to seeing human life as it is), poetic largeness
(witness the hackneyed instance of the ending of *The Dunciad*),
and insight (no poet has it keener). Some passages even have
benignity if it comes to a pinch (Pope certainly claimed that
satire 'heals with Morals what it hurts with Wit'[2]), though
benignity would seem the most eccentric desideratum of the
four. But the piling up of abstract terms does not take us very
far. It is more helpful to look at the couplets.

If all of them were like the couplet Arnold quotes, we could
call Pope, for all his versification, a prose writer. But even that
prosy couplet (I am viewing it as an isolated poem since that
is what Arnold, for the occasion, makes it) is not the blankest
prose. Even that couplet exhibits a stealing out, if not a darting,
of the 'spirit', a perceptible stirring of the 'soul'. The mood of the
couplet begins as though Pope were merely versifying a scrap
of, say, Defoe's *Complete Tradesman*, but it becomes complicated
at the end, and the syntax with it. (Pope's method of complication owes something to Milton's method in *Paradise Lost*:
cf. ix. 433:

> From her best prop so farr, and storm so nigh;

and ix. 1106 f.:

> . . . a Pillard shade
> High overarch't, and echoing Walks between.)

The couplet derives from one of the *Imitations of Horace*, and, in
the couplet quoted, Pope is adapting Horace quite pointedly since
mutton and chicken, besides being typical English meats (Horace's
meats were chicken and kid), were exactly those meats to which
Pope had restricted Lord Oxford on the occasion of their dining

---

[1] *Essays in Criticism Second Series*, 1888, pp. 40 ff.
[2] *Imitations of Horace*, Ep. II, i. 262.

together a few years earlier.[1] But in the Latin there is no flicker of tenderness like that with which Pope ends his simple couplet. That small subtlety is insinuated at a point where his poem is demanding as blank a prose as he could write. It demands blank prose because at this point it demands fact. (The closing paragraphs of Newman's *Apologia* are of interest here. Though they are planned as a great musical dedication, Newman does not hesitate to introduce at length the cacophonous names of his fellow Oratorians, aesthetic considerations being suspended as a matter of course where facts are sacred.) Pope's poem demands the fact whether poetical (in the ordinary sense) or not. Facts which happen to be more poetical (in the ordinary sense) follow in the next lines:

> From yon old wallnut-tree a show'r shall fall;
> And grapes, long-lingring on my only wall;

but their superior 'beauty' is not the first reason why they are there, either for Horace or for Pope. And yet, the fact of chickens is expressed with a stealing out of the spirit. So that I should hesitate to say that even the Hounslow Heath couplet was altogether conceived and composed in the wits. In the same way, to switch to a bigger matter, I should hesitate to say that the prose writings of the eighteenth century, which Arnold praised with such filial admiration, were conceived and composed in the wits, though Arnold assumes that this is so, assumes that prose is an absolute thing, prose. Even the prose of Swift is sometimes near to poetry—it rouses intense emotions of an aesthetic kind, though of a severely aesthetic kind. (If we look at Swift's escritoire, photographed in Elrington Ball's edition of the *Correspondence*, we see a thing which is eminently useful but also so strikingly perfect in its proportions that it gives tense pleasure.) And there is as much of the poet as of the prose writer in the writings of, say, Berkeley, Johnson, Goldsmith, Sterne, and Burke. But if the Hounslow Heath couplet of Pope has its small element of 'soul', what about the thousands of couplets Arnold did not cite which have that element in plenty? Arnold's word is, of course, too vague for us to be confident that we understand it in the sense he intended (though his use of the word in such a poem as 'The Palladium' offers help), but I should have thought that, in any possible sense of the word,

---

[1] See the Twickenham edition, iv. 66.

'soul' exists in Pope's poetry. And since it is a poet we are dealing with, there is a more concrete check on its presence: we can usually approach the 'soul' of a poet by way of observing the quality of his senses: and Pope's senses are as fine, amorous, immediate, and voracious as Keats's (though they range more widely and are much more under control).

Since I am concerned to show that, whatever else he was, Pope was a poet according to Arnold's own tests and standards for a poet, there is another quality which it would be well to claim for him if possible. In the lectures on Celtic literature Arnold distinguishes what he calls 'natural magic':

in the magical [handling of nature], the eye is on the object, but charm and magic are added.[1]

Arnold's instances of this quality are various, and imply the inclusion of some of Pope's poetry. Pope's way, of course, is not to drown a poem in 'natural magic'. It is there like all the elements in his poetry when the poem reaches the point of needing it, or, rather, the point of needing the cluster of elements of which it is one. But, as if he were giving Arnold and his like every chance not to miss it, Pope sometimes indulges its stay a little: his hands, like those of the village organist, sometimes dwell a little longer than is strictly necessary on the trembling chords. The one instance I give is from the passage which describes the decline and fall of the young aristocrat on the grand tour, a passage from which I select the following:

> Europe he saw, and Europe saw him too.
> There all thy[2] gifts and graces we display,
> Thou, only thou, directing all our way!
> To where the Seine, obsequious as she runs,
> Pours at great Bourbon's feet her silken sons;
> Or Tyber, now no longer Roman, rolls,
> Vain of Italian Arts, Italian Souls:
> To happy Convents, bosom'd deep in vines,
> Where slumber Abbots, purple as their wines:
> To Isles of fragrance, lilly-silver'd vales,
> Diffusing languor in the panting gales:
> To lands of singing, or of dancing slaves,
> Love-whisp'ring woods, and lute-resounding waves.
> But chief her shrine where naked Venus keeps,
> And Cupids ride the Lyon of the Deeps;

[1] *On the Study of Celtic Literature*, 1867, p. 164.
[2] The goddess Dulness.

Where, eas'd of Fleets, the Adriatic main
Wafts the smooth Eunuch and enamour'd swain.
Led by my hand,[1] he saunter'd Europe round,
And gather'd ev'ry Vice on Christian ground.[2]

The lines of 'natural magic' exist in this passage not only, of course, because of the luxury they pour on the senses, but also because of their necessary contribution to the account of the rake's progress: Pope rises to the poetic occasion now that he encounters it in the course of the observed biography (that is the best way of putting it since a satirist is dependent on what materials offer themselves). And his display of 'natural magic' is as authentic as anything in Shakespeare or in Keats.[3] The same thing happens whenever his poem demands it (or whenever he demands it for his poem), which is fairly often.

An opportunity for understanding Pope's use of 'natural magic' was provided for Arnold by his own experiences over the 'New Sirens'. That poem, unlike any poem of Pope's, is drowned in 'natural magic'. (It is the poem of which the final stanza is known to all readers of nineteenth-century poetry:

Pluck no more red roses, maidens,
Leave the lilies in their dew—
Pluck, pluck cypress, O pale maidens,
Dusk, oh, dusk the hall with yew! . . .)

Arnold's friends could not make out the gist of the poem, and Arnold writes penitently to Clough:

Cumin also advises a running commentary for the New Sirens: and Shairp finds them cloudy and obscure: and they are, what you called them, a mumble.[4]

Arnold supplies a commentary, but without any confidence in its remedial power: '. . . your word is quite just—it is exactly a

---

[1] The hand of his tutor, who is speaking.

[2] *Dunciad*, iv. 294 ff.

[3] The reader may object to Pope's use of 'silver' with 'lilies' as having too metallic a light. If so, it is worth noting that Arnold would probably not have agreed with him. He himself ascribed something metallic to flowers. Austin Dobson quite rightly drew attention to the line from 'Thyrsis',
              Roses that down the alleys shine afar,
commenting, 'it may be questioned whether "shine" is absolutely inevitable as applied to a rose' (*A Bookman's Budget*, 1917, p. 129). Like any big flower, a rose can be seen from a distance, but not seen as shining. The same verb is used of the rhododendron in one of the late letters (*Letters*, 1895, ii. 341), but here Arnold may be describing its leaves rather than its flowers.

[4] *Letters . . . to Arthur Hugh Clough*, 1932, p. 104.

mumble'.[1] He did print the poem, but only in his first volume (1849). And that was the end of the matter till Swinburne's repeated plea prevailed on him in 1876 to reinstate it. The moral is clear. Arnold and his friends of 1849 did not consider 'natural magic' a sufficient ground for a poem's existence: sense, too, was necessary, and this, in the 'New Sirens', Arnold had attempted but failed to supply. When the poem is readmitted into the canon, it is mainly to please Swinburne, that is, to please one who was never happier than when isolated from everything except 'natural magic'. After this experience, and because of Arnold's general views on how poems should be put together, one would have expected him to value the achievement of Pope, an unusual one for an English poet: that of commanding this 'magic' into being, and that of limiting its life to the service of the larger matter in hand.

VIII

Arnold does not seem to have given Pope's poetry the attention necessary for experiencing it as it is. And one reason for this may well have been his dislike of the heroic couplet. This dislike was clearly formulated by 1862, the date of his essay on Maurice de Guérin. After depreciating the French alexandrine, Arnold continues:

The same may be said of our own poets of the eighteenth century, a century which gave them as the main vehicle for their high poetry a metre inadequate (as much as the French Alexandrine, and nearly in the same way) for this poetry,—the ten-syllable couplet. It is worth remarking, that the English poet of the eighteenth century whose compositions wear best and give one the most entire satisfaction,—Gray,—hardly uses that couplet at all: this abstinence, however, limits Gray's productions to a few short compositions, and (exquisite as these are) he is a poetical nature repressed and without free issue. For English poetical production on a great scale, for an English poet deploying all the forces of his genius, the ten-syllable couplet was, in the eighteenth century, the established, one may almost say the inevitable, channel. Now this couplet, admirable (as Chaucer uses it) for story-telling not of the epic pitch, and often admirable for a few lines even in poetry of a very high pitch, is for continuous use in poetry of this latter kind inadequate. Pope, in his *Essay on Man*, is thus at a disadvantage compared with Lucretius

---

[1] Ibid. p. 107.

in his poem on Nature: Lucretius has an adequate vehicle, Pope has not. Nay, though Pope's genius for didactic poetry was not less than that of Horace, while his satirical power was certainly greater, still one's taste receives, I cannot but think, a certain satisfaction when one reads the Epistles and Satires of Horace, which it fails to receive when one reads the Satires and Epistles of Pope. Of such avail is the superior adequacy of the vehicle used to compensate even an inferiority of genius in the user! In the same way Pope is at a dis-advantage as compared with Addison. The best of Addison's com-position (the 'Coverley Papers' in the *Spectator*, for instance) wears better than the best of Pope's, because Addison has in his prose an intrinsically better vehicle for his genius than Pope in his couplet.[1]

We can take it that the main reason for Arnold's dislike of the heroic couplet is its art, which, since variations between small units can be appreciated readily, is art that is patent rather than art that is hidden. In this matter we come up against a stolid deficiency in Arnold, a deficiency no doubt compensated by the presence of a complementary virtue. The pleasure which he derived from art was insignificant in comparison with the pleasure he derived from nature. By 'art' I mean things ac-counted beautiful at the time concerned (in this instance the nineteenth century) and in the making of which human beings have played a decisive part. For all his humanism, Arnold does not value art. This lack is shown most clearly in his letters. Aesthetically he experiences almost nothing when hearing music, and not very much when seeing painting (he only begins to be excited by painting when he finds that the Italian galleries give dates on their labels and so allow him to exchange the burden of aesthetic contemplation for the lively interest of constructing a private history of the art). And he freely states that he can never see anything in pottery and china. Only to architecture does he respond adequately (he responds also with remarkable catholicity, admiring Grecian buildings in Birmingham and Liverpool as well as dreaming spires and the cathedral at Florence).[2] If you do not care for art except when it reaches the scale of cathedrals and town halls, it is unlikely that you will care very much for the heroic couplet (or the French alex-

---

[1] *Essays in Criticism*, ed. 1869, pp. 78 ff. Cf. *The Six Chief Lives from Johnson's 'Lives of the Poets'*, ed. 1915, p. xxiii.

[2] *Letters*, 1895, ii. 163: 'to my feeling the most beautiful church in the world, and it always looks to me like a hen gathering its chickens under its wings, it stands in such a soft, lovely way with Florence round it.'

andrine). There is no need, at this date, to show up Arnold's mistaken estimate of the heroic couplet. If the heroic couplet is what Arnold thought it, a mechanical means of achieving the prose virtues of 'regularity, uniformity, precision and balance', Pope, blessed with a darting spirit, would not have used it throughout his career. Nor is Arnold's citation of Gray to the purpose. Gray used the heroic couplet for subjects and 'kinds' which needed it: for the satire on the Rev. Henry Etough and for the fragmentary 'essay' on education. But, like Pope, he did not use it for the odes and lyrics of which his best work, unlike that of Pope, mainly consisted.

IX

I have written at length of Arnold's estimate of Pope because it is easier to defend an individual against charges that are vague than to defend a century against them, and because a defence of Pope contributes to a defence of the eighteenth century itself, since his poetry is a unique instance of how thoroughly a poet's work can penetrate the thinking and feeling of a country during a hundred years. Of his own country and also of the countries of Europe; and during a hundred years and beyond: it could be readily shown, for instance, that Arnold's own thinking was not without its debt to Pope. Perhaps Arnold also owed him a debt on the score of feeling. On that score, at any rate, Pope's own century owed him a heavy one: even those poets and critics who moved on to give their warmest admiration to other sorts of poetry than the *Essay on Man* first met and admired those other sorts of poetry in the poems of Pope.

A LIST OF THE WRITINGS OF
DAVID NICHOL SMITH[1]

1896

Review of Oliphant Smeaton's *Allan Ramsay*.
The Liberal Budget. A Monthly Journal of Politics and Literature. Printed and Published for the Proprietors by W. H. White and Co. Ltd., Riverside Press, Edinburgh. Vol. 1, No. 4, April 1, 1896, p. 63. This severe review of Smeaton's book was D. N. S.'s first publication. It is not signed.

1898

BRUNETIÈRE'S ESSAYS IN FRENCH LITERATURE. A SELECTION. TRANSLATED BY D. NICHOL SMITH. WITH A PREFACE BY THE AUTHOR SPECIALLY WRITTEN FOR THIS, THE AUTHORISED ENGLISH TRANSLATION. LONDON: T. FISHER UNWIN. 1898.
Preface by M. Brunetière, pp. vii–xi; note by the translator, pp. xiii–xiv; text of seven essays (selected by M. Brunetière) translated by D. N. S., pp. 1–255.

BOILEAU, L'ART POÉTIQUE. EDITED WITH INTRODUCTION AND NOTES BY D. NICHOL SMITH, M.A. CAMBRIDGE: AT THE UNIVERSITY PRESS. 1898.
Pitt Press Series. Introduction, pp. vii–xxxii; text, pp. 1–36; notes, pp. 37–98; index, pp. 99–104. The edition has been several times reprinted.

1899

KING HENRY THE EIGHTH. EDITED BY D. NICHOL SMITH, M.A. LONDON: BLACKIE & SON. 1899.
The Warwick Shakespeare. Introduction, pp. vii–xxxi; text, pp.1–80; notes, pp. 81–136; appendixes, pp. 137–57; glossary and indexes, pp. 158–67. The edition has been several times reprinted.

THOMAS BABINGTON, LORD MACAULAY. THE LAY OF VIRGINIA. WITH INTRO-DUCTION AND NOTES. LONDON: BLACKIE & SON. 1899.
Blackie's English Classics. Introductory note, pp. 3–5; text, pp. 6–16; notes, pp. 17–24. The editor's name is not given. The edition has been several times reprinted.

1900

DRYDEN'S ESSAY OF DRAMATIC POESY. EDITED WITH INTRODUCTION AND NOTES BY D. NICHOL SMITH, M.A. LONDON: BLACKIE & SON. 1900.
Introduction, pp. v–xxiii; text, pp. xxiv–xxviii, 1–79; notes, pp. 81–117; appendixes, pp. 118–45; index to notes, pp. 146–8. The edition has been several times reprinted.

[1] Compiled by F. P. Wilson. The titles of books and editions are printed in small capitals; the titles of contributions to works of composite authorship and to periodicals (other than reviews) are printed in roman type within inverted commas.

MACAULAY, LIFE OF JOHNSON. BY D. NICHOL SMITH, M.A. WILLIAM BLACKWOOD AND SONS: EDINBURGH AND LONDON. MDCCCC.

An edition in Blackwoods' English Classics of the life contributed by Macaulay to the eighth edition of the *Encyclopaedia Britannica*. Introduction, pp. ix–xlii; chronological tables of Macaulay's life and Johnson's life, pp. xliii–xlviii; text, pp. 1–67; notes, pp. 68–95; appendix of illustrative extracts, pp. 96–104.

1901

HAZLITT, ESSAYS ON POETRY. BY D. NICHOL SMITH, M.A. WILLIAM BLACKWOOD AND SONS: EDINBURGH AND LONDON. MCMI.

Blackwoods' English Classics. A selection of ten essays. Introduction, pp. ix–xxxix; chronological table, pp. xl–xliii; text, pp. 1–207; notes, pp. 208–50.

1902

KING LEAR. EDITED BY D. NICHOL SMITH, M.A. LONDON: BLACKIE & SON. 1902.

The Warwick Shakespeare. Introduction, pp. vii–xxvii; text, pp. 1–95; notes, pp. 97–143; appendixes, pp. 144–60; glossary and indexes, pp. 161–74. The edition has been several times reprinted.

1903

EIGHTEENTH CENTURY ESSAYS ON SHAKESPEARE. EDITED BY D. NICHOL SMITH, M.A. GLASGOW: JAMES MACLEHOSE AND SONS, PUBLISHERS TO THE UNIVERSITY. 1903.

Introduction, pp. ix–lxiii; text, pp. 1–303; notes, pp. 304–48; index, pp. 349–58. The authors reprinted are Rowe, Dennis, Pope, Theobald, Hanmer, Warburton, Johnson, Farmer, and Morgann.

BLACKIE'S STANDARD SHILLING DICTIONARY. BLACKIE AND SON. 1903.

The Dictionary (pp. 1–406), but not the Preface and the Appendixes, is by D. N. S. It is based mainly on Charles Annandale's revision (1898) of John Ogilvie's *The Student's English Dictionary*.

'William Hazlitt.'

Chambers's Cyclopaedia of English Literature, New Edition by David Patrick, LL.D., vol. iii (1903), pp. 79–85.

1904

Review of *The Collected Works of William Hazlitt*, edited by A. R. Waller and Arnold Glover.

The Scottish Historical Review, vol. i (April 1904), pp. 331–2. A brief notice of the Index volume is printed in vol. iv (January 1907), p. 226.

Review of William Barry's *Heralds of Revolt*.

The Speaker, New Series, vol. xi (29 October 1904), pp. 109–10.

1905

'Literary Criticism.'

An article in *The Harmsworth Encyclopaedia*, originally issued in fortnightly parts in 1905 and published by the Amalgamated Press, Ltd., London, and Thomas Nelson and Sons of Edinburgh. The article, which is not signed, is to be found under 'Criticism', vol. iii, pp. 1713–17. This and the following article were reprinted in Nelson's *Encyclopaedia* (1911–12), vol. vii, pp. 349–57 ('Criticism'), and vol. i, pp. 409–11 ('Ancients and Moderns').

'Quarrel of Ancients and Moderns.'

An unsigned article in *The Harmsworth Encyclopaedia* (see above), vol. vii, pp. 5005–7.

Review of W. J. Courthope's *A History of English Poetry*, vols. iii and iv.
The Scottish Historical Review, vol. ii (January 1905), pp. 194–7.

Review of Charles Whibley's *Literary Portraits*.
The Speaker, New Series, vol. xi (18 February 1905), p. 491.

Review of Edmund Gosse's *French Profiles*.
The Speaker, New Series, vol. xii (15 April 1905), pp. 46–7.

1906

Review of W. J. Courthope's *A History of English Poetry*, vol. v.
The Scottish Historical Review, vol. iii (April 1906), pp. 374–5.

Review of H. M. Trollope's *The Life of Molière*.
The Speaker, New Series, vol. xiv (5 May 1906), pp. 121–2. The review is not signed.

1907

Obituary estimate of Ferdinand Brunetière.
The Bookman, vol. xxxi (January 1907), pp. 176–8.

Review of Charles Crawford's *Collectanea*, First Series.
The Bookman, vol. xxxi (January 1907), pp. 188–9.

1909

THE FUNCTIONS OF CRITICISM. A LECTURE DELIVERED BEFORE THE UNIVERSITY ON FEBRUARY 22 1909 BY D. NICHOL SMITH, M.A., GOLDSMITHS' READER IN ENGLISH. OXFORD: AT THE CLARENDON PRESS. 1909.
Pp. 1–24.

MACAULAY, ESSAY ON JOHNSON. OXFORD: AT THE CLARENDON PRESS. n.d.[1909].
Oxford Plain Texts. The unsigned introduction (pp. 3–6) to this reprint of Macaulay's review of Croker is by D. N. S.

Review of *Critical Essays of the Seventeenth Century*, edited by J. E. Spingarn.
The Oxford Magazine, vol. xxviii (18 November 1909), pp. 93–4. The review is not signed.

1910

JEFFREY'S LITERARY CRITICISM. EDITED WITH INTRODUCTION BY D. NICHOL SMITH. LONDON: HENRY FROWDE. 1910.
Oxford Library of Prose and Poetry. Introduction, pp. v–xxiv; text,

pp. 1–208; appendix—list of Jeffrey's articles in the *Edinburgh Review*, pp. 209–16.

Review of J. M. Robertson's *Montaigne and Shakespeare*.
The Oxford Magazine, vol. xxviii (24 February 1910), p. 230. The review is not signed.

Review of W. J. Courthope's *A History of English Poetry*, vol. vi, and Arthur Symons's *The Romantic Movement in English Poetry*.
The Oxford Magazine, vol. xxviii (28 April 1910), pp. 279–80. The review is not signed.

Review of W. J. Courthope's *A History of English Poetry*, vol. vi.
The Scottish Historical Review, vol. vii (July 1910), pp. 406–8.

1911

Review of *The Cambridge History of English Literature*, vols. v and vi.
The Oxford Magazine, vol. xxix (26 January 1911), p. 162. The review is not signed.

Review of Ernest Law's *Some Supposed Shakespeare Forgeries*.
The Scottish Historical Review, vol. ix (October 1911), pp. 88–90.

Review of *Biographia Epistolaris, being the Biographical Supplement of Coleridge's Biographia Literaria*, edited by A. Turnbull.
The Oxford Magazine, vol. xxx (9 November 1911), pp. 75–6. The review is not signed.

1913

'Johnson and Boswell.'
The Cambridge History of English Literature, edited by Sir A. W. Ward and A. R. Waller, vol. x (1913), chap. viii, pp. 157–94; bibliography, pp. 459–80.

Review of Mrs. Stopes's *Burbage and Shakespeare's Stage*.
The Scottish Historical Review, vol. xi (October 1913), pp. 102–4. See also, ibid. (January 1914), p. 231.

1914

THE LETTERS OF THOMAS BURNET TO GEORGE DUCKETT 1712–1722. EDITED BY DAVID NICHOL SMITH. OXFORD: PRINTED FOR PRESENTATION TO THE MEMBERS OF THE ROXBURGHE CLUB. MDCCCCXIV.
Introduction, pp. xi–xlii; letters, pp. 1–175; later documents, pp. 179–206; notes, pp. 209–93; publications of Thomas Burnet and George Duckett, pp. 295–311; index, pp. 313–25. The book was presented to the Roxburghe Club by the Marquess of Crewe.

Review of Mary Sullivan's *Court Masques of James I*.
The English Historical Review, vol. xxix (January 1914), pp. 190–1.

1915

A BIBLIOGRAPHY OF SAMUEL JOHNSON. BY WILLIAM PRIDEAUX COURTNEY. REVISED AND SEEN THROUGH THE PRESS BY DAVID NICHOL SMITH. OXFORD: AT THE CLARENDON PRESS. 1915.

    Preface by D. N. S., pp. vii–viii; bibliography, pp. 1–174; index, pp. 175–86. The book was revised and augmented at the desire of the Delegates of the Clarendon Press. A reissue of this edition, limited to 350 copies and illustrated with facsimiles, appeared in 1925.

Review of A. W. Verrall's *Lectures on Dryden.*
    The Oxford Magazine, vol. xxxiii (12 February 1915), p. 196. The review is not signed.

Reviews of Mrs. Stopes's *Shakespeare's Environment* and Ernest Law's *More About Shakespeare 'Forgeries'.*
    The Scottish Historical Review, vol. xii (April 1915), pp. 319–20.

Review of C. D. Stewart's *Some Textual Difficulties in Shakespeare.*
    The Oxford Magazine, vol. xxxiv (5 November 1915), pp. 45–6. The review is not signed.

1916

SHAKESPEARE CRITICISM. A SELECTION. WITH AN INTRODUCTION BY D. NICHOL SMITH. HUMPHREY MILFORD: OXFORD UNIVERSITY PRESS.

    The World's Classics. Introduction, pp. v–xxvii; text, pp. 1–416.

'Authors and Patrons.'
    Shakespeare's England. An Account of the Life and Manners of his Age. Clarendon Press: Oxford. In the Tercentenary Year (1916), vol. ii, chap. xxii, pp. 182–211.

Review of *Jacke Jugeler* edited by W. H. Williams.
    The Oxford Magazine, vol. xxxiv (4 February 1916), pp. 165–6. The review is not signed.

Review of *Henry Tubbe* edited by G. C. Moore Smith.
    The English Historical Review, vol. xxxi (April 1916), pp. 336–7.

1917

Review of Ethel M. Portal's *The Academ Roial of King James I.*
    The English Historical Review, vol. xxxii (April 1917), pp. 310–11.

1918

CHARACTERS FROM THE HISTORIES & MEMOIRS OF THE SEVENTEENTH CENTURY. WITH AN ESSAY AND HISTORICAL NOTES BY DAVID NICHOL SMITH. OXFORD: AT THE CLARENDON PRESS. MDCCCCXVIII.

    The book appeared in a series (without name) of which D. N. S. was general editor. Essay on the Character, pp. ix–lii; Characters, pp. 1–258; notes, pp. 259–322; index, pp. 323–31. The book has been several times reprinted.

JAMES COLIN MACLEHOSE. 2ND LIEUT., RIFLE BRIGADE. 1897–1917. GLASGOW: PRINTED FOR PRIVATE CIRCULATION AT THE UNIVERSITY PRESS. 1918. Pp. 7–36.

Review of *Documentary History of Yale University, 1701–45,* edited by F. B. Dexter.
> *The English Historical Review,* vol. xxxiii (October 1918), pp. 548–9.

1920

A TALE OF A TUB. TO WHICH IS ADDED THE BATTLE OF THE BOOKS AND THE MECHANICAL OPERATION OF THE SPIRIT. BY JONATHAN SWIFT. . . . THE WHOLE EDITED WITH AN INTRODUCTION, AND NOTES HISTORICAL AND EXPLANATORY, BY A. C. GUTHKELCH AND D. NICHOL SMITH. OXFORD: AT THE CLARENDON PRESS. MDCCCCXX.
> Introduction, pp. ix–lxxv; text and notes, pp. 1–291; appendixes, pp. 292–353; index, pp. 355–70. The edition was completed at the desire of the Delegates of the Clarendon Press. D. N. S. 'revised and supplemented the introduction and added much new matter to the notes'. The eight original designs prepared for the fifth edition of 1710 are reproduced here for the first time.

1921

WORDSWORTH, POETRY & PROSE. WITH ESSAYS BY COLERIDGE, HAZLITT, DE QUINCEY. WITH AN INTRODUCTION BY DAVID NICHOL SMITH AND NOTES. OXFORD: AT THE CLARENDON PRESS. 1921.
> In the Clarendon Series of English Literature of which D. N. S. is general editor. Introduction, pp. v–xviii; text, pp. 1–192; notes, pp. 193–212. The notes are by D. N. S. and A. M. D. Hughes.

Review of *Old English Ballads, 1553–1625,* edited by H. E. Rollins.
> *The Oxford Magazine,* vol. xl (17 November 1921), p. 96. The review is not signed.

Review of *Peacock's Four Ages of Poetry: Shelley's Defence of Poetry: Browning's Essay on Shelley,* edited by H. F. B. Brett-Smith.
> *The Oxford Magazine,* vol. xl (8 December 1921), pp. 156–8. The review is not signed.

1925

DRYDEN, POETRY & PROSE. WITH ESSAYS BY CONGREVE, JOHNSON, SCOTT AND OTHERS. WITH AN INTRODUCTION AND NOTES BY DAVID NICHOL SMITH. OXFORD: AT THE CLARENDON PRESS. 1925.
> The Clarendon Series of English Literature. Introduction, pp. v–xiv; text, pp. 1–176; notes, pp. 177–204.

1926

THE OXFORD BOOK OF EIGHTEENTH CENTURY VERSE. CHOSEN BY DAVID NICHOL SMITH. OXFORD: AT THE CLARENDON PRESS. 1926.
> Preface, pp. v–xii; text, pp. 1–713; indexes, pp. 715–27.

'The British Grenadiers.'

An account of the origin of the Song, with a facsimile of the issue of 1780. Printed in *The Household Brigade Magazine*, Summer 1926, pp. 202–5, and reprinted in the *Journal of the Society of Army Historical Research*, January 1927, and in *The Faugh-A-Ballagh* (1927, pp. 69–72), the journal of the Inniskilling Fusiliers. Further articles by D. N. S. appeared in *The Household Brigade Magazine*, Winter 1926–7, pp. 31–3 (reprinted in *The Faugh-A-Ballagh*, 1927, pp. 136–8), and Summer 1927, pp. 194–6.

Preface to *The Letters of Sir Walter Raleigh (1879–1922)* edited by Lady Raleigh and published in 1926 by Methuen and Co. in two volumes.

The preface (vol. i, pp. v–xx) gives a short biography and appreciation of Sir Walter Raleigh. It was reprinted in the second and cheaper edition published in 1928 and, in condensed form, in a selection from the letters also published in 1928.

Introduction to *The Ashley Library. A Catalogue of Printed Books, Manuscripts, and Autograph Letters Collected by Thomas James Wise. Vol. viii. London: Printed for Private Circulation Only. 1926.*

Pp. vii–xi.

1927

Life of William Aldis Wright (1831–1914) contributed to *The Dictionary of National Biography 1912–1921* edited by H. W. C. Davis and J. R. H. Weaver and published by the Oxford University Press in 1927.

Pp. 595–7.

Review of Walter Graham's *The Beginnings of English Literary Periodicals*. *The Modern Language Review*, vol. xxii (July 1927), p. 361.

1928

SHAKESPEARE IN THE EIGHTEENTH CENTURY. BY DAVID NICHOL SMITH. OXFORD: AT THE CLARENDON PRESS. 1928.

Pp. 1–91. Three lectures delivered at Birkbeck College in November 1927, the first mainly on the performances of Shakespeare, the second on the editors of Shakespeare, and the third on the critics.

'Johnson's Revision of his Publications especially *The Rambler, Rasselas,* and *The Idler.*'

A paper read before the Johnson Club, 17 March 1926. Printed in *Johnson & Boswell Revised By Themselves and Others. Three Essays by David Nichol Smith, R. W. Chapman, and L. F. Powell. Oxford: At the Clarendon Press. 1928.* Pp. 7–18.

1929

'Johnson's *Irene.*'

Essays and Studies by Members of the English Association, vol. xiv (1929), pp. 35–53. The essay was published separately, with revisions and additions, at the Clarendon Press in 1929 (pp. 1–27), and is incorporated with omissions and alterations in *The Poems of Samuel Johnson* (1941), pp. 233–44.

WARTON'S *HISTORY OF ENGLISH POETRY.* BY DAVID NICHOL SMITH. WARTON LECTURE ON ENGLISH POETRY, BRITISH ACADEMY. 1929. PRINTED AT THE UNIVERSITY PRESS, OXFORD.

> Pp. 1–29. The lecture is also printed in the *Proceedings of the British Academy*, vol. xv (1929), pp. 73–99.

1930

JONATHAN SWIFT. A LECTURE DELIVERED IN ABERCROMBY HOUSE IN THE UNIVERSITY OF LIVERPOOL. 23 MAY 1930.

> Pp. 1–20. The lecture was printed without publisher's name by C. Tinling and Co. of Liverpool.

1931

'The Degree of Doctor of Philosophy (Ph.D., or D.Phil.).'

> *Fourth Congress of the Universities of the Empire 1931. Report of Proceedings* (1931), pp. 83–8: a paper read on 8 July 1931. The paper was reprinted as a pamphlet (pp. 1–8) at the University Press, Oxford, in the same year.

1932

ANCIENT SONGS CHIEFLY ON MOORISH SUBJECTS. TRANSLATED FROM THE SPANISH BY THOMAS PERCY. WITH A PREFACE BY DAVID NICHOL SMITH. OXFORD: PRINTED BY JOHN JOHNSON FOR HUMPHREY MILFORD AT THE OXFORD UNIVERSITY PRESS, AMEN HOUSE, WARWICK SQUARE, LONDON. M.DCCCC.XXXII.

> The book, which was in proof in 1775, was first published in 1932 with a preface (pp. v–xviii) and notes (pp. 53–6) by D. N. S. The text runs from p. 1 to p. 51.

1933

'The Newspaper.'

> *Johnson's England. An Account of the Life & Manners of his Age. Edited by A. S. Turberville. Clarendon Press, Oxford*, vol. ii, chap. xxvii, pp. 331–67.

1934

'The Contributors to *The Rambler* and *The Idler*.'

> Article in *The Bodleian Quarterly Record*, vol. vii, no. 84 (4th quarter 1934), pp. 508–9.

1935

THE LETTERS OF JONATHAN SWIFT TO CHARLES FORD. EDITED BY DAVID NICHOL SMITH, MERTON PROFESSOR OF ENGLISH LITERATURE IN THE UNIVERSITY OF OXFORD. OXFORD: AT THE CLARENDON PRESS. MCMXXXV.

> Introduction, pp. vii–xlvii; letters of Swift and Ford, pp. 1–175; poems among Ford's papers, pp. 179–215; fragment of a pamphlet, pp. 216–17; letters to Ford from Gay, Pope and Parnell, Bolingbroke, and the Duchess of Ormond, pp. 221–41; index, pp. 243–60. The notes are printed at the foot of the page.

'Jonathan Swift. Some Observations.'
> A paper read before the Royal Society of Literature, 13 March 1935. Printed in the *Transactions* of the Society, vol. xiv (1935), pp. 29–48, and reprinted in pamphlet form, pp. 1–20.

1937

Life of Sir Walter Raleigh (1861–1922) contributed to *The Dictionary of National Biography 1922–1930* edited by J. R. H. Weaver and published by the Oxford University Press in 1937.
> Pp. 701–4.

SOME OBSERVATIONS ON EIGHTEENTH CENTURY POETRY. BY DAVID NICHOL SMITH. MERTON PROFESSOR OF ENGLISH LITERATURE IN THE UNIVERSITY OF OXFORD. TORONTO: THE UNIVERSITY OF TORONTO PRESS. 1937.
> The Alexander lectures delivered at the University of Toronto in 1937: I. 'Pope—Poetic Diction' (pp. 9–30). II. 'The Heroic Couplet—Johnson' (pp. 31–55). III. 'Thomson—Burns' (pp. 56–81). The book is also issued with the imprint 'Oxford University Press. London: Humphrey Milford. 1937.'

1938

'Robert Burns.'
> A lecture delivered at the Sorbonne, 19 January 1938, and printed in *France–Grande Bretagne Bulletin Mensuel des Relations Franco-Britanniques*, nº 173, Février 1938, pp. 29–40.

1939

'Edmond Malone.'
> *The Huntington Library Quarterly*, vol. iii (October 1939), pp. 23–36. A revised version of a lecture delivered before the University of London, at Birkbeck College, on 10 May 1938.

1940

BYRON, POETRY & PROSE. WITH ESSAYS BY SCOTT, HAZLITT, MACAULAY, ETC. WITH AN INTRODUCTION BY SIR ARTHUR QUILLER-COUCH AND NOTES BY D. NICHOL SMITH. OXFORD: AT THE CLARENDON PRESS. 1940.
> The Clarendon Series of English Literature. The notes are on pp. 180–207.

Bibliographies of Samuel Johnson and James Boswell contributed to *The Cambridge Bibliography of English Literature*, edited by F. W. Bateson and published at the Cambridge University Press, 1940, vol. ii, pp. 613–28 and 650–4.

1941

THE POEMS OF SAMUEL JOHNSON. EDITED BY DAVID NICHOL SMITH AND EDWARD L. MCADAM. OXFORD: AT THE CLARENDON PRESS. 1941.
> Introduction, pp. ix–xxvi; text, introductions to particular poems, and notes, pp. 1–403; indexes, pp. 404–20.

'The Early Version of Shenstone's *Pastoral Ballad.*'
> Article in *The Review of English Studies,* vol. xvii (January 1941), pp. 47–54.

1943
'Samuel Johnson's Poems.'
> An address to the Johnson Club, 11 December 1941, printed in *The Review of English Studies,* vol. xix (January 1943), pp. 44–50.

'Hazlitt's Depth of Taste.'
> An overseas broadcast, especially for Indian students, 15 January 1943. Printed in *The Listener,* vol. xxix (28 January 1943), pp. 118–19.

'Thomas Warton's Miscellany: *The Union.*'
> Article in *The Review of English Studies,* vol. xix (July 1943), pp. 263–75.

1944
Review of A. T. Hazen's *A Bibliography of the Strawberry Hill Press.*
> *The Review of English Studies,* vol. xx (July 1944), pp. 244–6.

1945
'H. C. K. Wyld.'
> *The Oxford Magazine,* vol. lxiii (15 February 1945), pp. 149–50. An obituary notice.

INDEX OF NAMES

PRINTED IN GREAT BRITAIN AT THE UNIVERSITY PRESS, OXFORD
BY JOHN JOHNSON, PRINTER TO THE UNIVERSITY